DOCTRINES AND GENIUS
OF THE
CUMBERLAND
PRESBYTERIAN CHURCH

Alfred Brashear Miller

Memphis, Tennessee
Cumberland Presbyterian Church
2014

Funded, in part, by your contributions to Our United Outreach.

This book was originally published in 1892.

First modern printing March 2014.

ISBN-13: 978-0615987439
ISBN-10: 0615987435

OUR UNITED OUTREACH
Made Possible In Part By Your Tithe To Our United Outreach

Rev. Alfred Brashear Miller, D.D., LL.D.
1829-1902

RESOLUTIONS IN MEMORY OF DR. A. B. MILLER[1]

Your committee begs leave to report that it finds that Alfred B. Miller was received into the communion of this congregation under the ministerial care of Rev. S. E. Hudson in December, 1845; that he afterward entered the ministry of the Cumberland Presbyterian Church; and during his life was given the honorary degrees of D.D. and L.L.D.; and that for many years he was president of Waynesburg College; and that at the time of his death he was president emeritus of that institution.

His association with the educational interests of our church for half a century has made his name familiar to active Cumberland Presbyterians everywhere and his life work a part of our denominational history, and with the church at large we note his death with profound grief.

After a life of toil and hope and anxiety and disappointment and success, he has left a record of great and manifold and fruitful labors to perpetuate his memory and to encourage and console the multitude of friends, brethren and associates, who mourn his loss.

Waynesburg College was his life, and it is his monument. He was called to many honorable positions in the church, involving educational, ministerial and literary labors, in all of which he proved himself the gentleman eminent for varied learning, refined taste and high attainment in all the graces of pure Christianity and enlarged philanthropy.

Enrolled as a member of Hopewell congregation nearly sixty years ago, today we make the final entry opposite his name on our records with the full belief that the name of Alfred B. Miller is enrolled on the

---

[1]*The Cumberland Presbyterian*, February 20, 1902, page 254.

Lamb's book of life. Coming to us a plain country boy, whose name was perhaps unknown beyond the limits of his own township, he leaves a name that warms in thousands of true hearts to-day, and that shall live as long as the history of the Cumberland Presbyterian Church is read. The difference between his boyhood and old age is due to his energy, adaptability, versatility, talent and breadth and variety of attainment, ballasted by an unwavering faith in our Lord Jesus Christ and a faithful consecration to his service.

Cherishing a profound veneration for the talents, virtues and services of the late Dr. A. B. Miller,

Resolved, That we set apart one page in our session record as sacred to his memory; that we tender his living children our sincere sympathy on the occasion of their irreparable loss; and that we furnish a copy of this paper to *The Cumberland Presbyterian* for publication.

T. M. HURST,
HAMILTON NEWCOMER,
JESSE O. COLDREN,
Committee.

A. B. MILLER, D.D., LL.D.[2]

The subject of this sketch was born near Brownsville, Pa., October 16, 1829. After receiving a common school education, he attended Greene Academy, at Carmichaels, and with the opening of the Waynesburg College in November, 1851, he entered as a student the institution with which all his after life was identified. After two years as student he was made professor of mathematics, and six years thereafter was elected president, which position he held for forty years, and on resignation therefrom was chosen president emeritus, which place he filled until his death, which occurred January 30, 1902.

From earliest childhood Dr. Miller was a student and thinker. His mature life was given to the college, with the one purpose of building it up. While he was a preacher of acknowledged ability, he made the ministry only subsidiary to his work as a teacher.

As a writer he was singularly clear and forceful. While he was editing "The Cumberland Presbyterian" he made it a power in the Church, and especially in the crucial days which followed the close of the Civil War. His only work of magnitude as an author was the **Doctrines and Genius of the Cumberland Presbyterian Church**. He was a firm believer in the doctrines of his Church, inheriting his views largely from the pioneer preachers of western Pennsylvania—Morgan, Bryan, and others.

He possessed the genius for work, and never spent an idle moment. Often in conversation with friends his mind was shaping a sermon or an editorial. Frail in health in his youth, he preserved his physical vigor by a temperate life, and lived to a goodly age.

---

[2]*The Cumberland Presbyterian*, December 3, 1903, pages 716-717.

Dr. Miller was genial in disposition, very cordial in the treatment of students, and so won his way to their hearts. His influence over them was absolute, for no one thought of questioning his statements.

The common opinion of all who knew him was expressed to my by a visitor within the past month, that "Dr. Miller was one of the ablest and best men the Cumberland Presbyterian Church has produced."

JAS. N. MILLER.

DOCTRINES AND GENIUS

OF THE

Cumberland Presbyterian Church.

By Rev. A. B. MILLER, D.D., LL.D.,
President of Waynesburg College, Pennsylvania.

NASHVILLE, TENN.:
CUMBERLAND PRESBYTERIAN PUBLISHING HOUSE,
1892.

INTRODUCTION.

"He that entertains himself with moral or religious treatises will imperceptibly advance in goodness."—*Samuel Johnson.*

"I have gained the most profit, and the most pleasure also, from the books which have made me think the most."—*Guesses at Truth.*

To one of the world's great reformers, equally eminent as a preacher and as a theologian, is attributed a frequent repetition of the obvious truth that "only a reading people can be a growing people." The Board of Publication of the Cumberland Presbyterian Church has acted wisely in proposing to publish and place in the hands of our people a series of good books. Of a denomination of Christians it is true, as of the individual Christian, that in the measure in which it reads will it be intelligent, free, liberal, and progressive. There may not be too much reading of newspapers and other transient and fragmentary matter, but there is certainly a pernicious tendency among Church members to neglect the reading of good books; and it is the writer's ardent wish that the special work undertaken by our board may have a salutary influence in correcting this tendency.

Though this work has been furnished in response to a request from the Board of Publication, the author was left free in the selection of a subject, and the selection was determined by a desire to produce, if possible, a plain and thoughtful book that would interest and profit the reader. To promote growth in grace, to enlarge our views of religious life and duty, and to broaden and strengthen the foundations of our Christian character, patient reflection on the great Bible themes discussed in this book have a potency that is known only to those who have experienced it. "All graces," says a thoughtful writer, "begin

(iii)

in knowledge and are increased by knowledge." By that patient reflection which brings truth into contact with the soul, and by that obedience which accepts truth as the law of our lives, are we transformed "from glory to glory."

To some of our readers it may seem that too little attention has been given to the support of our positions by Scripture references, but it has been our aim rather to show the *reasonableness* of the fundamental doctrines accepted by all Christians, and of the doctrines which distinguish us as a denomination. Theology as a science must be, if true, a reasoned correlation of the teachings of the Bible in a system harmonious in all its parts. A system in opposition to man's reason can not be from Him who made man, and such a system man must ultimately reject. For the Cumberland Presbyterian system we claim this high and final sanction of *reasonableness.* In the mother Church, because of a system at war with man's consciousness and reason, there is unrest from center to circumference.

To "search the Scriptures" is the surest way to a satisfying faith in the Scriptures as a rule of moral and religious practice whereby human life may realize the highest possible good, and it is hoped that, on this broader plane, the chapters which follow may stimulate to more extended research on a subject so vitally related to our present and eternal welfare.

> "The Christian faith,
> Unlike the timorous creeds of pagan priest,
> Is frank, stands forth to view, inviting all
> To prove, examine, search, investigate,
> And gives, herself, a light to see her by."

The author aimed at a faithful statement of the historical and current sense in which the Church interprets its Confession on the subjects herein treated. In view of the recent discussions as to the accepted doctrine of the Church touching the Atonement, he has been at pains to ascertain the views of a number of the older ministers of the body, which he would gladly have cited had space permitted. The brief chapter on that subject, which is rather a simple statement of the prevailing view of our theologians than an attempt at an argument in support of the view itself, accords thoroughly with the views collated in the manner above named.

It is due the Board of Publication that it be here stated that the responsibility for the delay of the appearance of this work rests wholly with the writer, and he takes occasion to acknowledge the patient forbearance of the board. The work has been written in such brief intervals as could be so appropriated amid the labors incident to the author's relation to Waynesburg College. As it was begun, so it is now finished and sent forth in hope that it may be in some measure a useful and acceptable offering to the Church to which the author has devoted many years of labor. A. B. MILLER.

Waynesburg, Pa., July 16, 1892.

CONTENTS.

PART I.

CHAPTER I.

PART II.—DOCTRINAL STATEMENT AND EXPOSITION.

CHAPTER I.

CONTENTS.

PART III.

CHAPTER I.

The inquiry after truth and the belief of truth is the sovereign good of human nature.—Bacon.

THE Cumberland Presbyterian Church, like the spiritual kingdom of which it is a humble branch, came not with imposing display. In the year 1810, in a plain rural dwelling in Dickson county, Tennessee, it was instrumentally set up by three devoted and godly ministers. From its inception until the present, its course has been a remarkable progress; but it has gone forward with silent rather than with resounding steps. Its ministers have been laborious toilers in the field, not makers of books. Our literature is notably meager, and has no circulation beyond our own people. Hence it is not a just ground of wonder or complaint that, while God is doubtless our father, other branches of Abraham's great family are ignorant of us, and that the writers of histories in Israel acknowledge us not. As a denomination we have been singularly, if not culpably, indifferent to the obligation to bring our doctrines and our work more fully before the Christian public, and to this conviction, deep, long cherished, and intensified by many facts which have come to the personal knowledge of the author, the pages which follow are to be attributed.

"I suppose your Church is very numerous about Cumberland?"

"Not at all," I replied. "In fact, I do not know that we have a congregation in the State of Maryland."

"Is it possible! Why, did your Church not originate about Cumberland?"

"By no means—we originated in Tennessee."

"How, then, did you get your name?"

This fragment of a conversation with a minister to whom I was introduced in my first field of labor indicates not only that even ministers in other great communions know but little of us, but also that it is a disadvantage to wear a name entirely devoid of significance as to doctrine, and to only a few persons indicative of even our geographical origin.

In illustration of the erroneous opinions prevalent in respect to our doctrinal views, it is in place to cite a passage from the *Philosophy of Sectarianism*, by Rev. Alexander Blaikie, of Boston. As the imprint of the book is 1855, it might be difficult at this date to ascertain the sources of his information—if he had any. Having noticed other Presbyterian Churches, he proceeds to say: "We have then the Cumberland Presbyterians, originating from the irregular conduct of a Presbytery of that name, which, in 1803, introduced some *fatal doctrinal errors;* and appealing from the Synod of Kentucky, to which it had been subordinate, its doings were condemned in 1810, when it proclaimed itself an independent Church. Not only holding some tenets gratifying to natural men, but also employing in its ministry men of a less acquaintance with science, the languages, and theology, than other portions of the Presbyterian Church, it has grown rapidly."

This language seems to indicate that its author believed our rapid growth attributable to "some fatal doctrinal errors," "some tenets gratifying to natural men," and an illiterate ministry, while we have been wont to attribute it to the Lord's blessing upon a faithful exhibition of the word he has ordained as the "infallible rule of faith and practice;" and if the chapters that follow contribute to a better understanding, on the part of members of other denominations, of our faith and spirit, one of the aims in their preparation will have been secured.

Unity of faith is at once a powerful bond, a condition of peace, and a source of denominational strength. If our membership, now exceeding one hundred and sixty thousand, can be more generally enlisted in reading plain expositions of the fundamental principles of our holy religion, most valuable results will be realized in a higher type of individual Christian life, and in our enlarged usefulness as a Church. To this end it is desirable that the number of our books be multiplied as speedily as possible, and all the more so because the pulpit ministrations of to-day are, as a rule, quite barren of doctrinal exposition.

There is among the Churches of this country a growing disposition to lay aside those strifes over doctrinal differences which in the past have occasioned much waste of energy and provoked feelings quite at war with a true Christian spirit. If now these Churches will sit down to the task of an impartial examination of one another's standards, it may result that the differences will be seen to be so much fewer, and of so much less importance than they were hitherto thought, as to bring about kinder fraternal sympathy, and helpful adjustment and co-operation in work, among numerous branches that in all essential doctrines have a like precious faith. The vast work now challenging the utmost energies of the Churches of America seems to demand such a movement as will most efficiently mass their forces against the common foe, and we are confident that, in the event of such a movement, Cumberland Presbyterians will be ready for what seems for the glory of the Master and the promotion of his kingdom.

It is with no purpose of an uncharitable attack upon other creeds that this exposition of our own is sent forth. Comparisons will be made, to show differences as well as agreements; and as the Confession of the Cumberland Presbyterian Church— as indeed the Church itself—is a *protest* against what are called the severer features of Calvinism, to note specially our departures from the Westminster Confession will be helpful in defining our doctrinal system. The earnest debate over those stern features of Calvinism—at this very hour engaging the profoundest learning and logic of the mother Church—seems to render the present a time peculiarly suitable for such a publication as is proposed, since, as the sequel will show, the vicious theology now so perplexing the mother Church our fathers saw and purged away at the beginning of the century.

Our Church owes to itself and the public a manifest obligation to aid in the production of a healthful current literature. With its 2,776 congregations, its 1,646 ordained ministers, its membership of 163,216, its numerous literary institutions, and its theological seminary, the Church has done and is doing comparatively little to furnish the periodicals and books demanded by the great reading public, and thus comparatively little to shape the great currents of contemporary thought. From the whole body, therefore, should come a cordial and liberal response to the important step on the part of our Board of Publication to throw upon the mind of the Church and upon the reading public generally a series of books setting forth the system of doctrine through which as a denomination we have received singular blessing and enlargement.

For reasons herein given, and for more general ones to be stated in the next chapter, when recently the writer was requested by the Board of Publication of his Church to contribute a volume to a series it is now issuing, the subject of this effort at once occurred to him as the one he could discuss with the most hope of some useful service to the cause of truth.

CHAPTER II.

RELATION OF DOCTRINE TO DUTY AND DESTINY.

Ye shall know the truth, and the truth will make you free.—John viii. 32.

No error can be more pernicious or more absurd than that which represents it as a matter of but little consequence what a man's opinions are; for there is an inseparable connection between faith and practice, truth and holiness; otherwise it would be of no consequence to discover truth or to embrace it. Our Savior has said, "A corrupt tree can not bring forth good fruit."—*Introduction to Cumberland Presbyterian Confession of Faith.*

God and truth are always on the same side.—*Theo. Parker.*

IN strict use of language, one's *creed* is that which he believes; his *doctrine*, that which he teaches. As a candid man's teaching is also his belief, "creed" and "doctrine" are with him one and the same thing. In a technical sense a creed is a summary of Christian belief. The creed, or confession of faith, of a Church embodies the summary of principles the Church professes to believe and to teach; and hence creed and doctrine may be used as synonyms, as hereafter in these pages.

Zoroaster, the Persian philosopher and the founder of Parseeism, is credited with saying: "Taking the first footstep with a good thought, the second with a good word, and the third with a good deed, I entered Paradise." The beginning of his career was a good thought, its end Paradise. It was because the beginning was a good thought that the end was Paradise. The inseparable connection between creed and conduct, principle and practice, doctrine and destiny is solemnly affirmed by consciousness, observation, and the word of God. "As a man thinketh in his heart, so is he." "Ye shall know the truth, and the truth shall make you free," declared the Great Teacher who came to speak to the world the words which the Father gave to him. So far as a creed embodies error, be it a social, political, moral, or religious creed, it will be vicious in its issues. Only upon truth can rest the well-being of rational creatures. Only out of truth can come the harmony of the universe. Hence the vast importance and the responsibility, whether it pertain to an individual or a Church, of formulating a summary of principles to be believed, practiced, and taught. Believers are "chosen to salvation, through sanctification of the Spirit and belief of the truth." What God hath joined together in the process of the soul's salvation let us be careful that our "creeds" do not put asunder.

In every soul there is capacity for a true life—a life that opens godward, that fits its possessor for the presence in which there is fullness of joy. How is that susceptibility awakened into activity in the true spiritual evolution? Through the quickening power of the Spirit it is made capable of upward impulses from the apprehension of the truth, but these initial processes and the subsequent daily renewal of the inner man are in harmony with psychological laws. The soul, spiritually quickened, holding under survey the various impulses to action, chooses as its supreme end, because of a perceived obligation, the law and the service of its God. Truth believed begets sense of obligation, obligation felt begets volition, volition issues in action, action repeated begets habit, habits aggregated constitute character, character determines destiny.

But the soul which has chosen salvation through Christ, and the commandments of Christ as the law of its conduct, starts upon its career but a babe in Christ, and hence needs the means of developing, strengthening, training, perfecting its powers. To such the direction is, "Desire the sincere milk of the word, that you may grow thereby." For such Christ prays the Father, "Sanctify them through thy truth; thy word is truth." It is truth apprehended, truth received by faith, truth digested by reflection, and assimilated by daily observance as a principle of action, that is "profitable for doctrine, for reproof, for correction, for instruction in righteousness," so that thereby "the man of God may be perfect, thoroughly furnished unto all good works." Simply to believe the truth is not enough. Devils believe, but are devils still. It is by embracing the truth as good, by doing it, by looking into it as into a mirror, that, "beholding therein the glory of the Lord, we are changed into the same image, from glory to glory, even as by the Spirit of the Lord." "Divine truth exerts upon the mind," says Caird, "at once a restorative and a self-manifesting power. As light opens the close-shut flower-bud to receive light, so the truth of God, shining on the soul, quickens and stirs into activity the faculty by which that very truth is perceived."

In the introduction to his valuable compend, *Theology Condensed*, Rev. T. C. Blake, D.D., well urges that theology should be taught as any other science is taught, and that "parents owe it to themselves and to their children to have in their own houses such helps as will enable them and their offspring to form correct conceptions of God and of the plan of salvation which he has revealed." In this effort to present briefly the relation of doctrinal soundness to a life of godliness here, and to man's eternal well-being hereafter, the writer must record his regret that on the part of professing Christians generally there seems to be so little disposition to read and ponder works setting forth the vital truths of our holy religion. Not only does the study of moral and spiritual truth lay the granite foundation for that character which infinitely outvalues all perishable treasure, it also imparts the strength, piety, stability, and vigorous activity which should characterize the Church of Jesus Christ. If "ignorance is the curse of God," indifference to the truth is a paralysis of our moral and spiritual powers. In this realm of knowledge especially "God and truth are always on the same side," and that truth is the strait gate into the narrow way leading up to heaven, and immortality, and God.

Having penned the paragraphs of this chapter in hope of contributing something to awaken interest in the study of those words which are pure words, as silver tried in a furnace of earth, and purified seven times, the writer can be pardoned for recording his grateful recollection that in his youthful days Abbott's *Corner Stone of Religious Truth*, *The Pilgrim's Progress*, *The Saints' Rest*, Nelson's *Cause and Cure of Infidelity*, and other religious works, afforded mental food which he devoured with eager relish, when "sensational literature," which had already begun to teem from the press, and has since become multitudinous as the locusts of Egypt, was either unknown to him or beyond his ability to procure.

If our people will encourage the present effort of the Board of Publication to engage the pens of the Church for the production of a sound theological literature, the result will be most fruitful of good. It has been well said that religion is subjective theology—the exemplification in the experience and the life of the light and power of the truths of religion clearly apprehended, believed, and obeyed. To all the other methods of work of the Christian Church, books are an aid of the greatest value, in their religious bearing as well as in other respects justifying the sentiment of Bartholin, that "without books God is silent, justice dormant, science at a stand, philosophy lame, letters dumb, and all things involved in Cimmerian darkness."

CHAPTER III.

OF THE SCRIPTURES AND THE PROGRESSIVE DEVELOPMENT
OF THEIR MEANING, AND THE USE AND
ABUSE OF CREEDS.

Truth is the daughter of time.—*Aulus Gellius.*

THE volume received as the word of God is made up of
sixty-six distinct books, and its authorship is attributed to
over thirty writers. From the production of the first to the production of the last of these books there intervenes a period of
nearly two thousand years. Some of the books are historical,
some devotional, some prophetic. Though all are inspired, yet
each receives a coloring from its author's mental peculiarities,
and from the customs of the people, from the morals, the civil
institutions, and the philosophy of its own age. Some of the
subjects discussed are of such a character that their complete
comprehension transcends the human mind, and the entire
course of events revealed therein stretches from the creation of
the heavens and the earth to the end of man's probationary
career. Besides, this book is God's revelation for all the ages,
and many of the "things yet to come" of which it speaks will
not be understood until the race shall look upon them in the
light of their own unfolding.

Such being the character of the Bible, it is not remarkable
that men of equal candor, erudition, and piety differ, and differ
widely, in their interpretation of its teachings. It would be
much more remarkable if they did not differ. This is apparent
when we consider that we arrive at the meaning of the Script-

ures as we arrive at the meaning of other books, by faithful
study and the comparison of part with part. The Great Teacher
commanded, "Search the Scriptures," and the inspired word
itself declares that in Paul's Epistles "are some things hard to
be understood," and that these difficult passages the unlearned
and unstable not only do not understand, but "wrest unto their
own destruction." One can so interpret the world about him as
to be a morose pessimist; and one may so wrest the teachings
of the word of God as to justify a wicked life—as we have
known men to do. Whoever will read the Bible with a reverent
mind, seeking the Spirit's guidance, will undoubtedly so far
understand it that it will be made to him the power of God unto
salvation. Utterly unreasonable are those who put aside the
whole question as to the claims of the Bible by saying to Christians, "Why, you can not yourselves agree what it means!" In
all the sciences and in all the arts men differ in their views; and.
yet the sciences contain truth, and the arts are useful. The
Bible is not contradictory in its teachings; but man's judgment
is fallible. In the study of the Bible we see what we bring the
power to see, and no more. As constitutional peculiarities and
the customs of his times give coloring to the writings of every
inspired author, it is likewise true that every individual student
of the word will see it, in a greater or less degree, in coloring
reflected upon its pages from his own mental idiosyncrasies, the
education he has received, his system of metaphysics, and the
preconceived theological views with which he sits down to the
study of the word. In every department of study men differ,
and none differ more widely than those justly esteemed the
world's great thinkers. It is related that an Englishman desired
to introduce his son, then an Oxford student, to the two greatest
living thinkers, as he esteemed them—Carlyle and Herbert
Spencer. Upon the close of the interview with Spencer the
father remarked that it was his purpose to take his son to see
Carlyle also, whereupon Mr. Spencer exclaimed: "Ah, Mr. Car-

lyle! I am afraid he has done more to propagate error than any other writer of the century." Upon the close of the interview with Carlyle the father remarked: "This will be a day for my boy to look back upon, Mr. Carlyle, for in it he has been introduced to two great men — yourself and Herbert Spencer;" whereupon Carlyle exclaimed: "Herbert Spencer! Herbert Spencer! an im-measur-able fool!" Yet were both these men great thinkers, each, in his sphere, seeing some truths more clearly than any predecessor had seen them, each contributing something to the general stock of knowledge.

The interpretation of the word of God, equally with the interpretation of the works of God, has been progressive. Newton knew more about the heavens than did Galileo, and the astronomers of to-day know vastly more than Newton knew; and we are constrained to believe that the sum of astronomical knowledge will yet be vastly increased. Similarly, we must believe that the concurrent theological thought of to-day more nearly represents the true meaning of the Bible than did the thought of any preceding age. And the advance in biblical interpretation comes much as does the advance of our knowledge of the world in which we live, in the science of government or of morals, and that is through the service rendered by those superior minds seemingly sent to guide the race up to greater heights of knowledge and improvement. To the interpretation of the Bible, the establishment of the Church, and the progress of Christian civilization, we may aptly apply the declaration of Carlyle, that "universal history, the history of what man has accomplished in this world, is at the bottom the history of the great men who have worked here;" and that all "things we see standing in this world are, properly, the outward material result—the practical realization and embodiment of thoughts which dwelt in the great men sent into the world." The idea that these great leaders may be divinely sent, to be the guides of the race in its march through and out of the wilderness of ignorance, seemed to impress the mind of Carlyle even, for he said: "The great man is the 'creature of Time,' they say; the Time called him forth; the Time did every thing; he nothing but what we, the little critic, could have done too! This seems to me but melancholy work. The Time calls him forth? Alas, we have known the Times call loudly enough for their great man, but not find him when they called! He was not there! Providence had not sent him; the Time *calling* its loudest had to go down to confusion and wreck, because he would not come when called." It is not more true in aught than in religion and in scriptural interpretation that one extreme begets another. A great mind set for the work of exposing and destroying a doctrinal heresy is liable to run into an extreme opposite the one he fights, as the history of theological opinions will show. Yet, upon the whole, there is progress; and we may not unreasonably indulge the belief that the great multiplication of facilities for the study of the sacred word, and the vastly increased number of competent critics now devotedly giving their erudition and their powers of logic to the investigation of that word, will gradually wear away the differences of doctrinal belief which now divide the Church into sects. The great work now before the Churches of this country, and their solemn responsibility in view of it, demand, as it seems to me, that they candidly consider, and at once, whether in many instances alleged doctrinal differences are not entirely too unimportant to justify the division they occasioned and still perpetuate, and whether because of these divisions there is not great waste of spiritual energy and of material agencies, both so greatly needed in the solution of the problem of the evangelization of the rapidly increasing numbers who never enter our places of worship.

As declared in the introduction to the Confession of Faith of the Cumberland Presbyterian Church, "the right of private judgment, in respect to religion, is inalienable." To search the Scriptures for himself is alike the right and the duty of every man who has the opportunity. No pope or council or creed can bind the conscience in this respect. Only the word of God is the rule of faith and practice, and it is such to every man in the sense in which he understands it through an honest effort to arrive at its meaning. This doctrine, common to Protestanism, is the key to progress in the interpretation of the Scriptures. To give it up is to go back to the spiritual bondage of the middle ages. The division and sub-division of Churches is preferable to the spiritual death in which men repose unquestioning faith in the opinions of a fallible man or a council of fallible men. A written creed, therefore, while it serves for a time a most important end, may become a most serious hindrance to the progress of truth, a very paralysis on the Church of which it is the bond of faith and practice. To say that any creed shall for all time express the faith of a Church is to claim that the creed is infallible, or that the Church holding it is incapable of progress. As a great thinker has said, if an oak be planted in an urn, the urn must break or the oak must die—a fact illustrated again and again in the history of the Christian Church. A creed is but a temporary halting place in the march of mind, indicating a position in advance of any previously reached; but knowledge multiplies, and directly the creed is out of harmony with the current of advanced thought, and unrest and agitation result in the revision of the creed or a secession that sets up a new one. The truths here hinted at in an imperfect way seem to me of the utmost importance, and to justify the insertion of the following excellent passage from Bishop Butler:

"And as it is owned the whole scheme of Scripture is not yet understood, so, if ever it comes to be understood, it must be in the same way as natural knowledge is come at—by the continuance and progress of learning and liberty, and by particular persons attending to, comparing, and pursuing intimations scattered up and down it, which are overlooked and disregarded by the generality of the world. Nor is it at all incredible that a book which has been so long in the possession of mankind should contain many truths as yet undiscovered. For all the same phenomena, and the same faculties of investigation, from which such great discoveries in natural knowledge have been made in the present and last age were equally in the possession of man-kind several thousand years before."

The following passage from the farewell address to the Plym-outh Pilgrims, by their pastor, Rev. John Robinson, sets in so clear a light the true spirit of the consistent student of God's word that I am confident the reader will be glad that it is here reproduced:

"Brethren, we are now quickly to part from one another, and whether I may live to ever see your face on earth any more, the God of heaven only knows; but whether the Lord hath appointed that or no, I charge you before God and his blessed angels that you follow me no farther than you have seen me fol-low the Lord Jesus Christ.

"If God reveal any thing to you by any other instrument of his, be as ready to receive it as ever you were to receive any truth by my ministry; for I am verily persuaded, I am very confident, *the Lord has more truth yet to break forth out of his Holy Word.* For my part I can not sufficiently bewail the con-dition of the Reformed Churches, who are come to a period in religion, and will go at present no farther than the instruments of their Reformation. The Lutherans can't be drawn to go beyond what Luther saw; whatever part of his will our good God has revealed to Calvin, they will rather die than embrace it. And the Calvinists, you see, stick fast where they were left by that great man of God, who yet saw not all things.

"This is a misery much to be lamented, for though they were burning and shining lights in their times, yet they penetrated not into the whole counsel of God; but were they now living would be as willing to embrace further light as that which they first received. I beseech you to remember it, 't is an article of your Church covenant, *that you be ready to receive whatever truth shall be made known to you from the written word of God.* Remember that and every other article of your sacred covenant. But I must here exhort you to take heed what you receive as truth. Examine it, consider it, and compare it with other scriptures of truth before you receive it, for 't is not possible the Christian world should come so lately out of such thick anti-Christian darkness, and that perfection of knowledge should break forth at once."—*Neal's History of New England.*

"It is evident," says Dr. Edwards A. Park in his "Duties of a Theologian," "that theology has been obviously improving within the last two centuries; and the comparison between the standard systems of the present day and those of Turretin, Ridgely, or Owen presents *a rich earnest of what is to come.* All these improvements have given and all future improvements will give new power to the essential doctrines of Jesus." I truly believe, as Dr. Park elsewhere adds, that "both the Testaments are more accurately interpreted at the present day than they have ever been since the days of John, the last of the unerring expositors;" to which may be added the expectant declaration of another equally distinguished critic, who says: "The time is coming (I can not doubt it) when *all the dark places* of the Bible will be elucidated to the satisfaction of intelligent and humble Christians. But how near at hand that blessed day is I do not know. 'The Lord hasten it in its time!'" In the same line of thought the following excellent words of Professor Shedd, author of *History of Christian Doctrine*, seem to indicate a hopeful expectancy of a convergence of the views of intelligent Christians in all evangelical branches of Protestantism, and the near approach of the better day when our great theological warriors will unitedly turn against the common foes of our holy religion the weapons hitherto employed for mutual overthrow: "All doctrinal history evinces," says Professor Shedd, "that just in proportion as evangelical believers come to possess a common scientific talent for expressing their common faith and feeling, they draw nearer together so far as regards their symbolic literature. While on the contrary a slender power of self-reflection and analysis, together with a loose use of terms, drives minds far apart within the sphere of theology who often melt and flow together within the sphere of Christian feeling and effort. Science unites and unifies wherever it prevails; for science is accuracy in terms, definitions, and statements." " Probably nothing in the way of means," adds the same writer, " would do more to bring about that universal unity in doctrinal statement which has been floating as an ideal before the minds of men amidst the denominational distractions of Protestantism than a thorough and general acquaintance with the symbols of the various denominations, and the history of their origin and formation."

The careful study of the influence of creeds in their relation to the progress of the interpretation of the Scriptures, and the history of Protestant Christianity will lead, we think, to the following conclusions:

1. That creeds are useful as depositories of the results of true progress in the interpretation of the Bible, treasuring the fruits of investigation by a master mind, or of an epoch of general quickening of thought.

2. As necessary to founding and perpetuating organizations by assimilating great numbers in faith and practice. We see, indeed, bodies of Christian believers who have no written creed, and for that very reason claiming to be *par excellence* Churches of Christ, as receiving only the Bible as their creed; but in these there is always an understood interpretation of the Scriptures, descending even to the detail of mode of baptism, which must be subscribed as a condition of fellowship. So it may be that there is most a creed where it is claimed there is no creed.

3. They are useful as tending to unify Christian belief, on the whole, by fixing definitely the meaning of theological phrases

and statements, whereby the means of comparison of views is furnished to the whole Church. "On all sides and for all minds," says Dr. Shedd, "more light would be poured upon the profound mysteries of a common evangelical Christianity, if theologians were in the habit of looking over the whole field of symbolic literature instead of merely confining themselves to the examination of a single system."

4. That creeds are harmful when they are so received as to discourage instead of promoting the study of God's word, and especially when put in the place of the only infallible standard, thus leading those who subscribe them to trust in man instead of God. If it was wrong for one to say, "I am of Paul," and another to say, "I am of Apollos," much more must it be wrong for one Christian of to-day to declare himself of Calvin and another to declare himself of Luther as to authority for their doctrinal views. Like the noble Bereans, the subscribers of all creeds should "search the Scriptures" to see whether these creeds speak according to the living oracles.

5. Creeds to be subscribed by the laity should be plain, brief summaries of only the essential doctrines of Scripture. For candidates for ordination, subscription to fuller formulas may be necessary in order to unity of doctrinal teaching in the pulpits of a denomination.

The Cumberland Presbyterian Church is fortunate in having but a brief creed. After a cursory view of it the learned Dr. Nelson, late of Lane Theological Seminary, said to the writer: "I see you have the advantage of us in one respect—you have less Confession of Faith; and if I had my way ours would be less still—there is no need of so much book."

A correspondent of *The Church Union* suggests this brief creed as a scriptural basis of Christian unity:

DOCTRINE.—" I believe that Jesus Christ is the Son of God."

PRACTICE.—" If we walk in the light, as he is in the light, *we have fellowship one with another*."

2

CHAPTER IV.

SOME ACCOUNT OF THE LEADING CREEDS OF THE CHRISTIAN WORLD.

"He that abideth in the doctrine of Christ, he hath both the Father and the Son."

IT seems desirable to introduce here, as required by logical continuity of our subject, a brief notice of the leading CREEDS of the Christian world, with such a general classification of them as may be interesting to the ordinary reader.

In his reply to the question of his divine Master, "But whom say ye that I am?" the Apostle Peter made a confession which seems entitled to the distinction of being regarded the first formal "confession of faith" under the Christian dispensation: "*Thou art the Christ, the Son of the living God.*" Whatever may be true in regard to the import of Christ's reply—whether the "rock" on which he said he would build his Church is Peter, or Peter's confession, or Christ himself—it is pertinent to notice that the confession of Peter recognizes Christ as the true Messiah and truly divine. As Lange observes: "It is a confession of Jesus Christ as the center and heart of the whole Christian system, and the only and all-sufficient fountain of spiritual life—as a true man and the promised Messiah, and as the eternal Son of God, hence as the God-Man and Savior of the world." It is not unsuitable to remark, in passing, that whatever be the import of the words of Christ conferring on Peter power to bind and loose in heaven (the Church), subsequently the same language (Matt. xviii. 18) was addressed to all the apostles; and that, as remarked by Rev. David Brown, D.D., in his commentary on the passage, " not in all the New Testament is there the vestige of any authority either claimed or exercised by Peter, or conceded to him, above the rest of the apostles—a thing conclusive against the Romish claims in behalf of that apostle."

Peter's open confession of faith in Christ as the Son of the living God, in his nature, his mission, his work, is the true door of admittance to the Church of Christ and the test of the fundamental orthodoxy of all subsequently formed creeds, as embracing the central idea, and life, and power of the gospel. As the sun in the solar system, so is the central truth divinely revealed to Peter, in its relation to all evangelical creeds, as is most suggestively illustrated in their contents—Christ " the way, the truth, and the life."

It is sufficient for our present purpose to classify creeds as those formed *before* and those formed *after* what is known as the Reformation, an event justly regarded a great dividing line in the history of the Christian Church.

A.—CREEDS FORMED BEFORE THE REFORMATION.

The confession of Peter seems to have been repeated by the early converts to Christianity upon their admission to the Church by the rite of baptism, as in the case of the eunuch baptized by Philip, whose solemn asseveration was, " I believe that Jesus Christ is the Son of God." (Acts viii. 37.) As commanded, the apostles baptized " into the name of the Father, and of the Son, and of the Holy Ghost ; " and this of necessity involved the convert's implied, if not a formally declared, confession of the doctrine of the Trinity, giving a second element in the faith on which primitive converts were baptized. Some writers upon the subject regard 1 Tim. iii. 16 as a " creed-form " current at the time it was penned, but it lacks formal confession of the Trinity, though the Trinity is implied in the summary of the person and mediatorial work of Christ. From these beginnings, through stages not now known, there was formed at a very early date what is known to the Christian world as

1. *The Apostles' Creed.*

Of this venerable creed Luther says: "This confession of faith we did not make or invent, nor did the fathers before us; but as a bee collects honey from the beautiful and fragrant flowers of all sorts, so is this symbol briefly and accurately put together out of the books of the prophets and apostles. . . . . And it has been in the Church from the beginning, since it was either composed by the apostles themselves or else brought together from their writings or preaching by some of their best pupils." Rufinus affirmed his belief at the end of the fourth century that it was made up of contributions from each one of the apostles, as the Greek word giving name to it (συμβολον) signifies "thrown in." The Latin title is *Symbolum Apostolicum,* and the first word of the symbol being *credo,* thence has come the ecclesiastical "creed." The more general belief is that it was made up from the formulas used by individual Churches, and that by common consent it had by the close of the second century come into general use as a formula for admitting into Church fellowship. By order of the English Parliament it was appended to the first authorized edition of the Shorter Catechism. This ancient creed, which, without modification, has been for seventeen centuries the symbol of the faith of those claiming one Father, one Savior, and one hope of life eternal, is here given in the version accepted by all English-speaking Christendom:

I believe in God the Father Almighty, maker of heaven and earth; and in Jesus Christ his only Son our Lord, who was conceived by the Holy Ghost, born of the Virgin Mary, suffered under Pontius Pilate, was crucified, dead, and buried; he descended into hell: the third day he rose again from the dead; he ascended into heaven, and sitteth at the right hand of God the Father

Almighty; from thence he shall come to judge the quick and the dead. I believe in the Holy Ghost; the Holy Catholic Church; the communion of saints; the forgiveness of sins; the resurrection of the body; and the life everlasting.

As there were in those early days only manuscript copies of the Bible, and these in the hands of very few, it is a reasonable supposition that the APOSTLES' CREED was generally memorized and frequently repeated. Thus this symbol comes to us, not only invested with the charm of antiquity, but with the hallowed association of having been on the lips of a vast multitude who have dropped their bodies on the shore of life's unresting sea!

As another index of the faith of the earlier days of Christianity, and as showing the agreement of the general teaching with the APOSTLES' CREED, the following is cited from a work of Tertullian, belonging to the end of the second century:

"The rule of faith is one only, unchangeable, and not to be amended, namely, the belief in one sole omnipotent God, the maker of the world; and in his Son Jesus Christ, born of the Virgin Mary, crucified under Pontius Pilate, raised from the dead on the third day, received into heaven, seated now on the right hand of the Father, and to come hereafter to judge the living and the dead, through the resurrection of the flesh."

2. *The Nicene Creed.* (A.D. 325–569.)

The circumstances giving rise to this creed are also the key to its doctrinal structure, and show how the Church has frequently found it necessary to expand a creed already in use. It contains a fuller statement of the doctrine of the Trinity, as the Father, the Son, and the Holy Ghost, an addition made necessary by the fact that heretical teachers sprang up who professed faith in *a* trinity, but denied the divinity of Christ and of the Holy Ghost. These teachers claimed, moreover, that they put on the Apostles' Creed the true construction, as also on the Scriptures. Hence, as Professor Shedd observes, this "symbol introduces scientific conceptions and technical terms, in order to preclude that possibility of two interpretations of language which was connected with the earlier symbol." The part of the creed relating to the divinity of Christ was formulated by a general council held in Nice, Bithynia, A.D. 325; the part relating to the divinity and personality of the Holy Ghost was added by a general council held at Constantinople, A.D. 381; and the part beginning with "filioque," supplied by a general council of the Latin Church at Toledo, Spain, A.D. 569. This creed was received by both the Greek and the Latin Churches, the former rejecting the last added part, and in modern times is, as Professor Shedd affirms, "the received creed-statement of all trinitarian Churches." By this ancient confession also, as by the Apostles' Creed, are we reminded of the essential unity and the unchangeableness of Christian faith in its fundamental elements. Systems of philosophy rise, flourish, and pass away; one system of government gives place to another, but the faith of God's people, like the word of the Lord on which it is founded, changes not. In its usual English dress the *Nicene*, or *Nicæno-Constantinopolitan Symbol*, is as follows:

"I believe in one God, maker of heaven and earth, and all things visible and invisible; and in one Lord Jesus Christ, the only begotten Son of God, begotten of his Father, before all worlds; God of God, Light of Light, very God of very God, begotten, not made, being of one substance with the Father, by whom all things were made; who, for us men and for our salvation, came down from heaven, and was incarnate by the Holy Ghost of the Virgin Mary, and was made man, and was crucified also for us under Pontius Pilate. He suffered and was buried, and the third day he rose again according to the Scriptures, and ascended into heaven, and sitteth on the right hand of the Father. And he shall come again with glory to judge both the quick and the dead; whose kingdom shall have no end. And I believe in the Holy Ghost, the Lord the Giver of life, who proceedeth from the Father and the Son, who with the Father and the Son together is worshiped and glorified; who spake by the prophets. And I believe in one Catholic and Apostolic Church; I acknowledge one baptism for the remission of sins; and I look for the resurrection of the dead and the life of the world to come."

Subsequent to the promulgation of the *Nicene* Creed there sprang up the heresy known as Nestorianism, which teaches that the human and the divine natures of Christ constitute two persons; to correct which a council held at Ephesus, A.D. 431, formulated the true doctrine of the two natures in one person. An opposite extreme taught that the two natures in Christ's person formed but one nature, which was condemned by a deliverance of the council of Chalcedon; and these two councils formulated the doctrine since received by the Christian world, of *two natures* in the *one person* of the Son of God. This creed is usually styled—

3. *The Chalcedon Symbol.* (A.D. 451.)

At this halting-place the Church has stood ever since. "The theological mind has not ventured beyond the positions established at this time, respecting the structure and composition of Christ's most mysterious person—a subject in some respects more baffling to speculation than that of the Trinity proper."— *Professor Shedd.*

4. *The Athanasian Creed.* (*Symbolum Quicumque.*)

"This creed," says Dr. A. A. Hodge, in his Commentary on the Westminster Confession, "was evidently composed long after the death of the great theologian whose name it bears, and after the controversies closed and the definitions established by the councils of Ephesus and Chalcedon. It is a grand and unique monument of the unchangeable faith of the whole Church as to the great mysteries of godliness, the Trinity of persons in the one God and the duality of natures in the one Christ." "It was drawn up," says Dr. Shedd, "in order to furnish a symbol that would be received by both the Eastern and Western Churches. . . . . It is most probable it originated in the school of Augustine and Hilary, whose trinitarianism it embodies."

Comparing these great creeds, beginning with the confession of the candidate for baptism, "Thou art the Christ, the Son of the living God," and coming on to this last, which brings us to the twilight of the Reformation, we see how in all of them there is imbedded a clear and unchangeable faith in the divinity of Christ, not less certainly than there are rocky strata in the crust of the earth—the element of faith essential to the great hope of humanity, that Jesus has power to forgive sins, and to give eternal life to all who believe upon him.

From the Athanasian creed that portion relating to the person of Christ is here given:

"27. But it is necessary to eternal salvation that he should also faithfully believe in the incarnation of our Lord Jesus Christ. 28. It is therefore true faith that we believe and confess that our Lord Jesus Christ is both God and man. 29. He is God; generated from eternity from the substance of the Father; man born in time from the substance of his mother. 30. Perfect God, perfect man, subsisting of a rational soul and human flesh. 31. Equal to the Father in respect to his divinity, less than the Father in respect to his humanity. 32. Who, although he is God and man, is not two, but one Christ. 33. But two not from the conversion of divinity into flesh, but from the assumption of his humanity into God. 34. One not at all from the confusion of substance, but from unity of person. 35. For as rational soul and flesh is one man, so God and man is one Christ."

We pass now a long interval which closed with the great transition event in the history of the Church, called the Reformation. A new birth of Christendom was to come—and was sadly needed. "The Lord's vineyard was a desert. The priesthood was grown worldly and even dissolute. The popes, overstepping all limits in their assumptions, led lives horrible and scandalous beyond measure. Church assemblies seemed held only for the Bacchanalian orgies that went with them." In the sky of this moral and spiritual night appeared such stars as John of Milic, Wiclif, and Huss, and directly there burst forth a resplendent constellation of such men as the world has rarely seen. Out of their labors came the Protestant Reformation, and out of the emancipation of thought attending the Reformation came a large number of confessions of faith, which may be designated

B.—CREEDS FORMED SINCE THE REFORMATION.

1. *Canons and Decrees of the Council of Trent.* (A.D. 1545–1563.)

A general synod, designed to counteract the progress of the Reformation, was called by Pope Paul, and met at Trent, December, 1545, continuing its sessions, with intermission, nearly eight years. This synod issued the creed known as *Canones et Decreta Concilii Tridentini.* A papal bull of Pius IV. confirmed the canons and decrees, and "forbade, under severest penalties, all clergymen and laymen from making explanations upon them." The "decrees" contain the papal doctrine, and the "canons" explain the decrees, and condemn the opposite tenets of the Protestant Church—ending always with "*anathema sit.*"

A catechism explaining and enforcing the canons of the council of Trent was promulgated A.D. 1556, by authority of Pope Pius IV.

In 1564 a bull of Pius IV. enjoined on all public teachers, all candidates for clerical or academical honors, and all converts from other Churches to subscribe the *Tridentine Profession of Faith*, which is made up of the Nicene Creed and the canons of the Tridentine synod.

The Papal Church has also the *Catechism of Bellarmine* (1603), the *bull Unigenitus* of Clement XI. (1711), the *Confutation of the Confession of Augustine*, the *Missale Romanum*, and the *Breviarium Romanum*, as "important auxiliary sources of the papal doctrine."

2. *Creeds of the Greek Church.*

The most important modern confession of the Greek Church is the *Orthodox Confession* drawn up in 1642 by Peter Mogilas, bishop of Kiew, to counteract Protestantism, which was published in Russian, modern Greek, Latin, and German. The *Confessio Dosithei* was prepared by a Greek patriarch of Jerusalem, exposing the errors of the Calvinistic system. The *Confessio Gennadii* was prepared at an earlier date (1453) by Gennadius, patriarch of Constantinople, being a summary of the fundamental truths of the Christian religion.

"This Church arrogates to herself pre-eminently the title of the 'orthodox,' because the original creeds defining the doctrine of the Trinity and the person of Christ were produced in the Eastern half of the ancient Church, and hence are in a peculiar sense her inheritance. Greek theology is very imperfectly developed beyond the ground covered by these ancient creeds, which that Church magnifies and maintains with singular tenacity."—*Dr. A. A. Hodge.*

Founding its doctrinal system on the Apostles' Creed and the decisions of the seven general councils previous to the division into the Eastern (or Greek) and the Western (or Latin) Church, the Greek Church rejects the decisions of all Western councils since the schism. The Greek Church, like the Roman, is Arminian in theology.

3. *The Lutheran Creeds.*

Luther and Calvin showed themselves leaders of theological thought, and the impress of their minds remains in the two great branches of the Protestant world, the Lutheran and the Reformed Churches. "The Lutheran Church," as remarked by Professor Shedd, "adopted with decision the Patristic results in the departments of theology and christology. But the doctrines of sin and redemption had been left, to some extent, undeveloped by the Patristic mind, and entirely without definite symbolic statement, and had been misstated by the papal mind at Trent; and hence the principal part of the new and original work of the Lutheran divine was connected with these." In the year 1530 a confession previously prepared by Luther, Melanchthon, and two other divines was submitted to the imperial diet at Augsburg, and, with slight modifications, was adopted. First in time, promulgated by an imperial diet, most important of all Lutheran symbols is this

(*a*) *Augsburg Confession.* (A.D. 1530.)

Summoned to the undertaking by Charles V., the papal theologians prepared a critical examination of this Augsburg Confession, which was read in an imperial assembly in August, 1530, and was approved by Charles, who thereupon demanded that the Protestants return to the doctrines of the Papal Church. A copy of this document was refused the Protestants, but Melanchthon, from notes taken by himself and others when it was read in the diet, prepared an able answer to the papal *Confutatio*, as it was called, which answer the Protestants desired to present to Charles, who declared, however, that he would neither hear nor receive any more documents from the Protestants. From the first this document, called the *Apology*, was regarded as of great authority in doctrine, and in 1537 it was formally subscribed, at Smalcald, as a doctrinal symbol, and is generally designated

(*b*) *The Apology for the Augsburg Confession.* (1530.)

After these principal symbols Lutheran theologians recognize (1) The *Larger and Smaller Catechisms*, "the first for the use of preachers and teachers, the latter as a guide in the instruction of youth," prepared by Luther (1529). (2) The *Articles of Smalcald*, prepared by Luther in 1536, and subscribed formally the next year. (3) The *Saxon Confession*, prepared by Melanchthon in 1551. (4) The *Wurtemburg Confession*, composed by Brenz in 1552, which, like the *Saxon*, was prepared for a council

of Trent, both being copies of the Augsburg Confession. (5)
The *Formula Concordiæ*, drawn up in 1557 by Andrea and others.
" It is a polemic document constructed by that part of the Lutheran Church hostile to the Calvinistic theory of the sacraments.
It carries the doctrine of consubstantiation into technical statement, teaching the presence of the divine nature of Christ in
the sacramental elements."—*Shedd.* The High Lutherans receive the *Formula Concordiæ ;* the moderate party reject it,
"content to stand by the *Augsburg Confession*, the *Apology*, and
the *Smalcald Articles.*"

4. *Reformed (Calvinistic) Confessions.*

Under the title of "Reformed Churches" are embraced all
the Churches of Germany subscribing the Heidelberg Catechism ;
the Protestant Churches of Switzerland, France, Holland, England, and Scotland ; the Independents and Baptists of England
and America ; and the various branches of the Presbyterian
Church in England and America.

The Reformed Churches represent that element of the Reformation which came most fully out, so to speak, of bondage to
papal traditions, and insisting most fully on the study of the
word of the Lord as the privilege and duty of every man. It is
but a natural sequence that we have creeds many and Churches
many, since theologians of this class went to work to determine
anew the teachings of the word, to the study of which they gave
themselves most earnestly. Passing by a number of confessions
having individual significance and some that were adopted by
quite limited numbers of individual Churches, we have the following list, which embraces the leading Reformed creeds:

(a) *The Thirty-nine Articles of the Church of England.*

Drawn up originally in A.D. 1551 by Cranmer and Ridley,
they were, in 1562, reduced by the bishops to their present number, at the order of Queen Elizabeth, and are the doctrinal
standard of the Episcopal Churches in England, Scotland, America, and the British colonies.

(*b*) *The Heidelberg Catechism.*

Prepared by Ursinus and Olerianus, A.D. 1562. "It was established by civil authority, the doctrinal standard, as well as instrument for the Churches of the Palatinate, a German State at that time including both banks of the Rhine. It is the Confession of Faith of the Reformed Churches of Germany and Holland, and of the German and (Dutch) Reformed Churches of America."—*Dr. A. A. Hodge.*

(*c*) *The Second Helvetic Confession.* (1564.)

"It was adopted by all the Reformed Churches in Switzerland with the exception of Basle, and by the Reformed Churches in Poland, Hungary, Scotland, and France."—*Professor Shedd.*

(*d*) *The Canons of the Synod of Dort.*

The synod of Dort (Holland) met in November, 1618, and continued its sessions until the next May. It was composed of sixty-eight Hollanders and twenty-eight foreign delegates, the latter representing England, Scotland, the Palatinate, Hesse, Switzerland, Nassau, East Friesland, and Bremen. The special object of the call of the synod was to oppose Arminianism, which had sprung up in Holland about the beginning of that century. The Arminians were represented by thirteen deputies, headed by Episcopius. "The English Episcopal Church, in which at that time the Arminian party was dominant, rejected the decisions of this synod, and a mandate of James I., in 1620, forbade the preaching of the doctrine of predestination."—*Shedd.* The deliverance of the synod embraces ninety-three canons, which constitute "a true, accurate, and eminently authoritative exhibition of the Calvinistic system of theology."

(*e*) *The Westminster Confession and Catechisms.* (A.D. 1643-1648.)

This doctrinal standard is the product of an assembly of divines called by the English Parliament for the purpose of settling the government, liturgy, and doctrine of the Church of England. The assembly met at Westminster, July 1, 1643, and sat until February 22, 1648, holding in all one thousand one hundred and sixty-three sessions. Chosen from the several counties of England, the members of the assembly represented the Presbyterian, the Episcopal, and the Independent Churches, Presbyterians being much in the ascendency. This doctrinal formula is adopted by "all the Presbyterian Churches in the world of English and Scotch derivation, and is of all creeds the one most highly approved by all the bodies of Congregationalists in England and America." The convention of Congregationalists called by Cromwell, in Savoy Palace, London, 1658, framed the *Savoy Confession*, which is so nearly the same as the *Westminster* that "the modern Independents have in a manner laid aside the use of it in their families, and agreed with the Presbyterians in the use of the assembly's catechisms." "All the assemblies convened in New England," continues Dr. Hodge, "for the purpose of settling the doctrinal basis of their Churches, have either indorsed or explicitly adopted this confession and these catechisms as accurate expositions of their own faith. The Cambridge (Mass.) Platform (1647-8), the Boston Confession (1679-80), and the Saybrook (Conn.) Platform (1708) are all of this Calvinistic type."

From the days of the great theologian whose name it bears Calvinism has largely dominated the thought of the Protestant world. It is a massive system, challenging the respect of pious souls by its exaltation of the sovereignty of God as displayed in an assumed unconditional eternal decree that determines whatsoever comes to pass, and hinging salvation on sovereign election thereto before the foundation of the world, and without any thing foreseen in the creature as a reason for the choice, and similarly attributing the damnation of the non-elect to the good pleasure of God in passing them by. It could not result otherwise than that an assumption so fundamental would largely affect the theology and the anthropology of a system of doctrine in harmony with it. And so it has been. But to this doctrine an early formal protest was made, and the constant growth of that protest furnishes a long and interesting chapter in the progress and emancipation of religious thought—a chapter not yet completed, New York, Chicago, and other places witnessing just now stormy theological discussions rising out of honest and irrepressible protest to Calvinism. This brings us to

5. *The Arminian Confessions.*

James Arminius, born at Oudewater, Holland, 1560, after a preliminary education spent six years in the university at Leyden, and subsequently studied at Geneva, where he had for his instructor one of the most distinguished scholars of the day, Theodore Beza, a Calvinist of the most rigid type. Here he incurred the displeasure of the "Aristotelians of Geneva," and in consequence was compelled to leave. Going to Basle, he "was offered by the faculty of divinity in the university the degree of doctor, gratis, which, however, he did not venture to accept, on account of his youth." Calvinism had already occasioned in the Netherlands "a passionate controversy, which ended in the split of the Netherland Reformed Church." Arminius was drawn into the controversy, and being commissioned to defend the doctrine of his instructor, Beza, regarding predestination, it is said he carefully examined both sides of the question, and with the unexpected result that "he himself began to doubt, and at last came to adopt the opinions he had been commissioned to refute." As Arminius is credited with a system of doctrine becoming so widely prevalent in the Christian world, his theological adherents find comfortable assurance in the abundant testimony to both his ability and his piety, one reliable authority declaring that "he was an extremely good man, as even his enemies allow; his abilities also were of a high order; his thinking is clear, bold and vigorous; his style remarkably methodical, and his scholarship respectable, if not profound."

The Arminians adopted no symbol or confession. The sources of their doctrines, as enumerated in Shedd's chapter on symbols, are these: (1) The writings of Arminius. (2) The Confessions of the Pastors called Remonstrants, by Episcopius. (3) The Remonstrance, by Peter Bertius, containing a specification of five points held by Arminius, in opposition to the well-known "five points" of Calvinism. (4) The writings of Grotius, Limborch, Wetstein, and LeClerc. In 1610 the Arminians ("Remonstrants") presented to the assembled states of the province of Holland a remonstrance containing the following five propositions, as being the logical results of the teaching of Arminius:

1. That God had indeed made an eternal decree, but only on the conditional terms that all who believe in Christ shall be saved, while all who refuse to believe must perish.

2. That Christ died for all men. If the efficacy of his death is restricted, it is by unbelief.

3. That no man is of himself able to exercise saving faith.

4. That without the grace of God men can not do any thing good, but that grace does not act in men in an irresistible way.

5. That believers are able, by the aid of the Holy Spirit, victoriously to resist sin; but that the question of the possibility of a fall from grace must be determined by a further examination of the Scriptures on this point.

The last point in the fifth item was a year later decided in the affirmative by the Arminians, their action adding to the fierceness of the controversy and causing the Calvinists to "put forth a strong 'counter-remonstrance' plainly asserting absolute predestination and reprobation." Politics added to the fury of the conflict, which reached such a stage of violence that the Calvinists refused to submit to an edict of the states for toleration to both parties, and the Arminians found it necessary to guard themselves from violence by the aid of a guard of militia-men, notwithstanding which several lost their lives, and the learned Grotius, with others, was cast into prison. The battles that followed have doubtless helped to give us the "purer air" and the "broader view" of our day, when Christians differing in faith exhibit a better spirit, and theological disputants show much greater zeal for truth, and less for party.   On all sides the progress of our race toward the better day has been through effort, struggle, sacrifice, and much seeming loss.   When the theological giants, equipped with all the armor that learning, logic and rhetoric could supply, strode forth to what seemed merely drawn battles, and retired mutually worsted, there was indeed apparent loss of most valuable moral power, but it now seems that through all the conflict theological thought was taking a set in the right direction.   To-day it is a deep, broad current, nowhere more obvious than with the denominations professing to hold to the Westminster Confession and Catechisms.   Having at our very origin taken our bearing far away from the troubled waters of Calvinism, as Cumberland Presbyterians we now may opportunely invite our brethren still "driven up and down in Adria" to examine the theological chart by which we find smooth sailing on a sea of divine mercy unlimited by a partial atonement or an eternal decree of unconditional reprobation.

In proof of the alleged drift of theological thought, the following action, just adopted by the Presbytery of New York, and passed with but three dissenting votes, is pertinent and, as indicating wide-spread demand, is hopefully significant of a near grouping of Protestant bodies into fewer organizations, and thereby, as we may believe, of greater efficiency in the common work :

" Furthermore, as germane to the subject which the assembly had in mind in referring these questions to the presbyteries, your committee recommends that this presbytery overture the General Assembly to invite the co-operation of the Presbyterian and Reformed Churches of America and of Great Britain and Ireland to formulate a short and simple creed, couched, so far as may be, in Scripture language, and containing all the essential and necessary articles of the Westminster Confession, which creed shall be submitted for approval and adoption as the common creed of the Presbyterian and Reformed Churches of the world. We believe that there is a demand for such a creed, not as a substitute for our Confession, but only to summarize and supplement it for the work of the Church. We would and we must retain our standards, which we have as our family inherit-ance and as the safeguard of our ministry and of our institu-tions. But a brief and comprehensive creed, at once interpret-ing and representing those standards, would be welcomed by our Churches as most helpful and beneficent for the exposition of what we have meant, through all these years, by the 'system of doctrine taught in the Holy Scriptures.' We want no new doc-trines, but only a statement of the old doctrines made in the light and in the spirit of our present Christian activities, of our high privileges, and of our large obligations—a statement in which the love of God which is in Christ Jesus our Lord shall be central and dominant."

The following is the *creed* of the illustrious orator and states-man whose name is subscribed, as he communicated it to a friend, August, 1807, saying, "Some time ago I wrote down, for my own use, a few propositions in the shape of articles, intending to exhibit a very short summary of the doctrines of the Christian religion, as they impress my mind." The reasons given for his belief of each article are omitted:

"I believe in the existence of Almighty God, who created and governs the whole world.

"I believe that God exists in three persons.

"I believe the Scriptures of the Old and New Testament to be the will and word of God.

"I believe Jesus Christ to be the Son of God. And I believe there is no other way of salvation than through the merits of his atonement.   D. WEBSTER."

CHAPTER V.

A FULLER ACCOUNT OF THE ORIGIN OF THE WESTMINSTER SYMBOLS.

BESIDES their relation to our own Confession and Catechism, the Westminster Standards are doctrinal formulæ of very great interest. The circumstances under which they were formed, their contents, and the extent to which for nearly two hundred and fifty years they have anchored the best theological thought of the world, will forever invest them with interest to the student of the progress of religious thought.

On June 12, 1643, what was called the Long Parliament issued an ordinance calling an assembly to meet at Westminster, on the first day of July. On the 22d of June the King issued a proclamation forbidding the meeting, declaring that no acts done by them ought to be heeded by his subjects, and threatening that if they should meet he " would proceed against them with the utmost severity of the law." This proclamation had the effect to deter the Episcopalian members from attending, and thereby really furthered the cause of Presbyterian polity and Calvinistic theology. The King and Parliament alike claimed the right to reconstruct the Church; but many, even then, believed it was no business of either.

" When the Parliament issued the ordinance for calling together an assembly of divines," says Hetherington's History of the Westminster Assembly, " there was, it will be remembered, actually no legalized form of church government in England, so far as depended on the legislature. . . . . The chief object of the Parliament was, therefore, to determine what form of church

government was to be established by law in the room of that
which had been abolished." The unhappy state of things in
England is charged, by the writer last quoted, on the Prelatic
system—"how Prelacy had *governed* and how Prelacy had
taught the English people." "At first it showed its tyrannical
tendency by imposing ceremonies not warranted by the word
of God, and associated with popery, and by enforcing these without the slightest regard to tenderness of feeling or liberty of
conscience. Advancing on its despotic career, it interfered with
the forms and the language of worship, prescribing to man after
what manner, and in what terms, he was to address his Creator,
without regard to that Creator's commands. At length it
reached its extreme limits, and presumed to exercise absolute
control over the doctrines which Christ's ambassadors were to
teach, thus rashly interfering not merely with man's approach to
God, but also with God's message to man."

The order convoking the Westminster Assembly delegated to
one hundred and fifty-one persons the right to membership
therein, namely, ten Lords and twenty Commons as lay assess-
ors, and one hundred and twenty-one divines. It seems to show
a wish of fairness on the part of the Parliament, as Hetherington remarks, that they named men of all shades of opinions in
matters of church government, and that there was an honest
purpose to secure a competent discussion of the whole subject.

"At length the appointed day came ; and on Saturday, the 1st
of July, the members of the two Houses of Parliament named
in the ordinance, and many of the divines therein mentioned,
and a vast congregation met in the Abbey Church, Westminster.
Dr. Twisse, the appointed prolocutor of the assembly, preached
an elaborate sermon from John xiv. 18 : 'I will not leave you
comfortless. I will come unto you.'" No business being in
readiness for the assembly, it adjourned until Thursday of the
next week. "This very fact," observes Hetherington, "points
out one peculiarity of the Westminster Assembly—it was neither

a convocation nor a Presbyterian Synod or General Assembly, and it could not be either the one or the other, for the Prelatic form of Church government had been abolished and there was no other yet in existence. The true theory of the Westminster Assembly comprises two main elements: (1) There was a Christian Church in England, but not organized; (2) and the civil power, avowing Christianity, had called an assembly of divines for the purpose of consulting together respecting those points of government and discipline which require the sanction of civil authority for their full efficiency."

By agreement all propositions were to originate with Parliament and go then to the assembly. Strict rules of procedure in business were adopted at the start, and such as seemed to aim at securing fairness on all questions and to all parties. To further secure the honest ends aimed at, it was resolved at the opening that every member of the assembly, whether a lord, common, or divine, should bind himself by solemn oath before taking a seat, which oath ran in this way: "I do seriously promise and vow in the presence of Almighty God that in this assembly, whereof I am a member, I will maintain nothing in point of doctrine but what I believe to be most agreeable to the word of God, nor in point of discipline but what I shall conceive to conduce most to the glory of God, and the good and peace of his Church," and it is recorded that this protestation was appointed to be read afresh every Monday morning, that its solemn influence might be constantly felt.

Preliminaries settled, the Parliament sent the assembly an order to "revise the Thirty-nine Articles, for the purpose of simplifying, clearing, and vindicating the doctrines contained therein." About ten weeks had been occupied in this discussion, only the first fifteen of the Thirty-nine Articles having been under discussion, when occurrences gave a new and unexpected turn to the deliberations of the grave body. Upon the first purpose to call the Westminster Assembly the Parliament

applied to the Scottish Church to send commissioners, and steps
toward granting the request were taken by the Church, which
appointed some ministers and elders to be in readiness. But
owing to delay in the meeting of the proposed assembly, or because of not wishing to interfere in the strife between the King
and his Parliament, the Scottish delegates declined to attend.
In consequence of this failure English commissioners attended
the Scottish General Assembly early in August, 1643, presenting
an appeal signed by seventy divines, "supplicating aid in their
desperate condition," which "letter," says one historian "was so
lamentable that it drew tears from many eyes." But how assistance could be given to England without jeopardizing Scotland
was the very difficult problem of the hour. The commissioners
had assured their minds with reference to the sincerity of the
Parliament, but "the Scottish statesmen and ministers could not
but perceive that if the King should succeed in subjugating his
Parliament he would then be able to assail Scotland with an irresistible force." Another difficulty grew out of the fact that the
English commissioners sought aid for the defense of the civil
liberties of both countries, while the entire spirit of the contest
in which Scotland had been engaged was of a religious character, and only in defense of religious liberty. The famous document known as the "Solemn League and Covenant" was the
result, which, combining the idea of mutual aid in defense of
civil liberty with that of aid in the defense of religious liberty,
claimed as its objects "the reformation and defense of religion,
the honor and happiness of the King, and the peace and safety
of the three kingdoms of Scotland, England, and Ireland." It
was passed unanimously on the 17th of August by the Scottish
Assembly, "amid the applause of some and the bursting tears
of a deep, full, and sacred joy of others; and in the afternoon,
with the same cordial unanimity, passed the Convention of
Estates."

A copy of the "Solemn League and Covenant" was forwarded

the English Parliament and the Westminster Assembly, and, with "slight verbal alterations" for the sake of explanation, it was agreed to by all the assembly "except Dr. Burgess, who continued to resist it and to refuse his assent for several days, till he incurred the serious displeasure of both assembly and Parliament, which he at last averted by yielding." Accordingly, on September 15, the Scottish commissioners consented to take seats in the Westminster Assembly, only six in all, who were welcomed with great kindness and courtesy in three successive speeches. On the 25th of September both branches of Parliament subscribed the "Solemn League and Covenant," and in the most impressive manner "the prolocutor read it from the pulpit, slowly and aloud, pausing at the close of every article, while the whole audience of statesmen and divines arose, and, with their right hands held up to heaven, worshiped the great name of God and gave this sacred pledge." Speaking of this event, a prominent member of the assembly declared it "a new period and crisis of the most great affair which these hundred years has exercised these dominions," and Hetherington adds that "he was not mistaken; it was indeed the commencement of a new period in the history of the Christian Church, though that period has not yet run its full round, nor reached its crisis— a crisis which will shake and new mold the world." The great principles set forth in this memorable "League and Covenant," while they may not justify the claim that "it is the wisest, the sublimest, and the most sacred document ever framed by uninspired men," certainly do render it a most remarkable deliverance in its spirit, its aim, and its clear enunciation of truths that are indeed new molding the religious world.

The course affairs had taken led the Parliament to direct the Assembly to lay aside the work of revising the thirty-nine articles, in order to prepare as speedily as practicable "such a discipline and government as may be most agreeable to God's holy word." The country was ecclesiastically, no less politically, in a state of the utmost confusion and unrest. Because Prelacy had been set aside or for other reasons "there had sprung up a great number of sects, holding all various shades of opinion in religious matters, from such as were simply absurd down to those that were licentiously wild and glaringly blasphemous. It is almost impossible even to enumerate the sectarians that rushed prominently into public manifestation when the overthrow of the prelatic hierachy and government rendered it safe for them to appear, and it would be wrong to pollute our pages with a statement of their pernicious and horrible tenets." The Presbyterians, the Independents, and the Erastians were the three principal parties as to theories of ecclesiastical polity, the Erastians claiming that all ecclesiastical power belongs to the civil authority. The debates, contentions, and intrigues by which these several parties sought to gain the ascendency make up a large part of the proceedings through which was finally reached a system of discipline and government which has gained wide acceptance. In October, 1647, both branches of the Parliament accepted the results of the labors of the Assembly, which was regarded as "the final settlement of the Presbyterian Church government, so far as that was done by the Long Parliament, in accordance with the advice of the Westminster Assembly of Divines." But this establishment of the Presbyterian government was only "until the end of the next session of Parliament," or about a year, before the expiration of which period "the Parliament itself had sunk beneath the power of Cromwell, whose policy was to establish no form of Church government, but to keep every thing dependent on himself, though his chief favors were bestowed on the Independents."

Of the reverses which in the immediate future awaited Presbyterianism in England our limits will not permit us to speak. The brief reference—too brief to be satisfactory—to some of the leading events of one of the most remarkable epochs in the world's history serves to indicate the heat of discussion in which was forged a system of ecclesiastical government at once compact, symmetrical, and efficient, and justifying perhaps, the high claim of its advocates, that it is, "of all systems that have ever existed in the Church, the most agreeable to the principles of Church government which may be deduced from Scripture."

Resuming the work of framing a Confession of Faith, the Westminster Assembly appointed a committee to prepare and arrange the main propositions which were to be discussed and digested into a system, who reduced the whole to thirty-two distinct heads, which heads were subdivided into sections. The committee resolved itself into sub-committees, "each of which took a specific topic for the sake of exact and concentrated deliberation." When the entire committee had agreed upon a report from a sub-committee, that article was reported to the Assembly, and "again subjected to the most careful and minute investigation, in every paragraph, sentence, and word." So the work was carried to completion. According to Hetherington, whose history of the Assembly is unquestioned authority, "throughout the deliberations of the Assembly while composing the Confession of Faith, there prevailed almost an entire and perfect harmony." On the doctrine of election they had "long and tough debates." The only other article that occasioned much debate is this: "The Lord Jesus, as King and Head of his Church, has therein appointed a government in the hands of Church officers distinct from the civil magistrate." This proposition was understood as condemning the spirit of Erastianism, and hence was bitterly opposed by the Erastian party, but was finally adopted, there being but one dissenting vote. Copies of the Confession were printed, that the members of Parliament might severally examine it, and in March, 1648, a meeting was held for comparing their opinions, both houses participating, the result of which is expressed by the following record: "The Commons this day (March 22), at a conference, presented the Lords with the Confession of Faith passed by them, with some alterations, viz., that they do agree with their Lordships, and so with the Assembly, in the doctrinal part, and desire the same may be made public, that this kingdom, and all the Reformed Churches of Christendom, may see the Parliament of England differ not in doctrine."

It has been well observed that the Westminster Confession deserves the attention of all students of theology, not only as a remarkable monument of Christian learning, but as the most representative expression of a great spiritual movement which has tinged the national thought of Britain, and modified the course of its history. Of its thirty-three chapters, only twenty-one are distinctly doctrinal. It makes the doctrine of the eternal, unconditional divine decree fundamental, subordinating all others to it. In the Reformed Churches it has evoked an amount of study and discussion second only to that bestowed on the Scriptures. It has divided Christian bodies and reunited them. What of its hold upon the Christian world of to-day?

Dr. C. A. Briggs, of Union Theological Seminary, who claims to have spared no time, labor, or expense necessary to the investigation of the question, declares that from the Westminster Standards, in their historical sense, "modern Presbyterianism has departed all along the line." After declaring the Westminster symbols "the most elaborate and definite of all the creeds of Protestantism," he adds: "But it is clear to any one who has studied the genesis of the Westminster Standards, and the doctrinal history of Great Britain and America, that the Presbyterian and Congregational Churches have drifted in many important respects from the Westminster orthodoxy." In his book suggestively entitled *Whither?* Dr. Briggs devotes several chapters to the proof of his assumption that "the American Presbyterian Church has drifted away from the Westminster Standards," and sums up the result in the declaration, "We have seen that the Presbyterian Church has departed from the nine chapters of the Confession considered in the present chapter, into serious error. In the whole realm of doctrine and practice contra-confessional views, that strike at essential and necessary articles, and destroy the Westminster system, are either entertained by large numbers of our ministry and people, or else are allowed to remain unchallenged by the orthodox, and are tolerated as if they were errors of small importance."

While I can not indorse the theological system of Dr. Briggs, I heartily commend his book for its fair and independent utterances, and as exhibiting much valuable research, upon which I shall have occasion to draw for illustration in the pages that are to follow. The following sentences embody truths of vast importance and of wide application in the great problem of the evolution of a system of theology in harmony with all truth, as one must be to be a true system: "None of the older divines gave the human reason its proper place in religion and theology." "The Bible . . . . does not war against the truths of nature, of the reason, or of history." . . . . "The sacred Scriptures are for the whole world, and for all time. As man grows in the knowledge of nature, of himself, and of history, he will grow in the knowledge of the Scriptures."

PART II.

Doctrinal Statement and Exposition.

DOCTRINAL STATEMENT AND EXPOSITION.

CHAPTER I.

OF THE HOLY SCRIPTURES.

THE system of doctrine held and taught by the Cumberland Presbyterian Church is comprised in its *Confession of Faith* and the appended *Catechism*. It is not proposed to present in these pages a systematic commentary on our standards, but rather to give prominence to the statement and discussion of such doctrines as set forth our *system* of theology, and especially as that system is distinguished from what is popularly known as the Calvinistic system. It will fall within my aim to treat more at length also any doctrines on which there is current discussion in our Church. Our Standards were revised so lately as 1873, and rather hurriedly for a procedure of so great importance in its relation to the peace and purity of the body. It could not have been otherwise than that time for careful examination of all the phraseology employed by the revisers would have developed differences of opinion as to the meaning of some of the doctrinal statements, and as to the propriety of some of the language used. It is a safe rule to hold that subordinate parts are to be interpreted in harmony with the system of doctrine embodied in the Confession, and all parts with reference to the Scripture passages cited as proof-texts.

The doctrinal statements of the Confession are grouped under thirty-six leading topics, under which heads are one hundred and fifteen specifications. Under the first general topic, the *Holy Scriptures*, we have these four specifications:—

"1. The Holy Scriptures comprise all the books of the Old and the New Testament which are received as canonical, and which are given by inspiration of God to be the rule of faith and practice." [Here follows an enumeration of the books of the Old and the New Testament.]

" 2. The authority of the Holy Scriptures depends not upon the testimony of any man or Church, but upon God alone."

" 3. The whole counsel of God concerning all things necessary for his own glory—in creation, providence, and man's salvation —is either expressly stated in the Scriptures, or by necessary consequence may be deduced therefrom ; unto which nothing at any time is to be added by man, or from the traditions of men ; nevertheless, we acknowledge the inward illumination of the Spirit of God to be necessary for the saving understanding of such things as are revealed in the word."

" 4. The best rule of interpretation of the Scriptures is the comparison of scripture with scripture."

The first item is doubtless intended for a definition of the Scriptures, but it serves to remind us that if the function of language be not " to conceal thought," words are often so collated as to express thought very imperfectly. The language implies that only as many of the books of the Old and the New Testament as " are received as canonical " are comprised in the Holy Scriptures. But are there in the Old and the New Testament any books not received as canonical ?

The Westminster Confession defines a little more clearly, thus, " Under the name of Holy Scripture, or the word of God written, are now contained all the books of the Old and New Testaments, which are these," the enumeration following.

Whether the added relative clause in our Confession, " and which are given by inspiration of God to be the rule of faith and practice," is further restrictive as to the books (of the two Testaments) that are to be comprised in the Holy Scriptures, or whether it is an independent assertion of the inspiration of the canonical books, it is difficult to decide. Notwithstanding its obscurity—a criticism indulged in no censorious spirit, and that may serve as an apology for obscurities in these pages—the first item sets forth three important propositions, namely:

1. Cumberland Presbyterians receive as canonical the thirty-nine books of the Old Testament, and the twenty-seven books of the New Testament, as these sixty-six books are held by all other Protestant Churches.

2. That the Holy Scriptures, comprised in the books specified, are " given by inspiration of God."

3. That they are given " to be the rule of faith and practice," or, in the stronger expression of the fifth section of the Introduction to the Confession, " the only infallible rule of faith and practice."

For the rejection of the books usually included in what is termed the Apocrypha received by the Roman Church, the following reasons are asigned: (1) The authors of these books do not claim inspiration; (2) the books contradict one another, and contradict also the books usually called canonical; (3) the Jews never acknowledged them to be inspired; (4) they were written after the days of Malachi, with whom, as the Jews believed, the gift of prophecy ceased; (5) they are never quoted by Christ or his apostles; (6) they were not received in the first ages of Christianity as canonical; (7) in the Roman Catholic Church they were not received by the most learned divines, until late in the sixteenth century the Council of Trent declared for the inspiration of the Apocryphal books.

There is wide difference of opinion as to what is meant by the statement that the Scriptures are " given by inspiration of God," some holding that only the doctrines contained in these books are divinely communicated, but that the writings are not inspired; while another view asserts such a divine guidance of the minds of the writers as secured an inspired statement of the divinely imparted doctrines; and a third view asserts verbal inspiration,

4

or that the very words in which a revelation was first made were suggested by the Holy Ghost. If there is in the Cumberland Presbyterian Church a current theory in regard to the exact import of the "inspiration of the Scriptures," the writer is unable to state it. It is possible for Christians to differ widely in respect to this point, and yet all hold that "all Scripture is given by inspiration," and all hold it in a sense that will render the Scriptures "profitable for doctrine, for reproof, for correction, for instruction in righteousness." Whatever may be the truth in regard to the original manuscripts through which inspired men first gave to the world a revelation of the will of God, not one of these manuscripts is known to be now in existence, and hence it is certain that we now can have but copies and translations that have come to us through the fidelity of pious and learned men who did not claim the gift of inspiration.

The following passage from Dr. A. A. Hodge's Commentary on the Westminster Confession presents the view of a plenary inspiration, extending even to "infallible expression in words:"

"The books of Scripture were written by the instrumentality of men, and the national and personal peculiarities of their authors have been evidently as freely expressed in their writing, and their natural faculties, intellectual and moral, as freely exercised in their production, as those of the authors of any other writings. Nevertheless, these books are, one and all, in thought and verbal expression, in substance and form, wholly the word of God, conveying, with absolute accuracy and divine authority, all that God meant them to convey, without any human admixtures or additions. This was accomplished by a supernatural influence of the Spirit of God acting on the spirits of the sacred writers, called 'inspiration,' which accompanied them uniformly in what they wrote, and which, without violating the free operation of their faculties, yet directed them in all they wrote, and secured the infallible expression of it in words. The nature of this divine influence we, of course, can no more understand than

we can in the case of any other miracle.   But the effects are plain
and certain, viz.: that all written under it is the very word of
God, of infallible truth, and of divine authority; and this infallibility and authority attach as well to the verbal expression in
which the revelation is conveyed, as to the matter of revelation
itself."

This doctrine of "verbal inspiration," taught by Hodge and
the Princeton theologians, is strenuously opposed by Dr. Briggs,
in his work already mentioned, as being a wide departure from
the historic teachings of the Presbyterian Church.   "These
Princeton divines risk the inspiration and authority of the
Bible," Dr Briggs goes on to say, "upon a single proved error.
Such a position is a serious and a hazardous departure from
Protestant orthodoxy.   It imperils the faith of all Christians
who have been taught this doctrine.   They can not escape the
evidence of errors in the Scriptures.   This evidence will be
thrust upon them whether they will or not. . . . . No more dangerous doctrine has ever come from the pen of men.   It has
cost the Church the loss of thousands.   It will cost us tens of
thousands and hundreds of thousands unless the true Westminster doctrine is speedily put in its place.   This false doctrine cir-
culates in a tract bearing the imprint of the Presbyterian Board
of Publication, among our ministers and people, poisoning their
souls and misleading them into dangerous error."

These conflicting views are cited to show, not only the extent
of the divergence of opinion with respect to the sense in which
inspiration may be held, but that scholars of high reputation,
who are accredited teachers in theological schools of the same
denomination, arrive at widely different conclusions in their investigation of this question.

Dr. T. C. Blake, in his compend of theology, after stating the
two principal theories of inspiration, adds that "the preponder-
ance of authority is certainly in favor of the latter method—
verbal inspiration," and proceeds to argue thus:

"It is a fact, which no one will .call in question, that we think in words. Words are the vehicles of *thought* as well as of *communication*. It is as impossible to *think* without words as it is to speak without words. This being true, how could God make a revelation to man without words? and if words were employed to convey the mind or will of God, the question arises, *whose* words were thus employed? Most certainly these were God's, else they could not be a revelation from him. The *ideas* could not have been given without the *words*, because without them they could not have been conceived."

If we allow that Dr. Blake's theory is true as to the original documents in which God revealed himself to man, it proves too much for any book that is now claimed to be a revelation, or, in other words, leaves the world without a revelation. If we have an English New Testament, what one of the many versions can lay claim to that distinction, according to Dr. Blake's test of inspiration?

The solemn practical question perplexing many pious minds doubtless is, whether modern criticism really leaves the world any scriptures that may be called a revelation from God in any sense that would constitute them an "infallible rule of faith and practice." Does it leave the world a Bible? In view of obvious facts there seems to be but one reasonable answer to this question, and that is in the affirmative. Not only so, but the versions of the Bible now extant in hundreds of the languages of the world, some exhibiting greater and some less fidelity to the text most approved by modern criticism, are all to be regarded as the word of God in every feature necessary to convey to men the will of God and the great scheme of gospel redemption. They produce like effect throughout the world. Through their instrumentality men are everywhere born into the same spiritual life, begotten unto the same blessed hope of salvation and everlasting life.

Dr. A. F. Mitchell, in his introduction to the Minutes of the

Westminster Assembly, declares that "if any chapter in the Confession was more carefully framed than another it was this, 'of the Holy Scriptures.' . . . And I think it requires only to be fairly examined to show that its framers were at more special pains than the authors of any other Confession: 1. To avoid mixing up the question of the canonicity of particular books with the question of their authorship, where any doubt at all existed on the latter point; 2. To leave open all reasonable questions as to the mode and degree of inspiration which could be consistently left open by those who accepted the Scriptures as the *infallible rule* of faith and practice; 3. To refrain from claiming for the text such absolute purity, and for the Hebrew vowel points such antiquity, as was claimed in the Swiss *Formula Concordiæ*, while asserting that the originals of the Scripture are, after the lapse of ages, still pure and perfect for all those purposes for which they were given; 4. To declare that the sense of the Scripture in any particular place is not manifold, but one, and so raise an earnest protest against that system of spiritualizing the text which had been too much countenanced by some of the most eminent of the Fathers, and many of the best of the mystics."

The best scholarship and thought lead to these conclusions touching this question of so very grave importance:

1. That plenary inspiration of the Scriptures as we now have them, or such inspiration as extends to the words of the Scriptures, and excludes the possibility of error in every particular, can not be defended. 2. That for all the purposes for which the Scriptures were given, namely, to "teach what man is to believe concerning God, and what duty God requires of man," they are truly inspired, having been given to the world through men who gave utterance as they were moved by the Holy Ghost, and that the Scriptures are thus an infallible rule of faith and practice. 3. That the claim for the plenary inspiration of the Scriptures as we now have them, whatever may have been true as to "the

ipsissima verba of the original autographs," is pernicious in its tendency, as being a claim not justified by the facts in the case, and thereby calculated to beget distrust in the intelligent mind, as to the general claim of the Bible to be the word of God. The evil tendency may not be so serious as would be inferred from the declaration of Dr. Briggs, that " no more dangerous doctrine has ever come from the pen of men," but with respect to this question, as to all others, it must be that the Church can build securely only as it builds on the foundation of truth. The sooner we come to rest upon the truth, the less will be the damage to be repaired.

As another illustration of the manner in which the docrine of plenary inspiration has impressed the minds of many of the profoundest thinkers of our times, we cite the following paragraphs from M. Guizot's *Meditations on Christianity :*

"And yet this is what is pretended by fervent and learned men, who maintain that all, absolutely all, in the Scriptures is divinely inspired, the words as well as the ideas, all the words used upon all subjects, the material of language as well as the doctrine that lies at its base."

"In this assertion I see but deplorable confusion, leading to profound misapprehension of the meaning and the object of the sacred books. It was not God's purpose to give instruction to men in grammar, and if not in grammar, neither was it any more God's purpose to give instruction in geology, astronomy, geography, or chronology. It is on their relations with their Creator, upon duties of men toward him and toward each other, upon the rule of faith and conduct in life, that God has lighted them by light from heaven."

" The Scriptures speak upon all subjects; circumstances connected with the finite world are there incessantly mixed with perspectives of infinity; but it is only to the latter, to that future of which they permit us to snatch a view, and to the laws they impose on men, that the divine inspiration addresses itself; God only pours his light in quarters which man's eye and man's labor can not reach; for all that remains the sacred books speak the language used and understood by the generations to whom they are addressed. God does not, even when he inspires them, transport into future domains of science the interpreters, or the nations to whom he sends them; he takes them both as he finds them, with their traditions, their notions, their degree of knowledge or ignorance as respects the finite world, of its phenomena and its laws. . . . . Whatever true or false science we find in the Scriptures upon the subject of the finite world, proceeds from the writers themselves or their contemporaries; they have spoken as they believed, or as those believed who surrounded them when they spoke. On the other hand, the light thrown over the infinite, the law laid down, and the perspective opened by that same light, these are what proceed from God, and which he has inspired in the Scriptures. Their object is essentially moral and practical; they express the ideas, employ the images, and speak the language best calculated to produce a powerful effect upon the soul, to regenerate and to save it."

But the question at the bottom of the whole discussion, and fundamental to the very idea of religion, is, Can we be assured that the writings we call the Scriptures are in a true sense inspired? Has God truly spoken to his rational creatures in this world? No question that engages our thoughts can have profounder interest than this one. Among the most intense yearnings of the human soul is its ceaseless petition for a revelation with respect to the unseen and that which is to be. "Show us the Father, and it sufficeth us!" Aside from the Christian Scriptures, the world knows no book whose claims to inspiration will at all stand the test of reason. Aside from these, the soul's cry for light as to duty and destiny is taunted with but an empty echo. But in these Scriptures themselves it is claimed that God spake to Moses, to David, to Isaiah, to Jeremiah, to Malachi; that in later times he spake to Peter, to James, to Paul, to John,

thus so filling up the measure of divine revelation as to make it
indeed an infallible rule of faith and practice. A firm conviction
that these Scriptures are from God is at once the most rational
support and the most powerful stimulus to good that can come
to a human soul. "I have read the sacred volumes over and
over again," says M. Guizot; "I have perused them in very
different dispositions of mind, at one time studying them as
great historical documents, at another admiring them as sublime works of poetry. I have experienced an extraordinary
impression, quite different from either curiosity or admiration.
I have felt myself the listener to a language other than that of
the chronicler or the poet, and under the influence of a breath
issuing from other sources than human. . . . . God is there,
always present, acting. It is the God One and Supreme, All
Powerful, the Creator, the Eternal. . . . . These books are really,
with respect to the religious problems that beset man's thoughts,
the Light and the Voice of God, revealing the duties which God
enjoins upon men in the course of their present life, and the
prospects which he opens to them beyond the imperfect and
limited world where this life passes."

Whoever will thus come to the earnest, candid, persevering
study of the Scriptures, yielding himself to a purpose to do the
will of God as that will becomes manifest, and opening his heart
to the guidance of the Holy Spirit, will most certainly experience that God is speaking to him through these Scriptures,
and that they are able to "make him wise unto salvation." So
he declared who came a Light into the world: "If any man will
(*honestly resolve to*) do his will (*as made known to him*), he shall
know of the doctrine (*I teach*), whether it be of God, or whether
I speak of myself." In his comment on this passage, the younger
Bengel says: "But that, in its turn, a more intimate access to
the truth is thrown open by the obedience of the will, both this
very declaration of the divine Savior, and the whole of Scripture
besides, openly testify." To the same sentiment testify the

passages, "He that followeth me shall not walk in darkness, but shall have the light of life," and, "If ye continue in my word, then are ye my disciples indeed; and ye shall know the truth."

Aside from this internal witness to the inspiration of the Scriptures, which springs from obedience to the truth as it is perceived, and from the illumination of the Holy Spirit, there is an intellectual assent to the inspiration of the Scriptures, which arises from the study of what are called the evidences of inspiration—a conviction that may come to the man who fears, rather than wishes, the Bible true, and is in willful rebellion against perceived obligation. Viewed in this light, the problem of inspiration is one which falls within the province of reason. What reason approves we accept; what it disapproves we must reject. Our intellectual and moral being knows no higher law. We can accept no book as inspired, on the simple ground that it claims to be inspired. In like manner the whole problem of Christianity falls within the domain of man's reason, according to the verdict of which it must be accepted or rejected. As one of the profoundest thinkers of the century has said: "If Christianity be not fundamentally in accord with our original constitution, and will not restore man to a true manhood, and the highest manhood, we can not accept it. . . . . Nothing that can be shown to be really in opposition either to reason or the moral nature of man, can be from God." It is true, also, that each generation must decide for itself the claims of Christianity and of the Bible. We do not accept even the propositions of geometry as true because Euclid declared them true, but we demonstrate them for ourselves.

That man has a moral nature is attested by his consciousness. He is, in fact, under moral law. It is equally true that he is endowed with what may be called a religious nature. In all time, everywhere man has worshiped. The history of the race is not more a history of any thing than of religious beliefs and ceremonies. Equally true is it that man has a longing for

immortality, and a perpetual craving for knowledge of the hereafter that awaits him. These things being true, if we assume
that there is an Infinite Intelligence, wise and good, who is the
Author of our being, a revelation of the will of that Creator
seems a most reasonable assumption, if not indeed a very
demand of reason. Such a revelation being clearly possible,
manifestly desirable, and absolutely necessary in order that man
may realize the highest good of which his moral and spiritual
faculties render him capable, we should come to the serious
investigation of this momentous question expecting to find a
revelation made through individuals of the race supernaturally
guided for that purpose.

If one were to happen upon a piece of mechanism unlike any
he had before seen, he might be helped to understand its object
and its value by learning when, and where, and by whom it was
constructed; but these items of information would be far less
satisfactory than that which would come from an investigation
of the structure and capabilities of the mechanism. From the
mechanism itself would he determine whether it were a phono-
graph, a chronometer, or a musical instrument. So, principally
and ultimately, the conclusion we reach in regard to the inspiration of the Scriptures must depend on what we find the Scriptures
to be, and what they are capable of doing for man. Given the
Scriptures as we have them, and the known capabilities of the
human mind, can the Scriptures be the product of uninspired
mind? Given man's moral and spiritual nature, and his need in
view of his own consciousness of being in a fallen state, is the
Bible fundamentally in accord with his constitution, and will it
restore him to the highest and happiest manhood of which he is
capable? Practically, Christianity is a daily, persistent miracle
of salvation from sin through the power of the Cross, bringing
peace and comfort and hope in prospect of a better and endless
life beyond the present unsatisfactory environment of mortal
life. Can this system of salvation have originated in the con-

ception of unaided human reason? One of the brightest intellects of England has said, " If the mind be vigorous and sane, it is incomparably easier to admit the divinity of Christ than to reject it, and read the Gospels without being perplexed and confounded." So, as it seems to us, we may justly say of the Scriptures, a series of writings given to the world through the long interval of fifteen hundred years, yet all harmoniously blending in one grand system developed as the ages passed, and revealing a grand consummation to which all parts are conspiring, it is incomparably easier to accept them as the products of minds divinely guided, than to account for them on any other hypothesis.

What are usually styled the "evidences of Christianity" embrace a great variety of proofs of the inspiration of the Scriptures, and these proofs have been, and to the end of time will continue to be, cumulative. With a better understanding of man's own nature, of the world about him, of the adaptation of the Bible to his need, and of the unfolding of the divine purpose revealed in the Bible, will come increased conviction of its harmony with all truth and of its divine origin and mission. Its inspiration has been argued from the claims of its writers to inspiration; from the fulfillment of prophecies contained therein; from the many miracles wrought by Christ in the presence of numerous competent witnesses; from the unity of its teachings; from its spotless morality; from the moral character of its writers; from its blessed effects upon individuals, society, and nations; from the dignity of its style and the sublimity of its language; from the correspondence between its teachings and what is called natural religion; from the inherent power of Christianity to propagate itself; from the absolute moral excellence of the Founder of Christianity, who was the fulfillment of the types and prophecies of the Old Testament, and from his life, teachings, work, death, and resurrection, which are the burden of the revelation of the New Testament.

Upon every one of these "evidences" volumes have been written, as also upon others not here enumerated. The last specified, or what we may designate "Christ's testimony to Christianity," is the central idea with which all must stand, or all be abandoned as fable or imposture. Spinoza, the Pantheistic Jew, of Amsterdam, perceived its logical relation to the system of Christianity when he declared, "If I could persuade myself that Jesus of Nazareth wrought one miracle, that he raised the dead, for instance, I would dash my system to pieces, and at once accept the belief of common Christianity." Christ is the perpetual unanswerable testimony to Christianity, and thereby to the inspiration of the Bible. Veiled in flesh that he might tabernacle with men, and pour into their souls his own thoughts and tender sympathies, at the appointed time Christ steps from the bosom of eternity upon the platform of earth, and starts the world upon a new career of thought and feeling and action. "One God, one Messiah, one Humanity! the whole race occupying one broad level of moral equality, with no recognized distinction in the sight of heaven but that of personal character! And yet this initial Idea of the new Era, so intensely hated, so simple that a child's mind can apprehend it when once stated, shining by its own light, touched and roused at once the popular heart, the common conscience, the universal reason and judgment of mankind, so as to win conviction, to revolutionize opinion, to uplift and reconstruct individual and social character throughout every rank and class of men and women, from the highest to the lowest, from the center of the metropolis to the hut of the wilderness. And so onward from that day to the present, this Messianic Idea has developed itself in history as the chief reforming power on the face of the earth." *

"How was it," asks the author of the foregoing extract, "that

---

* *Self-witnessing Character of the New Testament*, by Rev. Wm. Hague, D.D.

this Galilean fisherman, who had so lately left his boats and nets, arose so quickly to this eminence as the teacher and prophet of the ages, inculcating in a few words the *one principle* that, despite the mightiest antagonisms, has been the life-power of the world's progress during the eighteen intervening centuries, and is recognized at once as the living force of the present, the hope of the future?"

To this question no infidel has been able to frame a reply at all so credible as that given by St. Peter when, before the multitude assembled in the house of Cornelius to hear of the wonderful words of Christ, he "opened his mouth and said:"

"Of a truth I perceive that God is no respecter of persons, but in every nation he that feareth him and worketh righteousness is accepted with him. The word which *God sent unto the children of Israel*, preaching peace by Jesus Christ (he is Lord of all), that word ye know, which was published throughout all Judea, and began from Galilee, after the baptism which John preached; how *God anointed Jesus of Nazareth with the Holy Ghost and with power ;* who went about doing good, and healing all that were oppressed with the devil; *for God was with him.* Him God raised up the third day and showed him openly. And he commanded us to preach unto the people, and to testify that it is *he which was ordained of God* to be the judge of quick and dead."—Acts x. 35, etc.

We can not give too much prominence to the thought that Christ is the most convincing testimony to Christianity, and thereby to the inspiration of the Book which bears to the world the teachings of Christianity. Never do the pages of that Book seem so luminous with inspiration as when read in the light of the Sun of Righteousness viewed in his life, his doctrine, and his functions as prophet, priest, and king. It is a matter of personal experience with the writer that the arguments which have produced the profoundest conviction of the inspiration of the Scriptures, have been, not learned homilies on the authenticity and genuineness of the several books, or on theories of inspiration, but plain scriptural sermons exalting Christ in his person and offices. The last time it was our privilege to hear that eloquent and earnest minister of precious memory in the Cumberland Presbyterian Church, Rev. A. M. Bryan, D.D., his text, John x. 27: "For him hath God the Father sealed," led him to discuss the divine attestation of the mission of Christ as the Redeemer of men, which attestation the speaker found in the prophecies fulfilled in Christ, in the miracles he wrought, in the circumstances of his death, in the stupendous fact of his resurrection, and in the power of his life and teachings to renew a world spiritually dead, all of which was presented with such clearness and such fervor as to beget profound conviction in his great audience. And so, as it seems to us, will it ever be that he who has most of Christ in his argument will have most power to convince men that the Bible is inspired, and that Christianity is of divine origin.

If we admit the inspiration of the Scriptures, it follows that we accept them as an infallible rule of faith and practice. It is for the specific purpose of instructing man as to what he shall believe concerning God, and how, as a rational creature responsible for his conduct, he shall behave toward his fellows and his Creator, that this supernatural revelation was made. Embodied in written language, that revelation has been transmitted through the centuries, and will be transmitted to the end of time, and through the printing-press these Scriptures may now find their way to every inhabitant of earth. It is altogether a thing possible that "the earth shall be full of the knowledge of the Lord, as the waters cover the sea."

The second item in the Confession, which declares that "the authority of the Holy Scriptures depends not upon the testimony of any man or Church, but upon God alone," is retained, in abbreviated form, from the Westminster Confession. It is designed to declare the doctrine of the Reformation and the

"boast of Protestantism" that every man should read and interpret the Scriptures for himself. Catholicism insists that an infallible Church is the source of all authoritative interpretation.
It makes "the Scriptures a product of the Church, while in fact
the Church is a product of the Scriptures." Individual independence and individual responsibility are of the very essence
of Christianity, and its legitimate product everywhere. Bondage
to "tradition" (things handed down) has been one of the heaviest
yokes on the neck of humanity, and especially with respect to
religion. When Christ was upon earth the Jews were serving
the "traditions of the elders;" between Roman Catholics and
the word of God stand the "traditions of the Church;" and
with too many Protestants there is manifest bondage to traditions of confessions, time honored standards, great names, the
fathers, etc. There is a conservatism that is healthful, and
a respect for the fathers that is becoming, and creeds, commentaries, decrees of councils, and systems of theology may be
helpful to the inquirer after truth, but beyond and above all
these stand the Scriptures, to which every man should come for
himself under a sense of solemn obligation to receive and defend
the truth as he believes it taught therein.

The third item of the section teaches :—

(a) That the Scriptures are a complete rule, as revealing the
whole counsel of God so far as it is needful for man to know
that counsel in order to secure his own salvation and rightly to
discharge the practical duties of life, so as to glorify God
therein.

(b) That to this completed revelation nothing is to be at any
time added by man or from the traditions of men.

(c) That "the inward illumination of the Spirit of God" is
necessary for "the saving understanding of such things as are
revealed in the word."

Cumberland Presbyterians believe that this illumination of the
Spirit necessary to the saving understanding of the Scriptures is

given to every man. As in Adam all died unto spiritual good, so in Christ are all made alive to the ability to hear, understand and believe the gospel. This Spirit of illumination is given to reprove the world of sin, of righteousness, and of judgment; and leaves without reasonable excuse all hearers of the word who reject it, since by submitting themselves to the bestowed Spiritual illumination—a gift co-extensive with the loss occasioned by the fall—they would be guided, through the instrumentality of this word, to faith, obedience, holiness, and heaven.

The fourth item contains what it denominates "the best rule of interpretation of the Scriptures," namely, "the comparison of scripture with scripture."

This rule assumes that the Scriptures are a grand unity, a system of truth harmonious in all its parts. As the Westminster Confession declares, "when there is a question about the true and full sense of any Scripture (which [sense] is not manifold, but one), it must be searched and known by other places that speak more plainly." Again and again in the history of interpretation do we see the mischievous effects of building a system of dogmatic theology on a passage or two of the Bible taken without reference to their logical relation to the scheme of revealed truth, and then proceeding to interpret the Bible by this preconceived theological system. Canon Farrar, in his *Early Days of Christianity*, charges Calvin with "explaining away" a passage that favors Arminianism, instead of "explaining" it, appropriately adding, "but the Calvinists had no monopoly in the distortion of the plain meaning of the sacred words—an error which belongs, alas! to all sects and all religious partisans alike."

An open Bible for all the world, is the genius of Protestantism. As in the Pentecostal baptism the disciples were endowed with miraculous power "to speak with other tongues, as the Spirit gave them utterance," in order that Parthians and Medes and Elamites and all other nationalities present might hear in their own tongues the wonderful works of God, so is it manifestly the divine purpose that an open Bible, revealing God, and the way of salvation through a Redeemer, shall be given to all the inhabitants of earth, and in the language wherein all may read for themselves. Thus building on the word of God, with their brief Confession outlining only the fundamental doctrines of that word, Cumberland Presbyterians do heartily subscribe the sentiment of Chillingworth, " The Bible ! the Bible ! the religion of Protestants." Never, seemingly, was the power of the open Bible more clearly perceived or more forcibly expressed, than by a writer of the Roman Catholic Church, who pronounced the English Bible the " stronghold " of what he chose to designate, referring to Protestantism, the " heresy in this country." " It is a part," he says, " of the national mind, the anchor of the national seriousness. Nay, it is worshiped with a positive idolatry. The memory of the dead passes into it. The potent traditions of childhood are stereotyped in its verses. The power of all the griefs and trials of a man is hidden beneath its words. It is the representative of his best moments ; and all that there has been about him, of soft, and gentle, and pure, and penitent, and good speaks to him out of his English Bible. It is his sacred thing which doubt has never dimmed and controversy never soiled. It has been to him all along as the voice of his guardian angel ; and in the length and breadth of the land there is not a Protestant with one spark of religiousness about him, whose spiritual biography is not in his Protestant Bible."

5

CHAPTER II.

OF THE HOLY TRINITY.

" SECTION 1.—There is but one living and true God, a self-existent Spirit, infinite, eternal, and unchangeable in his being, wisdom, power, holiness, justice, goodness, and truth.

" SECTION 2.—God has all life, glory, goodness, and blessedness in himself; not standing in need of any creatures which he has made, nor deriving any essential glory from them; and has most sovereign dominion over them to do whatsoever he may please.

" SECTION 3.—In the unity of the Godhead there are three persons of one substance, power, and eternity: God the Father, Son, and Holy Spirit."

The answers to the fourth, fifth, and sixth questions in the Catechism embody the same doctrine as the foregoing sections of the Confession.

These sections assert or imply the following propositions:—

1. The existence of a being called God.

2. That there is but one such being.

3. That God is a self-existent Spirit.

4. That he is, in his being and attributes, infinite, eternal, and unchangeable.

5. That God possesses in himself all perfection absolute and relative, is completely independent of all creatures, and has sovereign dominion over them.

6. That the Godhead exists in Trinity, implying:

(a) Three persons of one substance, power, and eternity.

(*b*) That the Father, the Son, and the Holy Spirit are each alike truly this one God.

1. The existence of the being we call God.

By logical sequence of parts, systematic theology will always start with the subject of the existence and attributes of God. Belief in the existence of God as a moral Ruler of the universe is fundamental to every thing that can be denominated a system of religion. So begins the most ancient of all creeds: "I believe in God the Father Almighty." So the Nicene Creed: "I believe in one God, Maker of heaven and earth, and all things visible and invisible." Similarly the Thirty-nine Articles of the Church of England give the first place to this section:

"There is but one living and true God, everlasting, without body, parts, or passions; of infinite power, wisdom, and goodness; the Maker and Preserver of all things visible and invisible. And in unity of this Godhead there be three Persons of one substance, power, and eternity: the Father, the Son, and the Holy Ghost."

No peculiarity of the Scriptures is more striking, than the clearness, fullness, and confidence, with which they reveal God, not, indeed, formally presenting any argument in proof of his existence, but everywhere assuming it, and declaring that only "the fool hath said in his heart, there is no God." The sublime declaration opening Genesis, "In the beginning God created the heaven and the earth," does not declare, but assumes the existence of God, and this fundamental idea of God is carried forward to the closing sentences of St. John's Revelation, correlating to itself all the other doctrines of the Scriptures. This very feature of the Scriptures seems to us a powerful argument for the existence of God—that an invisible superior intelligence poured upon the world, through the minds of the sacred writers, this flood of light on a subject which so radically concerns the behavior, the hopes, and the destiny of man.

Again, since it must be admitted that man can not foresee

future events which depend on contingencies, if the Scriptures contain prophecies that have been fulfilled, they thereby afford proof of the existence of some intelligence superior to man, and endowed with prescience. In like manner if the Scriptures establish beyond question that a miracle took place—that is to say, that an event occurred which could not be an effect of what is called the "course of nature," then a power above nature must be assumed. In these and other ways the Scriptures may be said to afford proof of the existence of God.

The proof-texts cited under the first section are very significant of the confidence and clearness with which the sacred writers assume the being and attributes of the Jehovah of the Bible:

Deut. vi. 4: Hear, O Israel: The Lord our God is one Lord. John iv. 24: God is a Spirit: and they that worship him must worship him in spirit and in truth. Ex. iii. 14: And God said unto Moses, I AM THAT I AM: and he said, Thus shalt thou say unto the children of Israel, I AM hath sent me unto you. 1 Tim. i. 17: Now unto the King eternal, immortal, invisible, the only wise God, be honor and glory for ever and ever. Rom. xvi. 27: To God only wise be glory through Jesus Christ for ever. Amen.

Rational theism embraces what may be known, without a divine revelation, as to the existence and attributes of God, and his relation to the world. On one extreme, some have held that aside from an antecedent supernatural communication of the idea of God, man could never have conceived that idea from the study of himself and the world in which he lives. Rev. J. Loughran, the first president of Waynesburg College, a man of very extensive reading, and a thinker of no ordinary ability, thus taught his classes, and with zealous assurance of the correctness of his theory. Assuming the natural inability of the human mind to frame even the conception of a Supreme Being, he drew from the widely prevalent belief in such a Being a proof of an original revelation, and thereby of the existence of God, holding that polytheism and other erroneous theistic beliefs are but corruptions of the primitive revelation given to the parents of the race. Whether or not the various notions of the existence and attributes of a divine being, found to-day among the nations destitute of the Bible, are to be regarded as "broken and scattered rays of original revelation," it is an interesting and significant fact that the oldest peoples of the world seem to have been monotheists before they were polytheists. Of ancient Egypt, M. Emanuel Rougé says: "The first characteristic of the religion is the unity of God, most energetically expressed: God, One, Sole, and Only; no others with Him. He is the only Being living in truth." So a competent scholar tells us that the words significant of a divine being "show the religion of the ancient Chinese as a monotheism. . . . Five thousand years ago the Chinese were monotheists." And so archæologists tell us that "in the period that lay behind the Homeric poems and the Vedas and the earliest Gothic and Scandinavian legends, when Greek and Roman, Indian, Celt, and Teuton, were still a single people, a single name for God was in use."

Positivism, as represented by Comte, Herbert Spencer, and others, which teaches that "the only principle of certitude is the senses," denies, not only man's ability to derive from the natural world any knowledge of the existence of God, but also his ability to receive such knowledge by supernatural revelation, and teaches that man can know nothing but the phenomena of the world about him, and the laws which govern them.

On the other extreme are those rationalists who assert that from the light of nature man may learn all that it is necessary to know about God's being and will, holding that the teachings of any supernatural revelation that may have been made are useful only because the teaching of nature is neglected. In its ultimate phase it denies revelation entirely, claiming that reason is adequate to account for every thing seemingly supernatural in religion.

The first Confession of Faith adopted by Cumberland Presbyterians begins the chapter on the Scriptures with the assumption that "the light of nature, and the works of creation and providence, do so far manifest the goodness, wisdom, and power of God, as to leave men inexcusable." In this opening sentence of our Confession is our first doctrinal departure from the Westminster Confession, which latter adds, to the words just quoted, this clause, "Yet they are not sufficient to give that knowledge of God, and of his will, which is necessary unto salvation." The two declarations combined leave those who have only the light of nature in the hopeless condition of having knowledge enough to render them inexcusable, but too little to render salvation possible. Some of the earnest advocates of revision of the Westminster Standards at the present time urge the same modification at this point that was made at the start by Cumberland Presbyterians, looking, as do other proposed changes, to the elimination of the sterner aspects of Calvinism. The passage in Rom. ii. 12–16 unquestionably teaches that it is possible for the Gentiles who have not the law (the revealed will of God) to do by the guidance of reason and conscience the things required by the law, and thereby to attain to merciful acceptance, through Christ's work in behalf of all mankind.

That man may attain the idea of the being and the moral attributes of God by the study of the world about him, and to such an extent as to render him accountable, seems to be clearly taught in many places in the Scriptures. The passage in Romans i. 19–23 declares that the reason why the wrath of God is revealed from heaven against the ungodliness and unrighteousness of the heathen world, then so sunken in abominable iniquities, is, "Because that which can be known of God is manifested in their hearts, God himself having shown it to them; for his eternal power and Godhead, though they be invisible, yet are seen ever since the world was made, being understood by his works, that they (who despised him) might have no excuse; because, although they knew God, they glorified him not as God, nor gave him thanks, but in their reasonings they went astray after vanity, and their senseless heart was darkened. Calling themselves wise, they were turned into fools, and forsook the glory of the imperishable God for idols graven in the likeness of perishable men, or of birds and beasts, and creeping things."

So when he stood in the midst of Mars' hill, Paul addressed the Athenian philosophers, not as " too superstitious," according to our common version, but as in all things " *religiously* disposed," reminding them, however, that the " unknown god" to whom they had erected an altar, and whom they ignorantly worshiped, is " God who made the world, and all things therein," and that "in him we live, and move, and have our being," skillfully enforcing his doctrine by appealing to a sentiment of their own poets, that men are the offspring of God. Of two poets to whom Paul is here supposed to allude, one is Cleanthes, a Stoic philosopher, who died about three hundred years before this remarkable appeal by Paul to the Stoic and Epicurean philosophers encountered at Athens. What is known as *The Hymn of Cleanthes*, composed in honor of Jupiter, abounds in sentiments so elevated and so nearly Christian as almost to compel belief that inspiration was its source. The following extract embraces the sentiment ascribed by Paul to their poets :

> "O under various sacred names adored!
> Divinity supreme! all-potent Lord!
> Author of nature! whose unbounded sway
> And legislative power all things obey!
> Majestic Jove! all hail! To thee belong
> The suppliant prayer and tributary song,
> To thee from all thy *mortal offspring* due.
> *From thee we came, from thee our being drew.*
> Whatever lives and moves, great Sire, is thine,
> Embodied portion of the soul divine."
> —*Translation by Gilbert West, LL.D.*

The following lines not only make the human will the source

of evil, but seem to suggest the poet's faith in a grand renova-
tion through the divine goodness:

> "Vice is the act of man, by passion tossed,
> And in the shoreless sea of folly lost.
> But thou what vice disorders canst compose,
> And profit by the malice of thy foes;
> So blending good with evil, fair with foul,
> As thence to model one harmonious whole,
> One universal law of truth and right."

Paul declares that through faith "we understand that the
worlds were framed by the Word of God;" but David, gazing
upon the vastly multiplied splendors of the sky as seen through
the crystal atmosphere of the hills of Judea, rapturously ex-
claims, "The heavens declare the glory of God, and the firmament showeth his handiwork!" So in every age the most gifted
and most thoughtful men have studied the goodly frame of the
universe, and from the dependence, harmony, and manifest
adaptations of its parts inferred the existence, wisdom, and
power of an infinite Intelligence presiding over and directing it.
That this universe should be the result of an accidental combination of atoms, or of any forces not guided by intelligence, and
hence of necessity working without design, seemed to poets,
philosophers, and moralists a thing utterly incredible. Thus
Cicero, in his treatise on "*The Nature of the Gods*," declares:
"I can not conceive why the man who thinks this possible,
should not also imagine that, if innumerable forms of letters,
whether of gold, or of any other kind, should be thrown together into some receptacle, there could be accidentally made
out of these, when shaken out upon the ground, annals capable
of being read; whereas I doubt whether chance could effect
any thing of the kind, even a single verse. But if a concurrence
of atoms can produce a world, why not a portico, a house, or a
temple? which would be less laborious, and indeed far easier."

Nicole, of France, a profound thinker of the Cartesian school,
wrote in 1670: "I am persuaded that these natural proofs do

not cease to be sound. . . . Whatever efforts atheists may make to efface the impression that the sight of this great world forms naturally in all men, that there is a God, the creator of it, they can not entirely stifle it, so strongly and deeply is it rooted in our minds. We need not force ourselves to yield to it, but we must do violence to ourselves to contradict it. Reason has only to follow its natural instinct, to persuade itself that there is a God."

We have dwelt upon this phase of the proof from natural religion in order to come more intelligently to the status of the argument as it is to-day. Men are ready to say, "We know that a watch must have been made by an artisan, and that a house implies a builder; but science has taught us that the world was not made as a watch is fabricated, or as a house is built." And so they tell us the "technic" theory is a failure, for no agent outside of and above nature has worked upon it as a mechanic does on the materials which he fashions and combines into a house; but an energy inherent in matter has developed all things, man himself, into what they are. The final stage of this doctrine is the resolution of the universe into a sum total of matter, force, and motion. In the language of another, the problem is thus stated and solved:

"The world now is—once was not; man and his works are—once were not. How and why did they come to be? Nature is uniform, works everywhere from within, grows, does not construct, bears and becomes, does not manufacture, and science, as her interpreter, expresses her method or process by development, evolution. The forms of inorganic matter have been developed by the operation of necessary mechanical laws; the forms of organic life have been evolved by the operation of natural forces. Variation, the struggle for existence, the survival of the fittest, explain the endless varieties of organized beings that have lived and are living upon the earth. The interactive play of organism and environment, the creature and the medium in which it lives, has resulted in man and his works."

Admit that the theory stated in the foregoing paragraph be established. that " evolution " expresses the process by which the world came to be as it is—a thing not at all proved—and the only result is that we must modify our notion of the relation of a Creator to the world. Not in the least does evolution diminish the demand of reason for an intelligent cause of the world as it is. Evolution claims to show us the *mode* in which a cause has acted, but not the cause. Evolution is a theory of a *method* by which ends have been reached, not of a cause which operated to produce those ends. The main question still recurs, to which evolution proposes no answer, Whence came the thing called nature, and the wonderful potencies inherent therein? What started and directed the long process of evolution? What determined the end to which the long evolving process should work, as that end is seen in the present goodly frame of this world with its countless harmonies, adaptations, and final causes? Could chance, through the mode or process called evolution, have produced the system we call nature? Evolutionists themselves have not been slow to perceive that their theory does not remove the demand of reason for a first cause, though many of them try to express that cause in terms seemingly chosen to conceal the God their reason demands. There is a story in Plutarch to the effect that a satyr strove to stand a dead man upright upon his feet, but gave over after many vain endeavors, saying, *Deest aliquid intus*—something is lacking within. So is it with a universe built upon any theory that leaves out God—something is lacking within, because of which lack it is a motionless, dead universe. The author of the " Origin of Species " felt the need of this power, and confessed its presence : " There is grandeur in this view of life, with its several powers having been originally breathed by the Creator into a few forms or one ; and that while this planet has gone cycling on according to the fixed law of gravity, from so simple a beginning endless forms, most beautiful and wonderful, have been and are being evolved."

Whatever may be the truth as to how belief in the existence of a Creator originated, it is unquestionable that this belief, already in the mind, is developed, modified, strengthened by the study of ourselves and the world in which we live. Profound philosophers ignorant of, or indifferent to, the teachings of the Bible, and devout Christians who base their faith implicitly on the Bible, have alike experienced and confessed their deepened sense of the presence of God as a result of their contemplation of the works of nature. If the universe, as limited, transient, and therefore necessarily dependent, compels belief in a changeless Being on whom it depends, the prevalence of design or final cause, throughout the universe, compels belief in the infinite intelligence of this changeless Being. Before me lies a watch, a very slight knowledge of which teaches me that it is a thing that is transient, that it is dependent, that it must have had a beginning, that it could not have produced itself. Not only must it be "wound-up" daily in order to "run," but it will necessarily "wear out," or cease to be a watch. So my reason asserts again and again that something or somebody made the watch. But the watch is a microcosm—a miniature cosmos. What is true of it is true of the universe, in the respect in which I have spoken. The insect is ephemeral, the flower fades, man returns to dust, the heavens wax old as doth a garment. Something must have been before the earth and the world were formed, something from everlasting to everlasting.

A closer survey of the watch convinces me that it not only was produced by some cause, but that it was made for a purpose —that a design existed in a mind, and that the watch is but the product of that design; in other words the watch must have had, not only *efficient* cause, but that a *final* cause determined *for what* it should exist. As a whole, it is ingeniously contrived to indicate the passage of time, marking the flight into seconds, minutes, hours. Further study of it convinces me that every part of it, no less than the mechanism as a whole, exists for a purpose that was first in the mind of the contriver, and I am able to see *for what* the hands, the case, the dial, the crystal, and every wheel, and lever, and screw are as they are and in the places assigned them. What is true of the watch is true of every work of man. A railroad that spans a continent, and the pen with which this sentence is written alike exist for a final cause, for an end foreseen as desirable, and therefore realized by the use of the necessary means. If now I lift my thought from my pen to the eye that guides the pen across the page, the numerous and varied parts of the eye, and their wonderfully nice adjustment to each other at once impress me that it is a much more complicated structure than the simple pen in my hand, and as to function, that of the eye infinitely transcends that of the pen. I *know* that the pen was made for the purpose of distributing ink in forms somewhat resembling the letters of the alphabet, and I *know* that the eye answers the wonderful end of a mirror to bring the outer world under immediate cognizance by my soul, so that, while I do not see the eye itself nor any images photographed in its chamber, I do "see" the table before me, the books upon it, the houses of the village, the distant hills crowned with forest trees, and still more distant clouds drifting away to the east. Must I then not believe that this wonderful eye was made for a purpose, and that the unconscious forces which, working in unconscious matter, however long the time required to evolve such an eye, were directed by an intelligence which first conceived and then purposed to construct such an organ to mirror the world to the soul? As these reflections engage my mind, I seem to myself as well assured that the world exhibits design, and therefore a designer, as I am of the truth of the demonstrable proposition, that the sum of the angles in a triangle is equivalent to two right angles. As I go on reflecting on the wonderful relation the eye sustains to the enjoyments and the practical affairs of life, how the "cloud-capt towers," the "gorgeous palaces" and all the other magnificent works of man could never have been but for the marvelous powers of this little organ called the eye, I say to myself, Only Infinite Wisdom could have designed and formed such an eye.

Final cause implies three things: (1) An end foreseen, (2) a determination to realize it, (3) such control of materials and forces as will realize the end perceived and chosen. Thus, one "studies out" a beautiful dwelling, and the *ideal* rests in his mind for a time. By and by he resolves to realize his ideal, or to build just such a house. Then comes the intelligent control of forces in their application to wood, iron, stone, etc., until, the scaffolding removed, the realized ideal delights its owner. The only possible alternative to final cause, or design, is chance. If a hundred brick be dumped from a cart, we say that their juxtaposition in the pile is simply a matter of chance, by which we mean that no mind controlled their motions according to a pre-determined order. If later we look upon the same brick and find them disposed in a pile counting 2 x 5 x 10, we say that "some one has piled them"—that is, has controlled their juxtaposition according to a preconceived plan.

Now, of our bodies and the material world in which we live, we must predicate final cause, just as necessarily as of the works of man. If there is one instance of design, there are millions. It is everywhere. The mind of the maker of a piano is in every key, and hammer, and wire in it, and equally is the mind of God in all his works. If a watch, a piano, a locomotive exhibits final cause, much more does the human body as a whole and in the structure and correlation of its parts, making it indeed a "hymn to God." In the works of nature as in those of man, we justly infer the final cause, or design, of any part, from its capacity or adaptation. Thus it is said that Harvey was led to the brilliant discovery of the circulation of the blood by reflecting on the observed adaptation of the valves of the heart to such an end. In other words, the adaptation discovered in the structure of the heart led the philosopher to grasp the final cause that lay in the

Infinite Mind by which man is "fearfully and wonderfully made."

Viewed in relation to final cause as everywhere displayed, the natural world brings God very near to us. It proclaims "God first, God midst, God last," and that "in him we live and move and have our being." It matters not how God made the world, whether according to the old mechanical conception, or according to the modern idea of a force within matter by which the cosmos is evolved, whether six days or millions of years have been occupied, and whether in the one mode or the other, it is equally true that in all its parts nature is working for the realization of ends which necessarily involve the supposition of a preordaining and directing intelligence.

We have thus briefly tried to make it clear that evolution, or the doctrine of the development of the universe by the agency of fixed laws working through vast periods of duration, by no means destroys, but rather in fact increases the force of the argument drawn from final causes. Just here, in the minds of many who have but slightly examined the doctrine of evolution, arises much of the skepticism of the day, from a secret belief that science has really proved that all things could have come to be as they are, through the processes explained by evolution, and without a superintending intelligence. If any such doubter should read these lines, his faith in God should find reassurance in the following concessions selected from the many such made by most thorough advocates of the doctrine of evolution:

Prof. Huxley says: "There is a wider teleology which is not touched by the doctrine of evolution, but is actually based on the fundamental proposition of evolution."

Prof. Asa Gray, as strenuous and intelligent an advocate of evolution as our country has produced, and as competent as any other to see its relation to the doctrine of final causes, declares: "What is lost in directness may perhaps be gained in breadth and depth. . . . The natural history of ends becomes consistent and reasonably intelligible under the light of evolution.   As the forms and kinds rise gradually out of that which was well-nigh formless into consummate form, so do biological ends rise and assert themselves in increasing distinctness and variety.   Vegetables and animals have paved the earth with intentions."

Prof. John Fiske, an enthusiastic advocate of Darwinianism, in his work, *The Destiny of Man*, says: " The doctrine of evolution does not allow us to take the atheistic view of man. . . . He who recognizes the slow and subtle process of evolution as the way in which God makes things come to pass, must take a far higher view. . . . The Darwinian theory, properly understood, replaces as much teleology as it destroys.   From the first dawning of life we see all things working together toward one mighty goal, the evolution of the most exalted spiritualities which characterize humanity."

The doctrine of evolution, if true, by no means eliminates final cause.   If, indeed, the conceived plan and the execution in its full development are so remote, and linked by a series of agencies so numerous, and working through periods so vast, even the greater seems the demand for intelligence as the author of such wonderful processes and results.   Behind the screen of natural forces patient thought finds imperative demand for God to conceive, ordain, and energize the vast scheme.   "We are, by the discovery of the general laws of nature," says Whewell, "led into a scene of wider design, of deeper contrivances, of more comprehensive adjustments.   Final causes, if they appear driven further from us by such extension of our views, embrace us only with a vaster and more majestic circuit.   Instead of a few threads connecting some detached objects, they become a stupendous network which is wound round and round the universal frame of things. . . . Our discovery of laws can not contradict our persuasion of ends."   "It would appear from modern discovery," says Canon Mozley, " that creative design was more distant and circuitous than the design of the human artificer in constructing a machine; was in less immediate contact with the result, and of earlier date in scheme; that it acted on a large scale by bringing things together from different and distant quarters, and by the use of contingent materials, whose place in the plan was seen only by the light of the end. . . . But creative design is not obscured on these accounts, but only appears the more subtle, powerful, and grand."

It is believed that the strongest of all proofs from final cause are to be found in the mind as endowed with intellect, sensibility, will, freedom, and a moral nature, man becoming thus a subject of moral law, and finding in himself thus endowed the data of a necessary belief in an Intelligent Creator and Moral Governor in whose image he is made. But upon this and other proofs commonly relied upon in the theistic discussion, the limits of this volume will not permit us to enter. After much study of the whole subject as one of absorbing interest and as sustaining a most important practical relation to morality, to the welfare of society, to science, and to religion, two conclusions force themselves upon us: (1) The universe is the product of an Infinite Intelligence, (2) we can know and interpret the universe only because we are made in the image of that Intelligence. The universe thus becomes intelligible as being itself a thought—a thought of the infinitely wise Thinker, and only because made in the image of that Thinker, could Kepler exclaim as he looked upon the visible world, "O God, I think Thy thoughts after Thee!" Science is but the interpretation of the thought of God as it is discerned in the world, all branches of science combining to exhibit nature as a grand unity which proves it the thought of one mind. In the forcible words with which Noah Porter concludes his work on *The Human Intellect:* "We analyze the several processes of knowledge into their underlying assumptions, and we find that the one assumption which underlies them all is a self-existent Intelligence, who not only can be known by man, but *must* be known by man in order that man may know any thing besides. We are, therefore, not alone justified, we are compelled to conclude our analysis of the human intellect with the assertion that its processes involve the assumption that there is an uncreated Thinker, whose thoughts can be interpreted by the created intellect made in his image."

Having given so much space to an attempt at stating a few of the grounds of theistic belief drawn from Natural Theology, we may most suitably close with some paragraphs from one of the most thoughtful and systematic works* of recent years, setting forth alike the advantages of Natural Theology, and the need of a supernatural revelation. After declaring that such studies "vindicate the great fundamental truth of the existence of God," the author affirms his conviction that "beyond all we can learn concerning God and his relation to the world from reason and nature, there is room and necessity for the light and teaching of a supernatural revelation," for—

1. "Natural Theology can give only a partial and incomplete view of God's character.

2. It leaves us in the dark as to man's specific end in life, and how he may accomplish it.

3. Its intimations, though they suggest hope for the future, fail to bring immortality to full light.

4. It does not explain the existence of sin and the depravity of our race.

5. It furnishes no remedy for sin—no way of forgiveness, or salvation from sin.

6. The history of mankind shows unquestionably that when left to the mere light of nature and reason men hold low and inadequate conceptions of, God, and are wanting in the knowledge necessary to a right, pure, and happy life.

7. A revelation from God gives a fresh and most impressive proof of his existence. The great questions of truth and duty are answered. In God's light we see light."

Natural Theology, by M. Valentine, D.D., LL.D.

2. The Confession asserts that there is "but one living and true God." The unity of God carries with it the idea of exclusion—that there is no class of beings of the kind. The true God existing in unity is the only true God. This doctrine is taught in many passages of Scripture, some of which have been cited. The monotheism of the Hebrews was in marked contrast with the polytheistic beliefs of the nations around them, and through this chosen people was revealed to the world the vastly important idea of the unity of God. Natural Theology infers the same doctrine from what it regards the necessary oneness of an absolute First Cause, from the personality of that First Cause, and from the unity of the universe, since the unity of thought pervading the universe implies that it is the product of one Mind. Men are therefore the offspring of one Father, and thus constitute one brotherhood.

3. That God is a self-existent spirit. In this are two propositions, (a) God is self-existent—that is, a being absolute and underived. Something must be self-existent. Whatever is not self-existent had a beginning, before which it did not exist. If nothing is self-existent, there must have been a time when nothing existed, and if so, nothing could have come into existence, for, as the old philosophers correctly reasoned, out of nothing nothing can come. Therefore either the universe is eternal, or a self-existent being must have produced it. The latter seems the only rational conclusion. Said the late Professor Henry of the Smithsonian Institute: "The simplest conception which explains and connects the phenomena is that of the existence of one spiritual Being infinite in wisdom, power, in all divine perfections, which exists always and everywhere." Out of the attribute of self-existence comes that of eternity. From everlasting to everlasting, God is God, without beginning, without end. (b) That God is a spirit. This refers to our conception of the essence of God, for he is a true being, an entity. It implies that he is not matter—that he is not possessed of material parts.

He is not the universe, nor a force, nor the sum total of the forces in the universe, but a person, spiritual in essence. Materialism, or the doctrine that there is in the universe no entity except that which we cognize by the senses, and call matter, is essentially atheistic. If all our thoughts, volitions, and feelings were millions of years ago in the " fire-mist," out of which they, equally with our bodies, have been evolved, then design is itself but a product of matter, and the universe is utterly destitute of any testimony to an intelligent author. Says Sir William Hamilton: " It is only on the supposition of a moral liberty in man that we can attempt to vindicate a moral order, and, consequently, a moral governor in the universe. . . . In the hands of the materialist, or physical necessitarian, every argument for the existence of a Deity is either annulled or reversed in a demonstration of atheism." Hamilton further argues, and rightly, that *free will* is the ultimate fact on which we are warranted in assuming a second substance that we call *spirit*. The distinction between matter and spirit is radical, and must be held, if we are to retain any rational basis for ideas of morality, religion, or God.

But some tell us they know matter, but they can not know spirit; that they know matter exists, but that they can not know that there is spirit. Sufficient reflection will teach us, however, that we may have as valid assurance of the existence of spirit, as of matter, yea firmer assurance. Strictly speaking we can *know* neither matter nor spirit. We know their attributes, and we by logical necessity infer the entities that make the attributes possible. I am conscious of reasoning, remembering, willing, and other mental processes, and I must believe there is a something capable of these processes. I am conscious of freedom. But if I am in any true sense free—that is, if what I call my mind, my very self, is endowed with the power of self-determination, then my volitions are not links in the chain of physical causation, and there is a something that is not matter. We are not conscious of matter, and not conscious of mind. We are conscious of what compels a conscious belief in the existence of both. I look upon an apple before me, and say it is red; touch it, and say it is cold; taste it, and say it is sweet. But "red" and "cold" and "sweet" as used in such a connection signify only mental states called sensations. Of the entity, the matter composing the apple, that something which occupies space, and is endowed with properties which under proper relations to my body will awaken the sensations of red, cold, sweet, *I know absolutely nothing*. I infer a something, a substratum beneath the properties, and call it matter. Similarly, I refer my sensations, emotions, volitions, and all the other contents of consciousness to a something, a substratum without which they could not exist. The attributes of the two substrata are so unlike, so utterly incapable of being converted the one into the other, and of any common standard of comparison, that if I call the substratum to one set *matter*, I must call the substratum to the other by a term significant of a nature essentially different— *spirit*. Then, since spirit possesses the attributes of intelligence, volition, freedom, purpose, and has power to know the properties of matter, to modify it in the relations of its parts, and to use it to realize intelligent designs, and since the material world is evidently the product of intelligence and design, the only admissible conclusion is that its Author is a spirit infinitely wise.

There are those who regard reasonings like the foregoing as unsatisfactory, and therefore profitless; but to the writer they are extremely helpful, and therefore satisfying, deepening conviction in the inmost recesses of the soul that an infinite Spirit, Spirit of our spirits, is everywhere and ever present "beholding the evil and the good," the Moral Governor of a vast economy of intelligences of which the human race is but a fractional part. "Whither shall I go from thy spirit? or whither shall I flee from thy presence? If I ascend up into heaven, thou art there; if I make my bed in hell, behold, thou art there. If I take the wings of the morning, and dwell in the uttermost parts of the sea, even there shall thy hand lead me, and thy right hand shall uphold me."

Remembering the golden rule that the comparison of scripture with scripture is the best rule of interpretation, since many passages clearly teach that God is a spirit, we will explain all the passages which represent him as possessed of bodily organs, or material parts, as simply employing modes of expression adapted to man's habit of receiving and imparting ideas through such organs. "And when the Scriptures speak," says Dr. A. A. Hodge, "of his repenting, of his being grieved or jealous, they use metaphorical language, teaching us that he acts toward us as a man would when agitated by such passions. Such metaphors are characteristic rather of the Old than of the New Testament, and occur for the most part in highly rhetorical passages of the poetical and prophetical books."

4. It is taught that God is infinite, eternal, and unchangeable in his being, and his attributes of wisdom, power, holiness, justice, goodness, and truth.

"When we speak of God as infinite, we mean that his being can not be brought under any limitations of space or time; nor can any of his attributes be classed as finite." To our minds, infinite being, infinite power, infinite wisdom, and the like, are terms which can not be grasped in their positive meaning, for the finite can not comprehend the infinite, and yet both reason and the Scriptures teach us that God is not subject to any of the limitations which render man finite. We must believe many things which we can not understand, and the infinity of God is manifestly one of them.

The divine Personality as *infinite* implies, (*a*) *Omniscience*, or unlimited intelligence, (*b*) *omnipotence*, or unlimited power, (*c*) *omnipresence*, or presence not limited in space—God everywhere, (*d*) *unlimited wisdom*, or that application of knowledge which always selects the best ends and the best means for accomplishing them.

Holiness is defined "the state of freedom from sin." But sin is "the transgression of the law." Therefore the infinite holiness of God, is the eternal and perfect consonance of his will with that moral law which necessarily imposes, on man and all other moral creatures, obligation to obedience. The love of moral rectitude, the hatred of sin, conformity of will to the law of righteousness make up the content of the term holiness.

5. The goodness of God is infinite, eternal, unchangeable. It is infinite in degree, knowing no limitation ; eternal, as existing always; unchangeable, admitting neither increase nor diminution.

Love and benevolence are terms used in the same sense as good. The idea involved is that of a disposition to seek the highest good of sentient creatures. But the highest good of a sentient creature is in that condition in which it perfectly realizes the end for which it exists. Man's chief end is to glorify God and enjoy him forever, and the choice of this end for a fellow-creature is goodness in the one so choosing. God not only endowed man with faculties rendering him capable of happiness, but, as infinitely good, he wills that every man, and every other sentient creature, shall attain the good of which he is capable. "Rational love, as a whole," says Mark Hopkins, "will include a choice by us for all other beings of their end and good, and (a choice) for ourselves of our end and good." So to choose for another is to love him according to the divine requirement. Because God is infinitely good he loves, and commands all rational intelligences to love. He who loves in this sense is born of God. Always to will in accordance with the law of love is to be holy, as well as good, and just, as well as good and holy.

No truth is more explicitly asserted in the Scriptures, or more variously and frequently repeated, than that God is good. The words "God" and "good" are, in fact, synonyms, implying that the very idea of goodness is that of likeness to God. In Anglo-Saxon, whence we get the word, God means the one who is good.

The divine goodness extends even to brute creatures, for he opens his hand to satisfy the desires of every living thing. Not a sparrow falls without his care. Whatever of pain may seem inseparable from the animal economy, it is, nevertheless, manifestly the will of God that earth, and sea, and air be theaters of happy life. Man's rational and moral faculties lift him into higher spheres of enjoyment in the acquisition of knowledge and the practice of virtue, thus raising him to companionship with angels and God himself. Also, and for the sole purpose, so far as we can see, of adding to our enjoyment, the divine goodness has endowed us with an æsthetic nature, which is kindled into conscious delight when through the senses the outward world is mirrored to the soul. Our social nature, also, as the source of friendship, affection, and other ties that bind souls in fellowships true and sweet, must be regarded as a fountain opened by infinite love. Thus within us and without us proofs innumerable give confirmation to the Bible doctrine of the infinite goodness of God—a doctrine which itself is a well-spring of peace to the soul receiving it in its fullness, causing it to sing amid all life's experiences:

> "God is love! his mercy brightens
> All the path in which I rove;
> Bliss he wakes, and woe he lightens—
> God is wisdom, God is love!"

Proofs of the goodness of God, from whatever source drawn, are strengthened when we remember that man's moral and spiritual faculties are deadened by sin, and that the divine goodness, as thus manifested to the unworthy and the undeserving, is gracious and merciful. As a moral being, man is a system in derangement, an organism whose head is sick and heart is faint; and in the light of this truth man's own experiences and the Scriptures must be interpreted. God made us to be perfectly good, therefore perfectly happy; but we have sinned, and so have brought upon ourselves spiritual death, with all its train of ills. Still, God loves us—is gracious, pitying us, and seeking our deliverance. Read in the one hundred and third Psalm the fervent and eloquent expressions of a soul flooded with a sense of the goodness of God, and of the mercy which is "from everlasting to everlasting."

The doctrinal system of the Cumberland Presbyterian Church places in the foreground the doctrine of the infinite goodness of God, making that love which wills the good of all the source of a merciful provision for the salvation of all. At the very start, our fathers cast out the vicious element of a decree which unconditionally predestinates some men to everlasting life, and ordains others to everlasting death. If such an unconditional decree is held, the infinite goodness of God must be given up. The two are logical contradictions. The great demand for a revision of the Westminster Standards at this time is based on an alleged necessity for a doctrinal statement that will bring into prominence the goodness of God. But the Calvinistic system, placing the universal, unconditional decree in the foreground, has no place for the infinite goodness. That system retained, no logic is competent to the task of putting goodness in the foreground, or of finding any place at all for infinite goodness. The Cumberland Presbyterian Confession and the Westminster Confession teach systems that are logical antagonisms, as will appear more fully in chapters to follow, and the contrast of the two systems will always appear when they are viewed in their relation to the love of God. One puts love at the head of the chapter, the other puts it in a foot-note. Those who rejoice in the truth, and especially those who long to see our sin-stricken humanity transformed by the power of faith in the infinite love of a common heavenly Father, will sympathize with all movements for such a revision of Christian creeds as will show God to the world as the loving Father seeking the happiness of all his creatures, rather than as an arbitrary and dread Sovereign inspiring the hearts of his creatures with awful fear or hopeless despair, in view of his absolute, eternal decree.

Dr. Howard Crosby's "The Good and Evil of Calvinism " presents an admirable outline of Cumberland Presbyterian theology, as the system of scriptural truth remaining after he has eliminated from Calvinism, as its "evil," every thing characteristic of it as a system. In the conclusion Dr. Crosby states in the same brief paragraph that *personally* he is content with the Confession, and also that it should be so modified as to conform to God's word: " But although we are personally content with our standards, yet, as the error referred to has undoubtedly been a stumbling-block to God's saints (we care nothing for what the world says), we feel the importance, nay, the necessity, of taking this stumbling-block out of the way. The Third and Tenth Chapters should be so modified as to conform to God's word, and not be a burden on the conscience of devoted and godly men."

In an interesting notice of Dr. O. W. Holmes at fourscore, in *The New England Magazine* for October, 1889, the writer says: "In another way Holmes has quite as much hope as Emerson had, and quite as strong a faith in the good the universe contains. His belief in the philosophy of joy has been at the heart of his severe criticisms of the old forms of theology. To him, as much as to Whittier, God is the eternal goodness; and he has not been able to think of God as wishing for any thing else than the happiness of his creatures." It is for God in this aspect of God as the eternal goodness, as the loving Father desiring the good of his creatures, and of all his creatures, that the heart of humanity yearns; and only a God of love can be preached to men with hope of winning them to God and heaven. To us it seems singular that Dr. Crosby should express indifference "for what the world says," for it is most certainly true that the very error he declares "has undoubtedly been a stumbling-block to God's saints," has no less certainly been a stumbling-block in the way

of sinners, over which multitudes have stumbled either into
downright unbelief or into secret bitterness of feeling toward the
supposed arbitrary Sovereign in the Father whose loving heart
yearns for the salvation of all. It is largely in the popular sentiment of the times, if we mistake not, that is found the confessed demand for a revision of the Calvinistic standards. A
foreign journal before me contains a brief editorial paragraph
from a North-western secular journal, seemingly penned in not a
very kind spirit, but characteristic of the popular demand named,
which paragraph, for that very reason, has twice crossed the sea:
"The Presbyterians have concluded to amend their Confession
of Faith. Sentences which have stood the buffetings of two
hundred years are to be changed, and little babies will be damned
no longer. The funniest part of yesterday's proceedings in the
New York Presbytery was the motion that they leave the wrath
of God and the damnation of the heathen and of infants in the
text, and put the love of God in a foot-note. This tearing away
of the old land-marks of the road to heaven is a severe blow to
the fathers in Israel, but nevertheless it is a mark of progress.
The God of the liberal Presbyterian is infinitely more divine
than the God of those who desire an avenger rather than a loving Father. The Presbyterian Church will be all the better for
the elimination from its creed of the crudities of former generations."

That which thoughtful men, both out of the Church and in the
Church, are demanding of Christianity is a creed in harmony
with man's own consciousness, the dictates of reason, and the
obvious teachings of the Scriptures as a whole. Cumberland
Presbyterians, making the infinite goodness of God the central
doctrine of their system, and to it subordinating all others in
their true logical relations, believe their creed consonant with
the Bible and the requirements of enlightened reason.

Finally, the Confession teaches that God exists in Trinity.
This is a doctrine we learn only from the Scriptures, neither

reason nor the world about us giving any intimation of it. It is fundamental to the system of redemption, which represents God as loving the world, and giving his Son to die for it; Christ as becoming incarnate, and assuming the functions of prophet, priest, and king; the Holy Ghost as sent to act in the office of Comforter of God's children, and to enlighten and reprove the world. Believers, according to the command of Christ, are baptized into "the name of the Father, and of the Son, and of the Holy Ghost," the "three that bear record in heaven." The concurrent Christian doctrine of the Trinity, as drawn from the Scriptures, is well expressed in the following propositions:—

1. "That Father, Son, and Holy Ghost are each equally that one God, and that the indivisible divine essence and all divine perfections and prerogatives belong to each in the same sense and degree.

2. "That these titles, Father, Son, and Holy Ghost, are not different names of the same person in different relations, but of different persons.

3. "That these three divine persons are distinguished from one another by certain personal properties, and are revealed in a certain order of subsistence and operation." *

These points may fitly conclude this chapter:—

1. Man is essentially a religious being. A God is the demand of his nature. "The universality of religion admits of but one explanation—the universal is the necessary. What man everywhere has done, he could not but do. His nature is creative of religion. And, so, religion is the fruit of faculties given in our nature."

2. The main source of the differences distinguishing the many religions of the world is in the conception and representation of the deity worshiped. Almost innumerable objects, from sticks and stones deified by fetichism, to the High and Holy One of the Scriptures, have received religious homage.

* Hodge's Commentary.

3. Man is influenced by nothing else so much as by religion. He who worships Buddha is like Buddha. "A nation's genius rises as its consciousness of God deepens. The point where the genius and culture of Greece culminated was the very point where it had come to realize most vividly the being and government of God." It is impossible for those living in a Christian land fully to estimate their indebtedness to Christianity. Even those who make no profession of Christianity, who may discredit its divine origin and authority, are unconsciously and wonderfully molded by its influence. A French infidel well said: "The best that is in me is from Christ."

4. The Hebrew and Christian conception of God as One, a pure Spirit, self-existent, infinitely good, wise, and just, is incomparably superior to any other theistic conception known to the world. The communication of the knowledge of this true and only living God to the world, through a selected people, who were surrounded by nations idolatrous, polytheistic, and given to the horrible rite of human sacrifices, seems to us a stupendous miracle. "This, then, was the gift of the Semitic race in its noblest branch to the world—faith in the righteous, living God. A gift so splendid might well hold in it the regeneration of the world, giving to it not only the idea of the Divine Unity, but religion changed into a mighty and commanding reality, which penetrates and inspires the whole man, dignifies him with the consciousness of a divine descent, gladdens him with the hope of a happy, because a holy, immortality, quickens him with the sense of omnipotence moving everywhere to the help of man in the soft guise of infinite gentleness. He who knows what these things mean will best understand that ancient saying, 'Salvation is of the Jews.'"*

---

* Studies in the Philosophy of Religion and History, by A. M. Fairbairn.

CHAPTER III.

OF THE DECREES OF GOD—A GENERAL VIEW OF THE SUBJECT.

NOTHING that can be said negatively of the doctrinal system of the Cumberland Presbyterian Church is more true or more characteristic of it than that it is *un*-Calvinistic. I am well aware that it is not uncommon with our people, some ministers included, to speak of our theology as "a mild form of Calvinism," "the Calvinistic system slightly modified," "Calvinism with the sterner features omitted," etc. With my views of the two doctrinal systems, I can only say that those who speak in such phraseology as the foregoing either have not carefully compared the two systems, or are very careless in the use of language which the facts in the case will not at all justify. The probable explanation of the mistake alluded to is to be found in the fact that those who organized the Cumberland Presbyterian Church had been Presbyterian ministers, the fact that our Confession is a (very radical) "modification of the Westminster Confession," and that the ordinary ministrations of the Presbyterian pulpit are, like Dr. Crosby's doctrinal exposition in *The Good and the Evil of Calvinism*, orthodox Cumberland Presbyterianism. The practical result of all this is that nearly all who leave us, ministers and laity, for reasons worthy or unworthy, go, as a matter of course, as it would seem, into the Presbyterian Church. Now, of this tendency among our people it is not at all the writer's purpose to speak complainingly, but reference is made to it in justification of his purpose to present, in the discussion of the subject of "Decrees," what he most thoroughly believes a very great and radical and very important difference between the two systems as contained in the two Confessions.

When the founders of the Cumberland Presbyterian Church made their first *protest* against the Westminster doctrines, that protest was against the teaching of Chapter III., by which first blow they completely struck the key-stone from the Calvinistic arch. The first proposition of their first published doctrinal statement contradicts a fundamental statement of this Chapter III. A little later, when they came to construct a Confession, they saw that in every vital point Calvinistic teaching was out of harmony with the fundamental principles they had already adopted. The Confession of Faith of the Cumberland Presbyterian Church, as adopted in 1829, and still more fully as revised in 1873, is in irreconcilable antagonism to the obvious and historical sense of the Westminster Confession; and this I desire so to exhibit that the difference may be fairly understood, the tendency of which will be finally to bring about, as I honestly believe, a better understanding between the two churches. On the one hand, our own people should better understand how distinctive is our doctrinal system; and on the other, our brethren of the Mother Church should candidly hear objections to the Westminster system, and not hastily charge us with misrepresenting it or wishing to exaggerate its less acceptable features.

With an exception or two, the Calvinistic theology is a system of most rigid logical coherence of parts. These parts are grouped necessarily about the doctrine of the eternal decree of the third chapter, and all of them must stand or fall as it stands or falls. As another expresses it: "The third chapter, *Of God's Eternal Decree*, may be said to be the key-note from which its most characteristic doctrines follow in immediate sequence and harmony." Therefore, I entreat the reader to consider once more, calmly and deliberately, this chapter, in which lies the spinal column without which the Calvinistic system can not stand. "Revision" is the order of the day, and it is hoped that a fair statement of revision, as embodied in the Cumberland Presbyterian Confession, may avail something to the advancement of the truth.

In fairness it is to be said that many Presbyterian ministers and laymen disclaim the doctrines that Arminians attribute to the Calvinistic eternal decree, as logically interpreted. They advocate revision, not, as a rule, acknowledging the errors of the Confession, but claiming that a re-statement is necessary " in order to tell the public what has been meant all the while by the Confession." By parity of reasoning another re-statement would be necessary to tell what the first re-statement meant, and so on. But the Westminster Confession was framed with much deliberation, every sentence, phrase, and word being used in a sense well understood, which sense is as readily ascertained to-day as when the Assembly concluded its work. Dr. Briggs, in his complaint that the Presbyterian Church is drifting, and his demand for a return to the true historic sense of the Confession, says: " There can be no doubt that the Westminster divines were Calvinists, that they held, in the main, to the Canons of Dort, and that they excluded Arminians and semi-Arminians from orthodoxy. The Westminster definitions were made with this end in view. They are sharp, hard, polemical, and exclusive; and, at the same time, apologetic, defensive, and guarding themselves from objections at every point. *I do not know where any such careful and admirable definitions can be found.* At the same time, it is my opinion that, in this respect, the Westminster divines went too far in their polemics. They sharpened their definitions into swords and spears that are as dangerous in the hands of unskillful Calvinists as they are to their Arminian foes. It is not surprising that these definitions have ever been regarded as hard and offensive, and that they have kept multitudes from uniting with the Presbyterian Church." (Italics ours.)

The two schools of theologians in the Presbyterian Church—

the Liberalists and the orthodox Calvinists, or those who favor and those who oppose revision—differ widely in their interpretation of some of the statements of the chapter on Decrees, as will be indicated by the following contrasted statements:—

Dr. Howard Crosby says: "Surely from these Scriptures we can safely say that any scheme of theology that makes God partial, resolving to furnish his grace only to some of those whom he invites, and willfully excluding others from all participation in it, is an unscriptural scheme, whatever may be its philosophical merits."—*Responsibility before the Gospel.*

Dr. A. A. Hodge says: "That as God has sovereignly predestinated certain persons, called the elect, through grace to salvation, so he has sovereignly decreed to withhold his grace from the rest; and that this withholding rests upon the unsearchable counsel of his own will, and is for the glory of his sovereign power."—*Commentary on the Confession.*

It will appear, on further investigation of the subject, that Dr. Hodge and his school are the consistent Calvinists, frankly accepting the conclusions of their own premises, and explaining the Confession in its obvious, logical, historical sense. Dr. Crosby and his school explain away the Confession, in order to be evangelical; the former explain away the Scriptures, as it seems to us, to be consistent Calvinists.

The divergence of the Calvinistic and the Cumberland Presbyterian doctrinal systems, which takes rise in the third chapters of the two Confessions, leads to logical results widely different in the interpretation of other important doctrines, and our attempt to bring these differences clearly and fully before our readers will begin with a brief statement of the

MEANING OF THE DECREES OF GOD.

In the last chapter reference was made to the harmony of the universe, the numerous adaptations of its parts, and the marks of design everywhere manifest, in proof that it must be the product of mind, of the Infinite Intelligence we call God. Further, we looked upon the world as full of proofs of the goodness of God, that the vast system of creation exists for the higher ends embraced in the happiness of creatures rational and sentient. As the earth is so insignificant a member of the universe that has limitless expansion on all sides of us, we must believe that we are but a handful of the great rational creation and moral economy of which God is the certain and rightful sovereign. Then, we must believe that, if this goodly frame is the product of a creative hand, it sprang from a purpose in the mind of God, which purpose we call his decree to create the world as it is, and to people it with such beings as are in it. If such a purpose was in the divine mind, it was always there, and so we believe God's decrees are eternal. Moreover, we must believe that he had a purpose, or will, as to how the creatures made in his own image should act; not necessarily that he decreed just what specific actions each one should perform, but the great principle or law of their behavior as beings intelligent and free. Thus the universe was a conception or ideal in the divine mind, the purpose to realize which is God's creative decree. From this definition of decree there will be no reasonable dissent.

"The will of God that any thing exterior to himself shall take place, is called his determination, or decree."—*Knapp's Theology*.

"By God's purposes (decrees) is meant his eternal and immutable pleasure, will, or choice concerning all creatures and events or whatever comes to pass in time or eternity."

The last definition has in it a very vicious element, in that it confounds the purpose, or decree, of God with his pleasure, will, or choice. We think of a divine decree as certainly efficacious, or never failing of fulfillment; but numerous passages of Scripture declare plainly and most positively that many things happen contrary to the pleasure of God. "Say unto them, As I live, saith the Lord God, I have no pleasure in the death of the wicked; but that the wicked turn from his way and live; turn

7

ye, turn ye, from your evil ways; for why will ye die, O house of Israel?" (Ezek. xxxiii. 11.)   Is it not amazing that, with the asseveration of God himself that he has no pleasure in the death of man, and the added pathetic importunity and remonstrance contained in this passage, that men, for the sake of a theory, will resort to the expedient of a *secret* decree by which the Lord brings about, as they affirm, the very thing he so solemnly declares contrary to his pleasure!   Will is used sometimes in the sense of pleasure or choice, sometimes in the sense of decree. It is the writer's will (pleasure) that Congress appoint a commission to investigate and report the extent of the evil suffered annually by the nation in health, morals, and business because of the liquor traffic; but he does not will (decree) that Congress do so, as such a decree would be futile; but were he an emperor, he would so decree, and say to Congress, "Do thus."

Calvinistic definitions of "decree" are, as a rule, illogical and unfair, since they add a limitation, that is no part of a definition, and such as begs the question at issue between the Calvinist and the Arminian.   The oft-repeated one, from *Buck's Theological Dictionary*, is an illustration: "The settled purpose of God foreordaining whatsoever comes to pass."   Whether God has decreed "whatsoever comes to pass," or whether men do many things contrary to the will of God, and which he, therefore, could not have decreed, is the very question at issue.   A decree of God is, then, simply his purpose to do whatever he does, for we can not suppose the divine action separable from determination to act.   If God called Moses to lead Israel out of Egypt, he determined (decreed) to call him.   Whether the divine decree respects whatsoever comes to pass, is quite another and very different question, before the discussion of which we may notice the

MODE OF THE EFFICACY OF THE DECREES OF GOD.

The event decreed is held to be dependent on the decree, and that it is made absolutely certain.   "The very reason why any thing comes to pass in time is because God decreed it" (Fisher's

Explanation of the Shorter Catechism).   In accordance with the foregoing, Dr. A. A. Hodge says, "The one eternal, self-consistent, all-comprehensive purpose of God at the same time determines the nature of the agent, his proper mode of action and each action that shall eventuate."   Again, he says that "they (decrees) render every event embraced in them absolutely certain."   A divine decree relating to man's final destiny is usually called predestination, and, as it relates to the salvation or the perdition of the person, it is called election or reprobation. Thus, Calvin says: " Predestination we call the eternal decree of God, by which he has determined with himself, what he willed to be done with every man.   For all men are not created in an equal condition (*pari conditione*); but eternal life is pre-ordained to some, eternal damnation to others.   Therefore, as every one was formed for the one end or the other end, so we say that he was predestinated to life or to death."

The point we desire specially noted is that the foregoing statements make the decree of God stand in the relation of an *efficient cause* to the thing decreed.   "The reason why any thing comes to pass," as above quoted, "is because God has decreed it."   "In the strict philosophical sense," says Dr. Reid, "I take a cause to be that which has the relation to the effect which I have to my voluntary and deliberate actions; for I take this notion of cause to be derived from the power I feel in myself to produce certain effects.   In this sense we say the Deity is the cause of the universe."   It is the opinion of Isaac Taylor also, one of the ablest of metaphysical writers, that in itself the mind comes to recognize "the first and only cause of which it has any knowledge," and that later, "in following the leadings of mathematical abstraction, and again in mastering the philosophy of the material universe, it establishes the fact of *its homogeneousness with the Supreme Creative Reason*."   The human mind is a cause.   The Infinite Mind is a cause.   Man *causes* a house, a telescope to be; God *causes* a universe to be.

If, now, we admit, for the sake of the inquiry in hand, that God has decreed whatsoever comes to pass, including, of course, the desires, volitions, and actions of men, how does the decree cause the event, how does it bring it to pass? For, since it is utterly incredible that every thing which comes to pass is an accidental correspondence with an eternal decree to bring about just such an event, we must believe, as I have attempted to show, that the procuring cause of the event lay in the decree, or, more strictly, in the mind putting forth the decree. If, now, I will to dismiss the train of thought engaging my mind, this volitional " down brakes " can bring about the event decreed. But if I will that the book nearest me lie at the farther end of my table, the decree is in no wise efficient—there is no conceivable *nexus* between the volition and the event willed. If, however, I will to rise and transfer the book to the designated place, the volition has an immediate efficiency to produce action in my body, and mechanical force transfers the book. Still, it is true that my volition is the cause of the change that took place, but it effected the change through what we call means. Similarly, if I decree that a mechanic shall build me a house, my decree is utterly inefficient to move his mind, but assurance of reasonable compensation will give efficiency to my decree, and the means in this instance we call a motive.

So, whether the divine decree effects immediately the event decreed, or effects it through means, or " proximate causes," it is equally true that the decree is the cause of the event. It is the accepted Calvinistic doctrine that God brings his decrees to pass through the agencies that are said to bring about the events naturally. Since the decree embraces, however, all the means necessary to effect the event, the use of the means makes God none the less the author of the event.

Says Dr. A. A. Hodge: " The decree of God is merely a purpose which he executes in his works of creation and providence. When it is said that all the decrees of God are certainly efficacious, it is not meant that they are the proximate causes of events, but that they render, under the subsequent economy of creation and providence, every event embraced in them absolutely certain." Again, "it (the decree) provides that free agents shall be free agents, and free actions free actions, and that a given free agent shall exist, and that he shall perform a certain free action under certain conditions." All that is very clear. The decree of God makes the *"shall"* in the performance of a free action under certain conditions. That is to say, God ordains the means to the end, namely, "certain conditions," which make the free agent's choice to perform the action an absolute certainty, "shutting up all other ways of acting." That is Calvinistic freedom—power to choose to do the thing decreed, without any power of contrary choice. If one were being swept over Niagara, *choosing* to make the awful plunge would be no relief to the one hopelessly borne to destruction. Choice without the power of contrary choice—the only theory of freedom logically consistent with the eternal causative decree —is "as perfect a fatality of choice," said Lyman Beecher, "as ever pagan, or atheist, or antinomian conceived."

THE CALVINISTIC DECREE MAKES GOD THE AUTHOR OF SIN.

However it may appear to other minds, to the writer it is most clear that no metaphysics, no theory of morals, can free the Calvinistic doctrine of decrees from the charge of making God the author of sin—decreeing not only every wicked act, but decreeing such a combination of "proximate causes" as will certainly cause the doomed agent to choose to do the act. But a few days ago, in this quiet town, a murderer suffered the penalty of death. Had it been shown to the court that a neighbor of the murderer had willed the death of the murdered man, and that he had purposely brought about a combination of circumstances that made it absolutely certain that the murderer would choose to commit the crime, and that any other choice would be impossible, the court should have released the prisoner on trial, and have convicted and hanged the person really guilty. It was in view of this grave difficulty which hopelessly besets the Calvinistic doctrine of a divine decree, which holds all human actions in the grasp of an absolute necessity, that Adam Clarke said: "He who leads another into an offense that he may have a fairer pretense to punish him for it, or bring him into such circumstances that he can not avoid committing a capital crime, and then hangs him for it, is surely the most execrable of mortals. What, then, should we make of the God of justice and mercy, should we attribute to him a decree, the date of which is lost in eternity, by which he has determined to cut off from the possibility of salvation millions of millions of unborn souls, and leave them under a necessity for sinning, by actually hardening their hearts against the influences of his own grace and Spirit, that he may, on the pretense of justice, assign them to endless perdition?"

That we have herein fairly represented the necessary relation of the will of God to the conduct and doom of the wicked, according to the doctrine that God has decreed whatsoever comes to pass, the following passage from the writings of the man whose name the system bears, may be cited in proof. Calvin says: "As by the efficacy of his calling toward the elect, God perfects the salvation to which he had destined them by his eternal decree; so he has his judgments against the reprobate, by which he may execute his counsel concerning them. Those, therefore, whom he created for the reproach of life and the destruction of death, that they might be organs of his anger, and examples of his severity, that they may come to their end, he sometimes deprives of the power of hearing his word, sometimes makes them more blind and stupid by the preaching of it. . . . . Therefore, that Supreme Disposer makes a way for his predesti- nation, when he leaves those in blindness, without the communi- cation of his light whom he has reprobated." So, again, "Let this be the sum; since the will of God is said to be the cause of

all things, that his providence is appointed to be the ruler in all
the counsels and works of men; so that it not only works its
power in the elect, who are governed by the Holy Spirit, but
also *compels the compliance of the reprobate.*"

All must admit that in one sense the creative decree of God
stands back of all other causes of human actions, for had God
not created man, the actions would not have taken place. But
that by no means necessitates the idea that God has decreed all
the actions of the rational creatures he decreed to make, but
Calvinism insists that he did so decree, and thus makes him the
primary cause in the sense of efficiency. Pictet, a Genevan Calvinist, in his work on Theology, bearing the imprint of the Presbyterian Board of Publication, says: " Moreover, the immutability of the decrees incontestibly proves that there are no *conditional* decrees—that is, such as depend on a condition which
may or may not be performed. . . . . It is not, indeed, to be
denied that the promises and the threatenings of God are conditional, but from these no conclusion can be drawn for conditional
decrees. For promises do not determine the future event, as
decrees do."

The doctrine of the foregoing is exactly what Dr. Crosby
declares the stumbling-block. He himself escapes the *fatality*
of the system by simply going (coming) over to the doctrine of
conditional decrees, declaring that " Pharaoh is hardened and
Moses has mercy shown him *after the two had either rejected or
accepted grace.* It is *then* God acts the potter, and does as he
pleases with the clay, making one vessel to dishonor and the
other to honor. If the allusion to the potter is to refer to any
thing else than God's action upon men *already decided in their
position*, then it must be interpreted as God's creation of some
men to be damned. *There is no alternative*" (italics here mine).
Certainly; that is what Cumberland Presbyterians have all the
while claimed to be the logical, inevitable conclusion of the
admitted Calvinistic premises of the universal, unconditional

decree of election and reprobation, without reference to any thing foreseen in the persons so elected or reprobated. Dr. Crosby says, speaking of justifying faith: "That first faith, the yielding to God's grace is man's own act, and not God's, and hence the formula in the gospel is, 'Thy faith hath saved thee.' It is a complete upsetting of common sense and a mystification of fruitless despair to put any thing behind the will of man when this faith is demanded of him by God." Certainly the theological world does move, when a recognized leader in a Calvinistic Church with a stroke of his pen demolishes what has been regarded as the stronghold of the doctrine of unconditional predestination, admits that the usual Calvinistic interpretation of Romans ix. involves the doctrine of God's creation of some men to be damned, and declares "*Paul never taught such a doctrine.*"

PERMISSIVE DECREES NO RELIEF.

To relieve the doctrine of universal decree from the odium of making God the efficient cause of sin, the advocates of the doctrine propose to call the decrees in relation to evil *permissive*, as distinguished from decrees relating to good. Thus, Pictet, who is high Calvinistic authority, explains: "Besides the *immutability* and *eternity* of God's decrees, we must say something of their *extent*. This is so great, that nothing takes place in the world which God hath not decreed should take place; still, it is certain that God is differently concerned in these events, according as they are either good or evil; the good he hath decreed to do, the evil only to permit." The following seems very contradictory: "And yet, since nothing can happen contrary to the will of God, we say that he permits evil, though he in no way approves it;" which amounts to this, that evil is according to the will of God, "since nothing can happen contrary to the will of God," but "he in no way approves of it;" which is to say that God in no way approves of that which is in accordance with his will! Whether the universal decree necessarily locates in the will of

God the efficient cause of evil, equally with the efficient cause of good, Pictet himself will thus testify, the italics being his own : " From this will be inferred what answer must be given to the following question—*Whether the end of every man's life is, with all its circumstances, so unchangeably fixed by the decree of God, that he can not depart out of life at any other period of time or by another kind of death, than that which actually falls to his lot ?* For if all that happens in the world was known to God from eternity, and if nothing could be foreknown by God which he did not also decree should take place, it follows that the end of human life is fixed and determined by God." Thus Pictet teaches not only that the divine decree has the same efficiency in relation to evil in the lives of men, that it has to good, but also to all the circumstances that are the proximate causes of the evil, as to those that are the causes of the good. By this teaching, the victim of the murderer falls at the very moment, in the very place, by the hand, the pistol, the very ball, decreed by God, who foreknew it would all happen, but could foreknow it only because he had decreed it. Thus, the murderer and the murdered, in the fulfillment of an eternal decree, were carried straight from their birth, one to his tragic end upon the scaffold, the other to his fall by the wayside, the chain of circumstances in both cases being alike divinely predetermined of such a character as inevitably to issue in the respective events. Such a theory leaves not a trace of a foundation for any just ideas of moral law, freedom, responsibility, or rewards and punishments.

That the practical bearing of the doctrine of universal decree is pernicious must be manifest, and facts sustain the decision. It is related that a Landgrave of Turing, being admonished that his vile conversation and wicked conduct were endangering his soul, made this defense: "*Si prædestinatus sum, nulla peccata poterunt mihi regnum cœlorum auferre; præscitus, nulla opera mihi illud valebunt conferre ;*" which may be thus rendered into English : " If I am elected, no sins can snatch the kingdom of

heaven from me; if reprobated, no good deeds can avail to procure it for me." Commenting on the foregoing circumstance, a
writer justly says, "It is an objection (to Calvinism) not more
old than common, but such, I must confess, that I have never
found a satisfactory answer to it, from the pen of Supralapsarian
or Sublapsarian, within the small compass of my reading." It
is not to be denied that good men have truly believed the doctrine here condemned as essentially pernicious in its practical
tendency. Nor may it be denied that a man of high moral purpose may be sustained in a virtuous life, and be stimulated to
extraordinary efforts for the good of mankind, by the conviction
that he is one of Heaven's elected favorites, notwithstanding his
belief that whatever is decreed must come to pass, and nothing
else can come to pass. To others, it is, as Dr. Crosby declares,
a "stumbling-block," and one over which multitudes stumble out
of all good into all evil, for time and eternity. The writer has
more than once remonstrated with a man endowed by nature
with extraordinary mental and physical parts, whom strong
drink has made a wreck and a charge upon the public, and the
remonstrance once drew from him the following significant
though irreverent reply: "Well, now, see here; what the Old
Man Above says has to be, that's got to be. He made you to be
a sober man, and me to be a drunken fool, and that's got to be."
He was firm in his philosophy, which he thought himself to be
practically illustrating, and to be a sufficient excuse for his
course as to any worthiness or blame. Really, a philosopher
could say the same—no less, no more, on looking over his record
for a day, a year, or a life-time: "I could not possibly have done
otherwise, for it was all eternally decreed just as it is, with the
proximate causes that gave absolute certainty to every event.
It is not necessary to take any concern about the future, for what
has been decreed concerning me will certainly come to pass, and
by no possibility can any thing else come."

SOURCE OF THE DOCTRINE OF THE UNIVERSAL DECREE.

There can be no question, we think, that the *fate* of the heathen world is the source of the universal unconditional *decree* of the Calvinistic theology.   The word *fate* (*fatum*) signifies "decree," that which is spoken, or commanded.   Leibnitz says that Mohammedan *fate* means an absolute necessity, such that an event must come to pass, even though its cause be avoided. The Stoical *fate* found its necessity in the "course of things," which, it was held, could not possibly be resisted.   "But it is agreed," adds Leibnitz, "that there is a *fatum Christianum*, a *certain destiny* of every thing, regulated by the foreknowledge and providence of God."

Man is a finite creature.   The horizon of his intellectual vision, like that of natural sight, is very limited.   The idea of the creation of the universe by an intelligent first cause, if conceived at all, prevails nowhere outside of those who have derived it from the Scripture.   Matter has been looked upon as eternal, and by many as having in itself the causes of all events.   Hence was easily imbibed the doctrine of an endless series of causes and effects, a chain that bound every thing—human actions, words, and volitions included—in an absolute, inevitable necessity.   Regarding their deities as themselves derived and as having material bodies, the heathen philosophers have held even their gods, in common with themselves, subject to the sway of fate,

"The fixed *decree* which not all heaven can move."

Poetry and mythology associated fate with a vague conception termed "destiny."   The Gnostics made sin an essential and eternal property of matter, and hence held that the contamination of a soul in a material body is fatal necessity.   Spinoza taught materialism and pantheism, making God the soul of the world, and the only agent in the universe, and yet himself, though the author of both good and evil, holiness and sin, subject to an eternal necessity of acting as he does.   Descartes found his fatality

in an atomic theory, making mental states the products of fortuitous combinations of atoms, volitions but resultants of concurrent material forces, and the universe destitute alike of design
and a designer. French fatalism, which banished God, inscribed
at the entrance to its cemeteries, " Death an Eternal Sleep," and
baptized the land in blood, taught that nothing *is* but matter,
and bowed to a fatality it found in an eternal succession of cause
and effect in the operation of material laws. So in one way or
another, all the nations who have not the Bible are accustomed
to believe in some source of an inexorable necessity which
causes every event to be just as it is.

In his *Intellectual System of the Universe,* Cudworth thus
classifies the teachers of *fatality : "First,* such as asserting the
Deity, suppose it irrespectively to decree and to determine all
things, and thereby made all actions necessary to us; which
kind of *fate,* though philosophers and other ancient writers
have not been altogether silent of it, yet it has been principally
maintained by some neoteric Christians contrary to the sense of
the ancient Church. *Secondly,* such as suppose a Deity that, acting wisely, but necessarily, did contrive the general frame of
things in the world; from whence, by a series of causes, doth
unavoidably result whatsoever is so done in it; which *fate* is a
concatenation of causes all in themselves necessary, and is that
which is asserted by the Stoics, Zeno, and Chrysippus, whom the
Jewish Essenes seemed to follow. And, *lastly,* such as hold
the material necessity of all things without a deity, which *fate*
Epicurus calls the *fate* of the naturalists, that is, indeed, the
atheists, the asserters whereof may be called also the Democrit-
ical *fatalists."*

Pictet urges, in support of the unchangeable fixedness of every
event, that "the heathen were fully persuaded of this truth."
Certainly, the heathen were persuaded that such a *fatality* pertains to every human life in its most trivial, as well as in its
important affairs. The passage from Seneca cited by Pictet, to

confirm a theological dogma by a dogma of heathen philosophy, is equally apposite as a proof of the unity of fatality in heathen philosophy and in the theological system of Pictet. Seneca says: "No one dies too soon, seeing that he never could have lived longer than he did; every one has his term fixed, which will always remain fixed where it is fixed, nor will any favor or endeavor make it longer."

This bit of fatalistic philosophy, that a time is fixed for every one's death, before which he can not possibly die, and at which he must die, "cause or no cause," as the Mohammedans say, has had wide currency in our literature. We still say, sometimes seriously, sometimes jocularly, "he can not die till his time comes," an expression we pass along without thought of the meaning in it, as we pass familiar coins without noticing date, image, or superscription. "He that is born to be hanged will never be drowned," was current in England a long time ago, a sentiment Shakespeare ingeniously employs in *The Tempest*, making Gonzales, the honest old counselor, find comfort, in the height of the storm, in what he regards evidence that the Boatswain is born to be hung: "I have great comfort of this fellow; methinks he hath no drowning mark upon him; his complexion is perfect gallows. Stand fast, good *Fate*, to his hanging! Make the rope of his destiny our cable, for our own doth little advantage! If he be not born to be hanged, our case is miserable."

FATALITY GRAFTED UPON CHRISTIANITY.

Referring again to Cudworth's grouping of fatalists in three classes, it will be seen that his first class embraces those who suppose Deity "irrespectively to decree and determine all things," and, thereby, as that author asserts, "make all actions *necessary* to us." We are aware that many Calvinists deny the sequence Cudworth asserts, as flowing from a universal decree determining all events, and so deny *fatality*, where Cudworth asserts it. But if the necessity arising from "the course of nature," or from "the nature of matter," or from a "fortuitous concourse of atoms," be properly called *fatality*, why may we not, with Leibnitz, call the necessity imposed by the eternal, universal decree, or the "*certain destiny* of every thing, regulated by the foreknowledge and providence of God," *fatality*, or, in the designation of Leibnitz, *fatum Christianum?* Surely, the decree of an omnipotent being—which decree is "the only reason why any thing comes to pass"—does not make events less certain or necessary than did the imaginary causes of the *fatality* of the heathen conception. If Calvinism teaches that (Pictet) "the end 'of every one's life, with all its circumstances, is so unchangeably fixed that he can not depart out of life at any other period of time, or by any other kind of death than that which actually falls to his lot," and the Stoics taught precisely the same, why should we call it *fatality*, when the necessity arises out of an eternal succession of cause and effect, as the Stoics taught, and deny that it is *fatality* when the necessity flows from an eternal decree of God, as Calvinism teaches? If it is *fatality* in one case it is in the other. Whatever is the practical bearing of the Stoic philosophy, that is logically the practical bearing of the Calvinistic doctrine of the divine decree of whatsoever comes to pass. Volition, indeed, there is, which consciousness asserts, but the *fatum Stoicum* and the *fatum Christianum* equally and utterly preclude the possibility of other volitions than those that come; so that, according to both these fatalistic theories, our volitions are not less fixed in their character, and in their places in an eternally-ordained series of sequences, than the flinty molecules in a granite boulder. We do not dwell upon this subject because of any supposed ability to suggest a new thought where almost unlimited discussion has engaged all the powers of logic and learning; nor simply to insist on calling things by their right names, as we understand them, and by names odious to brethren who differ with us; but to come at an understanding of the very foundation on which rests the difference, a difference great and vastly important, between the system of theology taught by the Cumberland Presbyterian Church and that system against which it is a protest.

Cudworth further asserts of deistic fatality that, "although philosophers and ancient writers have not altogether been silent of it, yet it has been maintained principally by some neoteric Christians, *contrary to the sense of the ancient Church.*" Not to the ancient Church only, but, as we verily believe, to the Scriptures also, is this doctrine in the most positive antagonism. The apostles warned the Churches, as in Colossians ii. 8, to " beware lest any delude them by means of an empty and deceitful philosophy," in connection with which passage Bloomfield observes that Paul condemns, and cautions the Colossians against, the Grecian philosophy as sure to deceive them in regard to religion; and the same writer quotes Warburton (*Divine Legation*) as saying that "the apostles always speak in terms of contempt or abhorrence of the Grecian philosophy," especially of the philosophy of the Gnostics and Stoics, both of whom were fatalists. The religion of the Gnostics, in the first centuries of Christianity, was a mixture of their philosophy and the teachings of the Bible, but so unsound and absurd that the "orthodox Fathers condemned their doctrines respecting grace, faith, election, and salvation as heretical and unscriptural." The effect of the apostles' warning in regard to the deceptive and dangerous tendencies of the fatalistic philosophies seems to have been to beget in the primitive Church a strong aversion to these philosophies, and even contempt for them. As a consequence, the writings of the Fathers show, as is asserted, no trace of fatalistic predestination before the time of Augustine. Calvin says (Inst. lib. ii., cap. 5, sec. 17), in defending his doctrines: " I know that they may quote Origen and Jerome in support of their exposition; and I, in my turn, could oppose Augustine to them." In commenting on this passage, a careful critic observes: " It appears from this passage that Calvin himself was aware that of all the ancients Augustine was the only one favorable to his opinions." In the same connection Calvin charges Augustine himself with inconsistency in saying that the hardening and blinding (of the reprobate) do not refer to the operation, but to the prescience of God.

AUGUSTINE THE AUTHOR OF THE DOCTRINE.

The introduction of the doctrine of predestination into Christian theology is usually ascribed to Augustine, who was born A.D 354. A passage in Cicero, relating to the worth and dignity of philosophy, is said to have first aroused his mind to earnest investigation, and for ten years he gave himself to the study of heathen philosophy, the simplicity of the Scriptures having no attraction for his taste. He became a professed Manichæan, which means a fatalist of the sternest type. Later he abandoned Manichæism, pronouncing it unsatisfying, and, after trying the Platonic philosophy for a short time, was led, through the influence of Ambrose, Bishop of Milan, to embrace Christianity. To the study of the Bible he betook himself, hoping to find therein "those truths which he had already made himself acquainted with from the Platonic philosophy." By and by he abandoned Platonic Christianity, and professed a most radical conversion to the faith and experience that only the direct power of God could save him from the downward tendencies of the ungodly impulses of his nature, the struggles of mind attending which part of his life are set forth in the eighth and ninth books of his *Confessions*.

Augustine has been regarded an indifferent scholar, critics asserting that, while he had studied the Latin authors well, he knew but little of Greek, and of Hebrew nothing. He was evidently a man of powerful impulses, his life exhibiting very great extremes and contradictions. When bad, he was "exceedingly dissipated." When he became a Manichæan fatalist, he avowed and taught his philosophy. Later, in Platonism his mind was led to the loftiest spiritual contemplations. When he abandoned Manichæism he bitterly opposed it. When brought to a realization of his condition as a sinner, prostrate under a fig-tree, and agonizing in prayer for pardon, he heard (he said), as from the lips of a boy or maiden, the command, " Take, read," which he interpreted to mean that by opening a copy of Paul's epistles he would learn his duty from the first passage that met his eye, which passage proved to be Romans xiii. 13. When he controverted the doctrine of the British monk Pelagius, who denied sin and guilt in the race as a result of Adam's transgression, and asserted man's self-determining power to enter on a life well-pleasing to God, Augustine went to the extreme of asserting the effect of the fall to be such that it is impossible for man to do any thing toward his salvation till after conversion, which he declared as much an act of God as the creation of a world is, and thence to the logical conclusion that, since only some were converted, God had eternally decreed to bestow converting grace on some, to withhold it from others, thus hinging man's destiny to everlasting good or ill on the absolute, unconditional decree, instead of the Manichæan fate which he had previously avowed and taught.

Some, however, ascribe to predestination an earlier appearance in the Church than the time of Augustine. Dr. E. De Pressense, in his *Heresy and Early Christianity*, attributes it to Valentinus, a Gnostic of the Second Century. According to the mixture of heathen philosophy and Scripture taught by Valentinus, human history, before it is enacted in our world of misery and darkness, is unfolded in the higher sphere of the ideal. The tragedy of existence is played in three parts: " First in the highest region, called the pleroma ; then in the intermediate sphere, and lastly upon earth." According to this mixture of the " most purely ethereal and most grossly material elements," every thing that transpires on earth is absolutely fixed in every respect,

8

being determined in the antecedent ideal sphere, and thus most inexorably fated to be as it is. The Gnostics, though reckoned a heretical Christian sect, put God far away from the world, in what they called the "abyss," confounding him with it. Around the "abyss" is the "pleroma," inhabited by the æons, who are emanations from God, and fulfill various functions. Of these æons some Gnostics held that there were three hundred and sixty-five. The one who created the material world was Demiurge. The redeemer of the world is the æon called Christ. They divide the human race into three classes, all of one class, and as many of the second class as have received a certain influence from the pleroma, being predestinated to salvation, and the remainder of the second class, with all the third, doomed to inevitable annihilation.

The Long Struggle with Philosophy.

In later periods we find many distinguished leaders in the Church so mingling heathen philosophy and Christianity as to evolve fatalistic and otherwise pernicious theological systems. Thomas Aquinas, born in 1224, is a representative of the Scholastic Philosophy, uniting Idealism and Realism, which philosophy Aquinas married to his theology. Nothing more fully exhibits the long, severe struggle of the simple truth of the gospel with these vain philosophies than the abstractions which employed the powers of the great disputants of the Middle Ages, when, as one has expressed it, "The strong undercurrent was Platonism, but the Aristotelic Philosophy the tide that flowed on the surface, propelled by every wind and storm that vexed the Church." Philosophy had arrived at the conculsion that the only things in the universe are *matter* and *form*, and that *form* has an actual existence apart from *matter*, and, then, that *forms* of all things have pre-existence, and that they are the *ends* to which nature, in all its operations and products, is instinctively and unceasingly working; and, so, that these eternal *forms*—"*ideas*" Plato called them—of necessity determined exactly what every material existence should be. Now, some of the Christian scholars of those times were competent to the task of reconciling Christianity with such a philosophy by simply transferring these eternal *forms* to the Divine Mind, calling them decrees, and finding there a creative energy that had to make the world exactly in the eternal molds. So theirs was a world under fatalistic necessity. It was the boast of the followers of Aquinas, called *Thomists*, that their leader, "St. Thomas," had "rescued Aristotle from atheism, and secured him for orthodoxy," which "reconciling" lay in identifying the eternal "forms" of the philosopher with the eternal "decrees" of God; and this made the *Thomists* Nominalistic in philosophy, Augustinian in theology. The process of "reconciling" theology with science—with cosmology, geology, evolution, etc.—is still in progress, and it is most manifest that with some of these peacemakers plain, scriptural theology is about all reconciled away. Yet man will study the problems of the world in which he lives, and rightly, and in the long run there has been a grand advance in the true reconciliation of our interpretations of God's two books of nature and revelation. That we have left behind us the abstractions of the Schoolmen—some of them so abstract as almost to make one dizzy in the effort to grasp them—let us thank God and breathe freer. The Church is certainly making progress in eliminating from her theology the heathen elements which crept in from the old philosophies, and if she does not bow to the materialistic tendencies of these times she will do well. Ignorance and error have caused countless wars, losses, and sufferings. "Knowledge is the wing wherewith we fly to heaven," said the greatest genius of his century, if not of all the centuries; and the divine Teacher declares: "Ye shall know the truth, and the truth shall make you free." On the rock of truth only can man come to permanent rest and abiding good. Truth abideth forever.

CHAPTER IV.

DECREES IN THE CREEDS OF THE CHURCHES.

THIS chapter is written with a sincere desire to arrive as clearly as possible at what is regarded very important truth. To the writer it seems of vital importance, at this juncture of affairs, that Cumberland Presbyterians stand fast in the liberty wherewith the truth has made them free, and that they be not in any wise entangled with the yoke of doctrinal bondage imposed by the Westminster Confession. There are good people who greatly dislike what is usually termed discussion, much preferring that you state your own views, without reference to what other people believe or teach. These good people forget that, by contrasting it with error truth is often much more readily seen in its simplicity, beauty, and consistency Tracing doctrines to their sources, comparing them with admitted truths, and noting carefully their logical sequences, are helpful means of forming a correct judgment as to their soundness. Christ himself reasoned much with those who attended his instructions, and sat in the temple, hearing the doctors and asking them questions. Stephen disputed with those who assembled in the synagogue of the Libertines, and Cyrenians, Alexandrians, Cilicians, and Asiatics, who "were not able to resist the wisdom and the spirit by which he spake." From the time Paul encountered the Athenians in the midst of Mars Hill, until this day, truth has been winning its way in the world through discussion, and thus will go on to whatever victories yet await it. President Garfield said that "unsettled questions have no mercy on the peace of nations," and another of our political sages said, with equal truth and significance, that "nothing is settled until it is settled right." The same things are equally true in regard to Churches; for doctrinal error in a creed will be a disturbing element, and an unsettled question, so long as it is not settled right. Questions rooting in the doctrine of decrees, in 1837, rent the Presbyterian Church into nearly equal parts. The subsequent reunion in 1869, when many of the leaders of the former great discussion had passed away, is now followed by a grander, but more peaceful, upheaval of thought, and by a seeming determination to break the yoke of theological bondage endured for generations.

AUGUSTINIAN PREDESTINATION.

It seems well established that through Augustine, early in the Fifth Century, the doctrine of predestination received its first public recognition in the Church. Various sects had existed, Simon Magus being supposed to have represented one, whose doctrines, as those of the Basilidians and the Valentinians, were fatalistic, making man's eternal destiny the issue of some power over which he could exercise no possible control; but these were all discarded by the Church as heretical. When Pelagianism sprang up, denying what is called original sin, and teaching that every man has in himself the power of choosing good or evil, and so can obtain salvation by choosing it and living for it, and that predestination to life is always founded on this choosing on man's part, Augustine appeared as the bitter opponent of these views, his own doctrine being formulated thus: "By the sin of Adam human nature became physically and morally corrupt. From it evil lust has come, which, since it has become the inheritance of all men by generation, has come to be original sin, in itself damnatory, and prevails so much over the will of the natural man that he can no longer will what is good, as he should do out of love to God, but sins continually, however his actions may externally appear. From this corrupt mass of humanity God resolved from all eternity to save some through Christ, and leave the rest to deserved perdition. Therefore, divine grace, alone and irresistibly, works faith in the elect, as well as love and power to do good. The others, to whom the grace of God is not imparted, have no advantage from Christ, and fall into condemnation, even an eternal one." These Augustinian views were formally sanctioned by the decisions of African synods, and by Zosimus in the West; "although their author," says Mosheim, "himself felt how dangerous they might be made to morals, and was able to bring them forward in instruction in no other than an inconsequential way." The same author states that "the Augustinian doctrine of grace was never adopted in the East," and that "even in the West, where this doctrine had been ecclesiastically ratified, there were never more than a few who held to it in its fearful consequences. Its injurious practical effects could not be overlooked, and appeared occasionally in outward manifestation."

Augustinian and Westminster Fatalism.

From the foregoing it will be seen that Augustine made the salvation of "some" to depend on an eternal decree and irresistible grace; that "the rest," by the divine purpose, utter inability of will to any good, and the withholding of irresistible grace, of necessity "fall into condemnation, even an eternal one." Why that doctrine is not really as *fatalistic* as Manichæism, or why it is a fatalism any better, it would be difficult to tell, especially if one were of "the rest" left to perdition. Rejoicing in the truth, we are glad to be able to quote such words as the following, from Dr. Crosby's tractate on Calvinism: "But Augustine, in his zeal against the errors of Pelagius, not only made the divine grace the foundation of man's salvation, but made it arbitrarily discriminate between man and man, contrary to the Scripture testimony that God wishes all men to be saved

(1 Tim. ii. 4).   He thus denies man's ability to accept the divine grace.   This Augustinian theology rendered man passive by making God to do all in the matter of salvation.   The gospel invitation addressed to all was (by it) not meant for all, but only for those whom God would compel to accept it.   The entreaties of God's word to sinners were thus rendered insincere, and our Lord's words, 'Ye will not come unto me that ye might have life,' should have been, 'God wills that ye should not come unto me that ye might have life,' or, 'God has not given you life whereby you can come unto me.'"   Most certainly the theological world does move!   For ascribing to Augustinianism the very errors here charged upon it by Dr. Crosby, Cumberland Presbyterians have been a thousand times declared inconsistent and unjust.   What is more remarkable still, Dr. Crosby charges upon the Westminster Confession the error of destroying the freedom of the will, which is exactly the same charge that Cumberland Presbyterians have always brought against that creed. Though it comes late, this testimony from the other side is gratifying, not only, however, as some justification of our protest against the Westminster Confession, but as an indication that the day may not be distant when the two Churches will see eye to eye on all the great doctrines of salvation.

"Calvin adopted the extreme views of Augustine," says Dr. Crosby, "and pressed them, as did Augustine, under the plea of logic, but it is just here, where these good men left God's word for their logical inferences, that they go astray.   The Semi-Pelagians were a rebuke to Augustine, and justly so.   The Arminians were still more justly a rebuke to the Calvinism of the Reformation.   The Heidleberg and Westminster Confessions (and no symbols can compare with them for clear statement of Scripture truth), with all their excellence, have the philosophic defects to which we refer, and which are the dead flies in the apothecary's ointment."   Now, in all kindness be it said, the very thing that Cumberland Presbyterians did with

Westminsterism was to cast the "dead flies" of the fatalistic philosophy out of the theological "ointment."

LOGICAL INFERENCES NOT TO BE DENIED.

The so-called "philosophical defects" attributed, in the foregoing concession, to the two Confessions named, seem to be that of pressing a doctrine to its "logical inferences." Yet, it seems incredible that so scholarly a divine can mean to ask us to accept a doctrine, if to follow it to its logical inferences requires us to leave God's word. Logical inferences must be true, if that of which they are inferences is true. If that law fails us, all is gone. Here, we may kindly suggest, a great deal of trouble has arisen, for Calvinists have written countless volumes to deny, and attempt to disprove, the "logical inferences" of their own premises. If God has unconditionally decreed whatsoever comes to pass, and any human being fails of salvation, it is not in the power of reason to avert the logical inference that God unconditionally decreed that the said human being should fail of salvation. The Calvinistic system utterly excludes conditional decrees, and conditions God's prescience on the absolute decree. He who accepts the premises of Calvinism must accept all its logical inferences, and if to follow these inferences is to leave God's word, then must we abandon the system with its inferences, or stultify reason. Truer words were never spoken than those of Bishop Tomlinson, touching this point: "But Calvinism, however modified or explained, while its characteristic principles are preserved, will always be found liable to the most serious objections ; and if those principles by which it is distinguished as a sect of Christianity be taken away, it is no longer Calvinism. Calvinism, in reality, will not bear defalcation or admit of partial adoption. It has, at least, the merit of being so far consistent with itself. Its peculiar doctrines, considered as a system, are so connected and dependent upon each other that if you embrace one you must embrace all; and if the falsehood of one part be proved, the whole falls to the ground."

In which is to be found inconsistency, the Calvinism of the times of the Reformation, or in that of the Nineteenth Century? Calvin and his adherents, indeed, pushed their premises to their legitimate conclusions, to their "logical inferences," and, in so doing, were true to the laws of human reason, which laws denied, no basis of knowledge remains. A few sentences from Calvin's writings will exhibit what Dr. Crosby probably means by the "extreme views" he attributes to both Augustine and Calvin:—

"Therefore, if we can not assign a reason why he (God) thinks his own worthy of mercy, except because it so pleases him, neither shall we have any other ground for his reprobating others, except his will."

"Many, indeed, as if they wished to repel odium from God, so acknowledge election that they deny that any one is reprobated; but too ignorantly and childishly; since election itself would not stand, unless opposed to reprobation. . . . Those, therefore, whom God passes over he reprobates; and for no other reason except that he chooses to exclude them from the inheritance which he predestinates to his sons."

Of the decree of reprobation he says: "I confess that it is indeed a horrible decree; no one, however, will be able to deny but that God foreknew what would be the end of man, before he formed him; and he therefore foreknew it, because he had so ordained by his own decree."

"Let this be the sum; since the will of God is said to be the cause of all things, that his providence is appointed to be the ruler in all the counsels and works of men; so that it not only exerts its power in the elect, who are governed by the Holy Spirit, but also compels the compliance of the reprobate."

"That the reprobate do not obey the word of God, when explained to them, will be rightly imputed to the wickedness and maliciousness of their own hearts, provided it be at the same time added that they are addicted to this wickedness because they are raised up by the just but inscrutable judgment of God, to illustrate his glory by their damnation."

The foregoing statements are supposed to indicate some of Calvin's extreme views: That reprobation is a necessary correlate of election, and that the two arise equally out of the good pleasure of God; that God, indeed, foreknew the end of man, that man would sinfully rebel, and foreknew it because he had "so ordained by his own decree;" that God's power exerts itself not only in his providence toward the elect, "but also compels the compliance of the reprobate;" that, while the reprobate do indeed reject the word of God through "the wickedness and maliciousness of their own hearts," yet "they are addicted to this wickedness because they are raised up by the just but inscrutable judgment of God, to illustrate his glory by their damnation." "Extreme views," surely—extreme views of a Creator proclaimed "gracious" and "merciful," yet raising up some men by his just and inscrutable judgments to illustrate his glory by their damnation for being carried by omnipotent power to the very end for which they had been created! What more extreme views could mortal mind conceive as to either the character of the God men are asked to worship, or the utter hopelessness of those reprobated for no other reason than because he chose "to exclude them from the inheritance to which he predestinates his sons?" But to these "extreme views" logical necessity drives those holding Calvinistic premises!

Now, if any good man is wounded by this presentation of a few of the hard sayings of Calvin, and will yet claim that, while he repudiates all such doctrines, he is a Calvinist, we must accept his repudiation of the extreme views, but equally must insist that "Calvinist" is, in his case, a misnomer. We desire, in this connection, to repeat and emphasize the fact that no Cumberland Presbyterian can be a "moderate Calvinist." Calvinism can be expressed in a very few words: God has unchangeably decreed whatsoever comes to pass. His decree respecting what shall be the end of every man is called predestination; and predestination is called election as it respects those predestinated to life, and reprobation in respect to those predestinated unto death. And God hath not decreed any thing because he foresaw it as future, or as that which would come to pass upon known conditions.

To the foregoing add the declaration of an enthusiastic advocate and competent interpreter of Calvinism: "Predestination is the all-ruling, all-conditioning soul of the Calvinistic system, upon which doctrine the admirable power, fullness, depth, and consistency of the system are directly grounded."

LOGICAL SEQUENCES OF PREDESTINATION.

Predestination, then, is the all of the Calvinistic system as respects the destiny of human beings—the eternal decree fixing what the end of every man shall be, carrying him straight to the mark. To us, the following seem to be unavoidable logical inferences of the system as taught by the Reformers and by the Westminster Confession:

1. That sin is according to the good pleasure of God.

Calvin seems to admit as much in this declaration—" I acknowledge that this is my doctrine, that Adam fell, not by the mere permission of God; but also by his secret counsel;" and in this, "I confess that I wrote that the fall of Adam was not accidental, but ordained by the secret decree of God."

To avoid this logical inference, Timothy Dwight makes this extraordinary shift: " To support the objection it must be shown that God can not will and accomplish the existence of voluntary agents, who, acting freely, shall, nevertheless, act in accordance with what is, upon the whole, his pleasure." That is to say, it is in the power of God to create beings with exactly such moral tendencies as will make it absolutely certain that they will do

freely the evil that is embraced in his decrees, for which evil
they are then to be eternally punished. Really, the vindication
seems worse than the charge in the logical inference, for it not
only makes God will the evil, but makes him create and endow
agents for the specific purpose of freely doing the evil, to which
agents other ways of acting are utterly shut up.

2. That the human will acts under a necessity that is rightly
called fatalistic.

It may be asserted that wicked men choose the wickedness
they commit. They certainly do so choose; consciousness tes-
tifies that. But Calvinism makes the actual choice the only possible choice. According to Dwight, they are so created and
endowed as to make it absolutely certain they will choose to do
the things decreed by an omnipotent Being. Could one be more
fated?

Upon this point we are able to quote the opinion of Dr.
Crosby, who thus charges the Westminster Confession with
teaching what he would call necessitated volition: "In order to
make God sovereign, these symbols make man a machine.
They in terms declare man a free agent, but in their statements
respecting God's sovereignty they deny this declaration. The
will to which God appeals, beseeching it to turn to him, they
state, is powerless to turn, unless God forces it to turn, thus
destroying the whole meaning of the appeal. . . . . Now, to say
that God's grace acts behind man's will as a compelling power,
in this acceptance, is to say that God accepts grace, and not
man. By no process of reasoning can man be made a free agent
in the matter, and the true declaration of the Westminster Confession (ch. iii., sec. 1) is contradicted, namely: 'Nor is violence
offered to the will of the creatures.'" [Dr. Crosby means that
ch. iii., sec. 1, of the Westminster Confession, is contradicted by
ch. vii., sec. 3.]

3. Limited atonement. For why should provision be made
for the salvation of those whom God "eternally predestinated to

death," as Calvin puts it, or whom he "passes by," as others more mildly say the same thing?

4. The salvation of only some infants ("elect infants") dying in infancy. If any human being predestinated to death or "passed by" in God's merciful provisions dies in infancy, such a one is surely not saved. But how can any one know or assert or possibly believe that not one of the "passed by" has died, or that one such never will die, in infancy? Yet that is the sole hypothesis on which an advocate of unconditional predestination can admit the salvation of all dying in infancy. If God's elective decree is not based on any thing foreseen in those elected, why should we suppose all dying in infancy are elect? There is simply no place in the Calvinistic system for such a supposition. Dr. Briggs says: "It seems plain that the adjective 'elect' limits 'infants,' as it does all other persons; and that the Westminster Confession teaches that there are some elect persons among infants," etc., thus frankly admitting that the Confession of his Church does not teach the doctrine of the salvation of all dying in infancy.

5. The certain final perseverance of all true believers, since an eternal decree of God predestinates them to life, and makes certain all the means necessary thereto.

6. That this life is not probationary.

It has long seemed to the writer that denial of probation to man here on earth is one of the most obvious logical sequences of the Westminster teaching. If an eternal decree has unchangeably determined that A is of the elected, and B is of "the rest of mankind," who have been "passed by," can it be said, in any proper sense of the term, that either A or B is in a state of probation? The destiny of each is fixed; and so is that of every human being, according to the Confession, since the angels and men predestinated and ordained, some to one class, some to the other, are "particularly and unchangeably designed," their number being "so certain and definite that it can not be increased or diminished." Beings thus " predestinated," " fore-ordained," and "particularly and unchangeably designed " by an eternal decree of an omnipotent God, are no more proba-tioners, in the ordinary acceptation of the term, than were Laz-arus and Dives when seen as separated by an impassable gulf. If God's omnipotent decree assigning men and angels particu-larly and unchangeably, some to the one class, some to the other, does not utterly preclude and exclude the predication of proba-tion of these men and angels, then one idea can not be logically exclusive of another. As destructive as must be this denial of probation, in its practical bearing on men's disposition toward an offered gospel, Dr. Briggs openly accepts it, saying: " The doctrine that this life is a probation, and that there is a private judgment at death are inseparable. Both are Arminian, and *neither can be reconciled with Calvinistic principles."*

Dr. Briggs in his recent work (*Whither?*) charges the Calvin-ists of to-day with going beyond the Reformers, and certainly shows that in some doctrinal aspects they do; while Dr. Crosby declares that the Reformers are the ones who were at fault in pushing their " logical inferences " too far. The seeming contra-diction is, doubtless, to be explained by the fact that in the days of Calvin, as now, those who held to predestination and cognate doctrines differed considerably in their views. The consistent Calvinists, as seems to us undeniable, are the hyper-Calvinists. A system of doctrine of any kind must be held responsible for its " logical inferences," and that, too, when pushed to "extreme views," provided that those views are " logical inferences." If we accept a geometrical proposition, we accept all its logical cor-ollaries, and to deny any of them would be to stultify ourselves. It has been very common, indeed, for Cumberland Presbyterians to be charged with the unfairness of attributing to Calvinists doctrines which they do not believe nor teach. As Cumberland Presbyterians discard Calvinism, it may be assumed that as a matter of course they view that system of doctrine in all its objectionable features, not excepting any truly logical inference it yields. This they are justly entitled to do so long as they state fairly the premises of the system, and in the sense put into the language by the authors of those premises. The writer is desirous at this point, not only to vindicate his own Church, but also to have our brethren of the other Church understand us. That all disputants upon our side have been always fair, is what can not be reasonably presumed; that as a rule they have been or at least meant to be so, our personal knowledge of these discussions does not permit us to doubt.

CALVINISM OF THE REFORMERS.

As an illustration of how the Calvinistic system was interpreted in the days of the Reformers, we subjoin what are known as *The Lambeth Articles*, proposed at Lambeth, England, November 10, 1595, by Archbishop Whitgift, and adopted by the divines from Cambridge along with others assembled for the purpose of defining the system:

"1. God from eternity hath predestinated certain men unto life; certain men he hath reprobated.

" 2. The moving or efficient cause of predestination unto life is not the foresight of faith, or of perseverance, or of good works, or of any thing that is in the person predestinated, but only the good will and pleasure of God.

" 3. There is predetermined a certain number of the predestinate, which can be neither augmented nor diminished.

" 4. Those who are not predestinated to salvation shall be necessarily damned for their sins.

" 5. A true, living and justifying faith, and the Spirit of God justifying, is not extinguished, falleth not away, it vanisheth not away in the elect, either totally or finally.

" 6. A man truly faithful—that is, such a one who is truly endowed with a justifying faith—is certain, with the full assurance of faith, by the remission of his sins, of his everlasting salvation by Christ.

" 7. Saving grace is not given, is not granted, is not communicated to all men, by which they may be saved if they will.

" 8. No man can come unto Christ, unless it be given unto him, and unless the Father shall draw him ; and all men are not drawn by the Father, that they may come to the Son.

" 9. It is not in the will or power of every one to be saved."

These Articles were not indeed authoritative, and are cited only in proof of the interpretation of Calvinism in the early days of its history. They were so displeasing to the Queen that she commanded the Archbishop speedily to recall and suppress them, " which was performed with such care and diligence," says an historian, " that a copy of them was not to be found for a long time afterward." Are not all these points embraced, in phraseology somewhat different, in the Westminster Confession?

The Church of England is largely opposed to the Calvinistic system, some of the strongest protests against it which have ever appeared having come from her learned divines. Bishop Sumner, commenting on the express and comprehensive command, " Go teach all nations, baptizing them in the name of the Father, and the Son, and the Holy Ghost," observes " that these words imply a benefit placed within the power of the whole nation generally, and not of a select part from each nation, can not at least be denied on the face of the words themselves, which convey the impression that Christianity was to be gradually diffused and the offer of the gospel made without reserve." Speaking of the Calvinistic tenet of man's inability to do any thing until that call is received which must always be effectual (*gratia irresistabilis*), Sumner says: " No one can be blind to the dangerous tendency of this doctrine ; no one, I should imagine, would incur the hazard, except from an overruling sense of duty, of thus promoting rashness, supineness, or despair. In St. Paul's mode of addressing the churches, in several passages he speaks of a co-operation, or at least an exertion on man's part, which is incompatible with his being a mere patient, working no more than dead, senseless matter in the artificer's hands, ... as when he encourages the Philippians to use their own power earnestly, from a consciousness of the grace by which they would be supported, '*Work out your own* salvation, for it is God that worketh in you.' "

DECREES IN THE THIRTY-NINE ARTICLES.

Article xvii. of this Symbol of the Church of England and of the Episcopalians of the United States, "Of Predestination and Election," reads thus: "Predestination to life is the everlasting purpose of God, whereby (before the foundations of the world were laid) he hath constantly decreed by his counsel secret to us, to deliver from curse and damnation those whom he hath chosen in Christ out of mankind, and to bring them by Christ to everlasting salvation, as vessels made to honor. Therefore, they which be endued with such an excellent benefit of God be called according to God's purpose by his Spirit working in due season ; they through grace obeying the calling; they be justified freely; they be made sons of God by adoption; they be made like the image of his only begotten Son, Jesus Christ; they walk religiously in good works, and at length, by God's mercy, they attain to everlasting felicity."

There is no allusion in the foregoing, and none in the remaining sections, to the reprobation of any portion of humanity, nor to their being passed by. Declaring the doctrine (our election in Christ) to be "full of sweet, pleasant, and unspeakable comfort to godly persons," the Article adds, "So, for curious and carnal persons, lacking the spirit of Christ, to have continually before their eyes the sentence of God's predestination, ... is a most dangerous downfall, whereby the devil doth thrust them either into desperation, or into wretchedness of most unclean living, no less perilous than desperation."

Bickersteth (*Questions on the Thirty-nine Articles*) says that the

9

words " to life " are inserted " to exclude the doctrine of *reproba-tion*." In further explanation of the doctrine of election as held by that Church, he adds that to be " chosen in Christ " means " only that God for his part had chosen them to be heirs of sal-vation, provided they on their part would ' put on the breast-plate of faith and love,' and so make their calling and election sure."

An eminent divine of the Episcopal Church declares that " by virtue of the dispensation of grace, under which human nature is now placed, no man is reprobate until he makes himself so by deliberate rejection of the grace of God, by driving from his soul the Holy Spirit, the source of all the good that is in man," and that "*the actual present state of human nature, through the mediation of Christ, and by the gift of the Holy Spirit, is that of probation, not of reprobation.*"

Every human being, a prisoner of hope, raised in Christ to a gracious probation, called of God to lay hold on eternal life freely and sincerely offered to all by the all-merciful Father who willeth not the death of any—such is the gospel we preach. These are the obvious, comforting gospel truths, pressed upon the judgment and consciences of men.

" We should," says Barrow, " adhere to those plain and posi-tive declarations whereby God representeth himself seriously designing and earnestly desiring that all men should come to the knowledge of the truth; that none should perish, but that all should come to repentance, not doubting but that his *declared mind* and his *secret providence*, although we can not thoroughly discern or explain their consistency, do yet really and fully conspire."

DECREES IN THE CANONS OF DORT.

As another illustration of the " extreme views " discarded and deprecated by Calvinists of the Dr. Crosby school, but asserted by more consistent Calvinists, as we must think them, to be "logical inferences" of admitted Calvinistic premises, we cite the summary of the Articles of the Synod of Dort, as it is given by Tilenus, and so far as it relates to the five points controverted between Calvinists and Arminians. This summary certainly shows that some men have been capable of a rugged faith indeed, if it could still trust and worship a God described as so decreeing in reference to his creatures:

"1. That God, by an absolute decree, hath elected to salvation a very small number of men, without any regard to their faith or obedience whatsoever; and secluded from saving grace all the rest of mankind, and appointed them, by the same decree, to eternal damnation, without any regard to their infidelity or impenitency.

" 2. That Jesus Christ hath not suffered death for any other, but for those elect only; having neither had any intent nor commandment of his Father to make satisfaction for the sins of the whole world.

" 3. That by Adam's fall his posterity lost their free will, being put to an unavoidable necessity to do, or not do, whatsoever they do or do not, whether it be good or evil, being thereunto predestined by the eternal and effectual secret decree of God.

" 4. That God, to save his elect from the corrupt mass, doth beget faith in them by a power equal to that whereby he created the world and raised up the dead; insomuch that such unto whom he gives that grace can not reject it, and the rest, being reprobate, can not accept it.

" 5. That such as have once received that grace by faith can never fall from it finally or totally, notwithstanding the most enormous sins they can commit."

" The *Canons of the Synod of Dort* constitute," says Professor Shedd (*History of Christian Doctrine*), "a highly important portion of the Calvinistic symbolism." These *Canons*, ninety-three in all, " combat the principal tenets of the Arminians, and develop the Calvinistic system," says Shedd, who adds that the Reformed Churches in various countries, and the Puritans in England, "received these Canons as the scientific and precise statement of Christianity." The English Episcopal Church rejected these Canons of Dort. It may be well supposed, indeed, that the circumstances giving rise to this Calvinistic symbol would produce a radical protest against Arminianism, which protest implies the greatest extreme possible in the direction of Calvinism. Yet, may it not be truthfully said that these harsh utterances all lie within the logical sequences of the Calvinistic premises? They are most assuredly but Calvinism "developed into precise and scientific statement." The foregoing summary may employ phraseology not justified by the Canons, but the ideas are necessarily in any true, scientific statement of Calvinism. Dr. Reid, the metaphysician, states that he was at first a firm believer in Locke's theory of ideas, but finding that consequences resulted from that theory "which gave him more trouble than the supposition of the non-existence of matter," he began to examine into the foundation principles of Locke's philosophy, and so to reject the hypothesis altogether. The trouble is with the fundamental premise of Calvinism, which premise adopted into our theological system, it is folly to deny the "logical inferences," or to attribute injustice and ignorance to those who declare the system chargeable with its logical sequences. Speaking of the evil tendencies of the Calvinistic system, Bishop Sumner declares: "It matters not that a pious Calvinist disclaims the natural results, or an acute disputant can explain them away : it is notorious that the illiterate enthusiast believes, and the sinner flatters himself with expecting, that, if he is one of the elect, he shall somehow or other be finally snatched out of the fire; and, if he is not, that no exertions of his can ever avail. Thus the real conclusion and the practical evil of the doctrine of election meet together." "I do not," he adds, "consider this as a matter of argument, but of historical experience." He refers for illustration to the passage in Burnet's *History of the Reformation :*

"The Germans soon saw the ill effects of the doctrine of decrees. Luther changed his mind about it, and Melanchthon wrote openly against it; and since that time the whole stream of the Lutheran Churches has run the other way; but both Calvin and Bucer were still for maintaining the doctrines, only they warned the people not to think much about them, since they were secrets that men could not penetrate into. Hooper and many other good writers did often exhort the people from entering into these curiosities; and a caveat to the same purpose was put into the Article about predestination." If Calvinism, then, has the tendency here ascribed to it, how must we think of it, if we apply the test set up by the infallible Teacher: "A good tree can not bring forth evil fruit?" This Calvinistic tree brings forth evil fruit; therefore—what? But theorists seem adequate to almost any task in the way of denying the "logical inferences," or of reconciling the pernicious consequences of their systems, in which art heathen philosophy showed no less skill than do theologians of some schools, as may be illustrated by the following passages from the fatalistic poet Manillus:

"The fates rule the world; arts and manners are alike given to created beings, and vices, and misfortunes, losses and gains in their affairs. None can want what is given him, nor can any have what is denied. Lo! parents destroy their children, and children their parents, and armed brethren inflict on each other mutual wounds. These are not the crimes of men; they are forced to such actions, and to incur their penalties and the laceration of their members." To this, his own statement, the poet opposes, what follows—a "yet not so as thereby": "Yet, crimes derive no defense from this statement, nor does it defraud virtue of its reward. . . . So, the praise of human merit is so much the greater that it comes from the will of Heaven, and, on the other hand, we hate those who do wrong, the more, because they are created for crime and punishment." Now, we must say of this fatalistic philosophy (as we should say of every fatalistic system of theology, which, by an eternal decree or any other agency, absolutely and unchangeably determines whatsoever comes to pass) that it utterly defies all honest effort at distinction between right and wrong in human conduct, and leaves not the semblance of a foundation on which to predicate the idea of moral government over rational creatures. Such a system, though Christian it calls itself, claiming to vindicate the glory of God by making whatsoever comes to pass an inevitable issue of his own absolute, eternal decree, in very truth robs him of the glory springing from the obedience, love, and adoration of a vast economy of free moral agents, created in his own image, loving, obeying, and adoring the Creator in whom they perceive all moral excellence.

The reader is again reminded that these paragraphs are not an intended discussion of what Dr. Crosby calls the " Evil of Calvinism," our purpose being simply to emphasize that *protest* (against the Calvinistic system) with which the Cumberland Presbyterian Church began its career, to which it has uniformly stood firm, which protest it should continue to maintain so long as the cause which first prompted it continues to exist. Most of all have Cumberland Presbyterians been charged with misrepresentation for insisting that the Westminster Confession teaches inferentially the (unpcpular) doctrine of

" INFANT DAMNATION."

To this subject Dr. Briggs (*Whither ?*) devotes over a dozen pages, to prove, not that Cumberland Presbyterians make a false charge, but that the Confession of Faith teaches exactly what Cumberland Presbyterians have always claimed it teaches, and that such is, as he shows beyond a reasonable doubt, what all the framers of the Confession understood it to teach, and meant to have it teach. Dr. Briggs also, at this point, charges the Presbyterian Church with forsaking the historic meaning of their Standards, adding; " This movement seems to have been begun by Dr. Archibald Alexander. In his youth he was greatly influ-

enced by the Baptists in Virginia; and when President of
Hampden and Sidney College, in 1797–99, he was .greatly
troubled about infant baptism, and for a while discontinued its
use.   These influences led him to abandon the Calvinistic doctrine of the damnation of non-elect infants."   Dr. Briggs quotes
Dr. Prentiss as saying, in *The Presbyterian Review*, that "the
change from the position generally held by Calvinistic divines
at the beginning, or in the middle of the Seventeenth Century,
to the ground taken by Dr. Charles Hodge, in 1871, in his *Systematic Theology*, is simply immense;" that it "amounts to a
sort of revolution."   "It is, however, *contrary to the Westminster Confession of Faith*," says Dr. Briggs, "*to believe in the salvation of all infants*, or to believe in the salvation of any of the
heathen who are capable of being outwardly called by the ministry of the word."   Again: "We are able to say that the Westminster divines were unanimous on this question of the salvation of elect infants only.   We have examined the greater part
of the writings of the Westminster divines, and have not been
able to find any different opinion from the extracts we have
given.   The Presbyterian Churches have departed from their
Standards on this question, and it is simple honesty to acknowledge it.   We are at liberty to amend the Confession, but we
have no right to distort it, and to pervert its meaning."   It is
due to Dr. Briggs to say that he courageously and avowedly dis-
cards his own Confession, saying: "We do not hesitate to express our dissent from the Westminster Confession in this
limitation of the divine electing grace.   We are of opinion that
God's electing grace saves all infants, and not a few of the
heathen."   Now that their interpretation of the Westminster
Confession touching the doctrine of infant salvation is fully
sanctioned by so eminent a scholar of the Presbyterian Church
as Dr. Briggs, Cumberland Presbyterians may feel reassured in
regard to the justice of their interpretation of that article in
the Confession, and equally in regard to their protest to the

article as thus interpreted, since not only Dr. Briggs is fully with us in interpreting and rejecting the "elect infants" article, but also that, as asserted by Dr. Prentiss, there has been a "revolution in theological opinion" along the very line of our departure from the Westminster symbols. Let us, then, in conclusion, state more definitely and authoritatively the

CUMBERLAND PRESBYTERIAN DOCTRINE OF DECREES.

By the end of three and a half years, the first organized Cumberland Presbyterian presbytery had grown to a synod, composed of three presbyteries. The "brief view" of doctrines and discipline approved at the first meeting of this synod is, so far as known to us, the first doctrinal statement put forth by the Cumberland Presbyterian Church. "As regards the doctrine of predestination and election, our fathers declared in the 'brief view' that they were pleased neither with the application that rigid Calvinists nor Arminians make of it. They thought that the truth of this, as well as of many other points of divinity, lies between the opposite extremes." * The "view" embraced these declarations as points of dissent from the Westminster Confession:

First—That there are no eternal reprobates.

Second—That Christ died, not for *part* only, but for *all* mankind.

Third—That *all* infants dying in infancy are saved through Christ and sanctification of the Spirit.

Fourth—That the Spirit of God operates on the world, or as co-extensively as Christ has made the atonement, in such a manner as to leave *all* men inexcusable.

These propositions are expressed in language that scarcely admits of being misunderstood. They embody doctrines fundamental, as to the relation of the gospel to the world, and vastly

---

* Origin and Doctrines of the Cumberland Presbyterian Church, by E. B. Crisman, D.D.

significant as determining factors in a theological system. These views, held in common, as it seems, by the members of the newly formed synod, had doubtless been frequently presented, defended, and enforced in the preaching so signally blessed in the years immediately preceding, so that they had come to be the well-understood views of the Cumberland Presbyterians. They are the *Creed* that antedates a Confession. In addition to the issue of this doctrinal statement, the synod appointed a committee "to prepare a Confession of Faith, Discipline, and Catechism, in accordance with the avowed principles of the Church." This committee "merely modified the Westminster Confession of Faith, expunging what they believed unscriptural, and supplying what they thought scriptural."* The committee's report, submitted to the synod at its next annual meeting, was approved and adopted as the Confession of Faith of the Church. It is not likely that this first revision of the Westminster Confession eliminated all the logical sequences of the rejected Calvinistic premises. With some amendments, the report of the committee was unanimously adopted—a fact quite significant of a well-understood rejection of the Calvinistic doctrine of decrees. The first General Assembly of the Church, held at Princeton, Ky., 1829, still further revised the revision adopted by the synod in 1814, and published it as "The Confession of Faith of the Cumberland Presbyterian Church," in which occurs the following statement of (Chapter III.) "The Decrees of God:"

"I. God did, by the most wise and holy counsel of his own will, determine to act or bring to pass what should be for his own glory.

"II. God has not decreed any thing respecting his creature man, contrary to his revealed will, or written word, which declares his sovereignty over all his creatures, the ample provision he has made for their salvation, his determination to punish

---

* Origin and Doctrines of the Cumberland Presbyterian Church, by E. B. Crisman, D.D.

the finally impenitent with everlasting destruction, and to save the true believer with an everlasting salvation."

How Our Fathers Viewed the Subject.

To the foregoing chapter on Decrees is appended, partly, no doubt, as explanatory of the brevity of the chapter, a lengthy note, of such value for clearness and doctrinal soundness, as to deserve preservation, especially as evidence of the views of our fathers on the subject under consideration. This note, with unessential parts omitted, we here insert:

"We think it better, under the head of Decrees, to write what we know to be incontrovertible from the plain word of God, than to darken counsel by words without knowledge. We are, therefore, free to acknowledge that in our judgment it is easier to fix the limits which man should not transcend, on either hand, than to give an intelligent elucidation of the subject. We believe that both the Calvinists and Arminians have egregiously erred on this point; the former by driving rational, accountable man into the asylum of fate; the latter by putting too much stress on man's *works*, and leaving too much out of view the grace that bringeth salvation, and thereby cherishing those legal principles that are in every human heart. We think the *intermediate* plan, on this subject, is nearest the *whole* truth. For surely, on the one hand, it must be acknowledged, the love of God, the merits of Christ, and the operations of the Holy Spirit, are the moving, meritorious, and active causes of man's salvation; that God is a sovereign, having a right to work when, where, how, and on whom he pleases; that salvation, in its device, in its plan, and in its application, is of the Lord; and that without the unmerited agency and operation of the Spirit of God, not one of Adam's race would or *could* ever come to the knowledge of the truth. . . . . But as it respects the salvation of the soul, God as a sovereign can only elect, or choose, fallen man in Christ, who is the end of the law for righteousness to every one that believeth. But it appears to us incontestible from God's word that God has reprobated *none* from eternity. That all men become legally reprobated by transgression is undeniable, and so continue until they embrace Christ. . . . . Reprobation is not what some suppose it to be, viz.: a sovereign determination of God to create millions of rational beings, and, for his own glory, damn them eternally in hell, without regard to moral rectitude or sin in the creature. This would tarnish the divine glory, and render the greatest, best, and most lovely of all beings most odious in the view of all intelligences. When man sinned, he was legally reprobated, but not damned. God offered and does offer the law-condemned sinner mercy in the gospel; he having from the foundation of the world so far chosen mankind in Christ, as to justify that saying in 1 Tim. iv. 10, 'Who is the Savior of all men, especially of them that believe.' . . . . For God declares in his word that Christ died for the whole world; that he offers pardon to all; that the Spirit operates on *all*, confirming by an oath that he has no pleasure in the death of sinners. Every invitation of the gospel either promises or implies aid by the divine Spirit. The plan of the Bible is grace and duty: God calls (grace), sinners hearken diligently (duty); God reproves, sinners turn; God pours out his Spirit, sinners resist not the light, but improve it; God invites, Wicked man, forsake your ways, your thoughts, and turn to the Lord (duty), and God will have mercy on you (grace), and God will abundantly pardon (grace)."

Without further comment thereon, we may be allowed to say that the foregoing seems to us to represent man's relation to the offers of the gospel, according to the obvious meaning of the Scriptures, and that it is conformable to the experience of those who have believed on Christ, and attained to a comfortable assurance of salvation.

THE CONFESSIONS COMPARED.

As revised and adopted in 1883, the Confession of Faith sets forth the doctrine of decrees, as held by Cumberland Presbyterians, in the following short paragraphs, which are here brought into juxtaposition with sections from the Westminster chapter relating to the same subject, the more clearly and efficiently to illustrate the material and radical departure of our theology from what is taught in the old symbols:

WESTMINSTER CONFESSION.

Of Decrees.

Chap. 3. God from all eternity by the most wise and holy counsel of his own will freely and unchangeably ordained whatsoever comes to pass; yet so as thereby neither is God the author of sin, nor is violence offered to the will of the creature, nor is the liberty or contingency of second causes taken away, but rather established.—*Sec.* 1.

Although God foreknows whatsoever may or can come to pass upon all supposed conditions; yet hath he not decreed any thing because he foresaw it as future, or as that which would come to pass upon such conditions.—*Sec.* 2.

By the decree of God, for the manifestation of his glory, some men and angels are predestinated unto everlasting life, and others foreordained to everlasting death.—*Sec.* 3.

The angels and men, thus predestinated and foreordained, are particularly and unchangeably designed; and their number is so certain and definite that it can not be either increased or diminished.—*Sec.* 4.

The rest of mankind God was pleased, according to the unsearchable counsel of his own will, where-

CUMBERLAND PRESBYTERIAN CONFESSION.

Of Decrees.

Chap. 3.—God, for the manifestation of his glory and goodness, by the most wise and holy counsel of his own will, freely and unchangeably ordained or determined what he himself would do, what he would require his intelligent creatures to do, and what should be the awards, respectively, of the obedient and the disobedient.—*Sec.* 1.

[The decrees of God are his purpose, whereby, according to the counsel of his own will, he hath foreordained what shall be for his own glory; sin not being for God's glory, therefore he hath not decreed it.—*Answer to Question 7 of the Catechism.*]

[God executes his decrees in the works of creation, providence, and grace.—*Answer to Question 8 of the Catechism.*]

by he extendeth or withholdeth mercy as he pleaseth, for the glory of his sovereign power over his creatures, to pass by and to ordain them to dishonor and wrath for their sin, to the praise of his glorious justice.—*Sec.* 7.

The doctrine of this high mystery of predestination is to be handled with special prudence and care, that men attending the will of God revealed in his word, and yielding obedience thereunto, may, from the certainty of their effectual vocation, be assured of their eternal election. —*Sec.* 8 *in part.*

Though all divine decrees may not be revealed to men, yet it is certain that God has decreed nothing contrary to his revealed will or written word.—*Sec.* 2.

The doctrine of decrees as set forth in the Cumberland Presbyterian Confession seems easily understood, and to embrace only what is conformable to enlightened judgment and to the obvious meaning of the Scriptures as a whole. (*a*) God's decrees are in accordance with the most wise and holy counsel of his own will. (*b*) They are put forth freely—attended by what we mean by volition absolutely uncoerced. (*c*) They are unchangeable, for an infinitely wise being could have no reason for changing his purpose. (*d*) They are conditioned on the manifestation of his glory and goodness. They must, therefore, embrace the actual or prospective existence of creatures rational and sentient to whom his glory and goodness would be thus manifested. It is a matter of fact that in the works of God men do behold manifestations of his glory and goodness. John declares, "God is love." Plato says, "God is beauty and love." What the philosopher beheld in nature was to the evangelist more fully manifested by the grace of God which bringeth salvation.

The Scope of the Decrees.

The *scope* of the decrees of God embraces:

1. "What God himself would do;" as, to create heaven and earth, and all creatures therein; to reveal to man a perfect rule of behavior, the law of love; to redeem man fallen, etc.

2. "What he would require his intelligent creatures to do." Though a slight ambiguity lurks, unfortunately, in these words, we do not doubt that their designed meaning is that God's decrees embrace what he desires his rational creatures, as moral agents, to do in the exercise of the freedom wherewith he has endowed them. It will include (a) man's behavior under law; as, to reverence his Maker, the observance of veracity, honesty, etc.; (b) specific assignments to men; as, Moses to lead Israel out of Egypt, Jonah to preach to the Ninevites, etc.

3. How he will deal with the obedient, and how with the disobedient.

The third specification, relating to the awards God has decreed to assign respectively to the obedient and the disobedient, asserts what is explained and declared throughout the Scriptures, that the final apportionments to men will be according to their behavior as subjects of moral law, and toward the gospel offer of mercy, and not in accordance with an eternal, unconditional decree, irrespective of man's behavior.

4. That God has decreed nothing contrary to his revealed will, or written word.

That we do *not* "know all the decrees of God," we must most certainly suppose, since man can be regarded as only a small fraction of a vast economy of rational creatures, and his dwelling-place but an insignificant orb in the universe of whirling spheres; but still we may suppose, and must suppose, that the God revealed to us in the Scriptures decrees nothing contrary to what he declares to be his will. There is in this view of decrees no necessity for reconciling God's "secret purpose" with his revealed will. God is truth. With him is no variableness nor shadow of turning. Infinite wisdom and infinite power are alike attributes of God. We can comprehend neither, but they need no reconciling. God foreknows all things, and man acts freely. The two statements need no reconciling, for they involve no antagonism of thought.

The decrees of God, as taught by Cumberland Presbyterians, mean but the divine purpose to do and permit that which infinite wisdom sees to be for the highest well-being of all sentient creatures. All the decrees of God made known to us are in perfect harmony with goodness and mercy, and such as to posit a rational basis for divine sovereignty, human agency, moral government, a gracious offer of salvation to all men, and a just final reward for the obedient and final punishment of the disobedient.

THE SCRIPTURES VERSUS UNCONDITIONAL PREDESTINATION.

Of the numerous plain passages of Scripture which, taken in their obvious import, underlie, as a granite foundation, this reasonable view of the decrees, but to which the Calvinistic decree is utterly unconformable, we may instance that wonderful epitome of the gospel found in 1 Timothy ii. 1–6: "I exhort, therefore, that, first of all, supplications, prayers, intercessions, and thanksgivings be made for all men ; for kings and all that are in authority, that we may lead a quiet and peaceable life in all godliness and gravity. For this is good and acceptable in the sight of God our Savior, *who wills that all men should be saved*, and should come to the knowledge of the truth. For (over all) there is but one God, and one mediator between God and men, the man Christ Jesus, *who gave himself a ransom for all men*, to be testified in due time." The translation by Conybeare and Howson is given, as more nearly expressing the sense of the relative clause, " who will have all men to be saved," still more literally, *who wills* ($\theta\acute{\epsilon}\lambda\epsilon\iota$) *all men to be saved*. Now, if an inspired apostle exhorts that prayer be made for all men, and on the ground that God wills that all men be saved, and that the one Mediator between God and men gave himself a ransom for all, how can it be believed that "God so ordains," as Calvin says, "by his counsel and his will, that some among men should be born devoted to certain death from the womb, to glorify his name by their destruction ; " or that, as the Westminster Confession puts it, "God was pleased, according to the unsearchable counsel of his own will, for the glory of his sovereign power over his own creatures, to pass by" these "some among men," and, by a decree unconditional, without reference to any thing foreseen in 'these "some among men," "to ordain them to dishonor and wrath?" If any one claims that he believes Paul, who declares that God wills the salvation of all men, and that he can, at the same time, believe Calvin and the Westminster Confession, he has prodigious capacity for believing; and he who claims to be able to reconcile the teaching of Calvin and the Confession with that of Paul in the passage cited, certainly claims the ability to reconcile logical contradictions; and the God pictured by the imagination of such a one must be, saying it reverently, a singular kind of a God for a rational creature to worship! The note of Dr. Van Oosterzee (in *Lange's Commentary*) on the passage under consideration, is so excellent that we subjoin it in full: "Paul teaches, not only here, but in other places (Rom. viii. 52; xi. 32; Titus ii. 11), that the desire of God to bless all sinners is unlimited, yet it can be only in the ordained way of faith. And here, perhaps, he affirms it, in order to maintain this doctrine plainly against every Gnostic limitation of salvation, as well as to give a fit motive for prayer. *For had God willed the contrary of what is here revealed, it would be foolish and fruitless to pray for the welfare of others, when perhaps this or that person might be shut out from the plan of salvation.* Yet more, the apostle speaks here of the θέλειν of God in general, not of the βούλημα, which regards believers (Eph. i. 11). It is, therefore, entirely needless, by any exegetical gloss, to limit the expression, all men, or to understand it in the sense of all classes of men (which would make verse 1 an absurdity)."

This plain and exceedingly precious passage, and a few others of similar import, may appropriately be placed in juxtaposition with an equal number of Calvinistic predestinarian utterances, to illustrate how thoroughly discordant the language of these utterances is to that of the Scriptures, and how utterly irreconcilable is the Calvinistic decree of predestination with the gracious message of the gospel. On the one side we shall have the idea of the absolute and dreadful sovereignty of God electing some of our race, without any thing foreseen in these as moving him thereto, to be heirs of the joys of salvation, and passing by the remainder of the same lump of fallen humanity, and appointing them heirs of inevitable wrath and destruction; but on the other side, the impartial compassion of a common heavenly Father who loved the world, the infinite compassion of the one Mediator who tasted death for all, and the universal invitation to that merciful provision the grace of God sets before all.

THE WORDS OF THE LORD.

"I exhort, therefore, first of all, that supplications, prayers, intercessions, thanksgivings, be made for all men; for kings and all that are in high place; that we may lead a tranquil and quiet life in all godliness and gravity. This is good and acceptable in the sight of God our Savior; who willeth that all men should be saved, and come to the knowledge of the truth. For there is one God, one Mediator also between God and men, *himself* man, Christ Jesus, who gave himself a ransom for all."

"As I live, saith the Lord, I have no pleasure in the death of the wicked, but that the wicked turn from his way and live."—Ezek. xxxiii. 11.

"And ye have not his word abiding in you; for whom he sent, him ye believe not; . . . . and ye will not come to me that ye may have life."—John v. 38.

"For God so loved the world, that he gave his only begotten Son, that whosoever believeth on him should not perish, but have eternal life."—John iii. 16.

THE WORDS OF MEN.

"Predestination we call the eternal decree of God, by which he has determined in himself what he would have to become of every individual of mankind; for they are not all created with similar destiny; but eternal life is foreordained for some, and eternal damnation for others. Every man, therefore, being created for the one or the other of these ends, we say he is predestinated either to life or to death."—*Calvin.*

"Since the will of God is said to be the cause of all things, that his providence is appointed to be the ruler in all the counsels and works of men; so that it not only exerts its power in the elect, who are governed by the Holy Spirit, but also *compels the compliance of the reprobate*" (compels their wicked course—their rejection of Christ). —*Calvin.*

"The rest of mankind (the nonelect) God was pleased, according to the unsearchable counsel of his own will, whereby he extendeth or withholdeth mercy as he pleaseth,

10

for the glory of his sovereign power over his creatures, to pass by and to ordain them to dishonor and wrath for their sin."—*Westminster Confession.*

"How often would I have gathered thy children together, as a hen doth gather her brood under her wings, and ye would not."—Luke xiii. 34.
"It was necessary that the word of God should first have been spoken to you; but seeing ye put it from you, and judge yourselves unworthy of everlasting life, lo, we turn to the Gentiles."—Acts xiii. 46.

"I will not scruple to own that the will of God lays a necessity on all things."
"Every action and motion of every creature is governed by the hidden counsel of God."—*Calvin.*

"The Lord . . . . is long-suffering to usward, not willing (not desiring —*New Version*) that any should perish, but that all should come to repentance."—2 Peter iii. 9.
"Let no man say when he is tempted, I am tempted of God; for God can not be tempted with evil, and *he himself tempteth no man;* but each man is tempted when he is drawn away by his own lust and enticed."—James i. 13, 14.

"God calls to the reprobates, that they may be more deaf; kindles a light, that they may be more blind; brings his doctrine to them, that they may be more ignorant; and applies the remedy to them that they may not be healed."—*Calvin.*

"Because I have called, and ye refused; I have stretched my hand, and no man regarded it; . . . . for that they hated knowledge, and did not choose the fear of the Lord. . . . . Therefore shall they *eat of the fruit of their own way,* and *be filled with their own devices.*"— Prov. i. 29-31. [Chalmers makes *their* ways and *their* devices the ways and devices of God.]

"Every step of every individual character receives as determinate a character from the hand of God, as every mile of a planet's orbit, or every wave of the sea. . . . . This power of God knows no exceptions; it is absolute and unlimited. It reigns and operates through all the secrecies of the inner man. It gives birth to every purpose, it gives impulse to every desire, it gives shape and color to every conception. It wields an entire ascendency over every attribute of the mind; and the will, and the fancy, and the understanding, with all the countless variety of their hidden and fugitive operations, are submitted to it."—*Dr. Thomas Chalmers*

CURRENT DISCUSSION OF THE SUBJECT.

We have dwelt upon this subject because it involves what is fundamental in the distinction between Calvinistic theology and Cumberland Presbyterian theology. The complete rejection of the Westminster doctrine of eternal unconditional predestination and its logical sequences is the distinguishing characteristic of the Cumberland Presbyterian Church, as a member of the Presbyterian family. It is also true, as before observed, that the doctrine that "God has decreed whatsoever comes to pass," which of necessity involves unconditional election, and its correlative, unconditional reprobation, identifies, shapes, and completely dominates the Calvinistic system. We can no more have Calvinism, if the eternal, universal unconditional decree is omitted, than we can have a vertebrate without a spinal column. In Calvinism there is no high and low, hard and soft, extreme and moderate. Calvin himself derided as silly all those who held to election, but rejected reprobation. In the discussion of the question of "revision" in the Washington (Pa.) Presbytery, the Rev. Dr. Cunningham, though opposing revision, declared that it is "only a limited intelligence that can not understand that preterition is the necessary consequence of election;" and that, "If we reject preterition, we must reject election." Rev. Dr. Moffat, President of Washington and Jefferson College, is reported as strenuously advocating revision, declaring that the "radical revisionists" are not confined to the New York Presbytery, but are all over the country, and that the New York men were only bolder, and had hung out their banner. The action of the Washington Presbytery was awaited with much interest. The territory embraced in the presbytery's limits is sometimes designated the "backbone of Presbyterianism," and includes an important seat of learning. After protracted and earnest discussion, the vote, forced by the call for the previous question, showed seventeen for and forty-two against revision. One member of the body is reported as declaring it " impossible to make verbal changes without making doctrinal changes." It is certainly true that the Calvinistic system could not well be stated in more carefully chosen language, and if that system is to be retained the entire discussion seems equally useless and meaningless. But the discussion is not meaningless. It is hopefully and immensely significant, as revealing in the laity and the ministry of that intelligent, numerous, and powerful Church, a large element fully determined so to modify the creed as to free the doctrine of the goodness of God from the frigid limitations of Calvinistic predestination. The following passage from the argument of Dr. Moffatt frankly states that the demand for revision arises out of dissatisfaction with the chapter on Decrees; but, like others, he demands only a change of phraseology, while, as is apparent, he proposes to retain the Calvinistic element that is the true source of the uprising protest of head and heart: " There is not a Presbyterian Church on the face of the globe that has not had trouble right here. To stand over the Confession and refuse to allow it to be touched is not loyalty. If this confession is capable of improvement, I feel bound to attempt that improvement. As to the decrees of God, in that chapter we are telling the world the character of God. . . . There is in the world the Calvinistic idea of God; we must say often to others, that they are mistaken as to those doctrines, and we have to explain those sections in chapter three. We want to avoid the suspicion of supralapsarianism, or the doctrine that God created men in order to damn them. Those old Westminster divines believed that, many of them, and preached it; but we do not believe it to-day, nor teach it. Any minister to-day may preach that doctrine, and be true to the confession : to me it is a damnable heresy. *My whole contention is right here.* The other proposed changes are unimportant." If this language is correctly ascribed to Dr. Moffatt, we are sure the reader will be amazed when told that, in the same connection, the speaker said

" Let any man propose a change which would subvert any great Calvinistic doctrines, and that man would be buried out of sight." The fundamental premise of Calvinism involves by logical necessity the very doctrine discarded as " damnable heresy," and yet a proposition " to subvert any great Calvinistic doctrines " would, in the Presbyterian Church, subject its author to " be buried out of sight ! " But again the speaker gets away from his Calvinism, affirming, " I have told men that if they go to hell, it is because they want to go. God does not want men to perish." Scriptural, but very *un*-Calvinistic.

THE OLD DOCTRINE MUST FALL.

The framers of the Westminster Confession certainly did believe, many of them, the doctrine ascribed to them by Dr. Moffat; and, by his own admission, " any minister to-day may preach that doctrine, and be true to the Confession." Then it must be in the Confession. It is most prominently there, fronting the Confession, in one of its longest chapters. To such a place it is entitled in any system of which it is an element, for it can not be subordinate. As a writer of the Calvinistic school puts it, " Election is the great fundamental institute of the gospel: it is that which in human states is called 'the supreme law;' which is both irreversible in itself, and requires that all inferior administrations may be accommodated thereto." Predestination is the ground-plan of the Calvinistic structure, determining the relations of all the parts, and constituting, as the advocates tell us, " the plot whereby God designs to himself the highest glory; " since, as they affirm, this unconditional assignment of one human being to heaven and another to hell, " is the sublimest act, and most apparent demonstration, of sovereign power concerning men. ' The following excellent words touching revision of the Westminster Confession are from the pen of the venerable Dr. McCosh: " I can not tell how glad I am in reading of the unanimous decision of the Presbytery of

New York in regard to the revision of the Confession. When I uttered my opinion on the subject, in my Presbytery, on October 1, I had no clear idea as to how Presbyterian sentiment was tending. . . . How pleased I am that the Presbytery of New York has come to the same conclusion that I did. It is clear that we are to have *the obnoxious passages in the Confession* withdrawn in the course of a year or two." According to their own statements, our brethren of the Presbyterian Church are embarrassed with doctrinal standards which, to say the least, and what they admit, are liable to perplexing and damaging criticism. It must be apparent, too, that a revision of its creed by a Church of the magnitude of the Presbyterian body, must be indeed a difficult work. All who sincerely desire the peace and prosperity of the common household of God, will pray that our brethren may, in this endeavor, come at last to such a result as will make the intelligence, the wealth, the numbers, and the prestige of this denomination a still greater power in our own land and throughout the world. With its wonderful equipment for every branch of Christian work, it has before it grand possibilities, which, through a wise and faithful improvement of this demand by thousands of its own people for the elimination of the vicious Calvinistic predestination, it may more than realize.

With the writer's earliest recollections of preachers and preaching are associated the frequent discussions of this subject by Rev. Milton Bird and other ministers who introduced into western Pennsylvania the doctrines of the Cumberland Presbyterian Church. Crowds of people thronged those discussions, to be convinced by the masterly arguments; and many were the converts through the gracious influences attending the urgent presentations of God's impartial love as manifested in the gospel provision and the gospel call to all men. Our early attempts at the perusal of theological discussions embraced *The Great Supper* by Rev. Archibald Fairchild, of the Presbyterian Church, and *Error Unmasked*, by Rev. Milton Bird, and the impression

then received, that in this controversy truth lies on the side of
Cumberland Presbyterian doctrine, has been strengthened by
much study of the questions involved. A calm and impartial
view of the doctrine of decrees as presented in the third chapter
of the Westminster Confession—as far as we are capable of an
impartial view, forces upon us these conclusions, as

LOGICAL SEQUENCES OF PREDESTINATION.

1. Upon the hypothesis of Westminster predestination (election and preterition), *the goodness of God*, as we are accustomed
to think of it, *can not be maintained*.

The Westminster Confession declares that God is "infinite in
being and perfection," and "abundant in goodness." If it is
meant that goodness is an attribute, it is infinite. Our Confession positively asserts that God is "infinite, eternal, and unchangeable" in being and attributes, *goodness* included in the latter. The Scriptures declare that "*God is love*" (1 John iv. 8).
This passage teaches, as Macknight justly observes, "that God
greatly delights in the exercise of benevolence, and perhaps that
his other perfections are exerted for the accomplishment of
his benevolent purposes;" and adds, that "the declaration that
'God is love' must afford us the greatest consolation, as it as-
sureth us that all God's dealings with us proceed from love, and
in the end will assuredly issue in our happiness, unless we refuse to co-operate with him." The relation of the idea of an unconditional decree electing a portion of humanity to salvation,
and passing by the rest, to the idea of the goodness, or love of
God, is a very plain one. If of two of my fellow beings exposed,
by their own fault, to imminent peril, I rescue one, and, of my
own good pleasure, pass the other by, when I could as readily
have rescued both, no one would claim that I had done as much
good as I could have done. Had both been entirely destitute of
claim upon my sympathy and interposition, so much the more
conspicuous would have been the goodness that prompted to the

rescue of both. "Turn this (Calvinistic) system as you will,"
says a vigorous thinker, "it sweeps away the mercy and goodness of God, and, in most cases, transforms even the invitations
and promises into scalding messages of aggravated wrath."
But we would not indulge in bitter words, whether our own or
borrowed. We most heartily sympathize with those who desire
so to revise their creed as to make prominent the love of God
now so overshadowed by the unconditional decree. The Bible
declares that "the love of Christ passeth knowledge," in other
words, that it exceeds human conception; but theologians have
certainly formulated systems which practically limit that love.
The following passage, from a transatlantic author, breathes so
good a spirit, and so conspicuously sets forth the ideas we would
present in this connection, that we commend it to the reader's
careful attention:

"You can not have a plainer statement of a fact than that
'God so loved the world that he gave his only begotten Son, that
whosoever believeth in him should not perish, but should have
everlasting life.' It sets before us the love of the Father and of
the Son in all simplicity and fullness; shows us the fact of a
divine love greater than we, if we try it, can comprehend. But
men have not been content with this. They have said, 'There
must be a reason for this, and we must find it. Love must work
according to a system, and we must lay it down.' And so we
meet with those who would teach us to believe, not in the love
of God as the first and greatest fact in the universe, but in what
they call the 'decree' whereby they say he, for his own pleasure
and own glory, elects some to eternal life, and lets his love rest
on them through Christ, and passes by others, also for his own
pleasure and glory, and lets his curse rest on them forever and
ever. Are we wiser when we have got this into our heads than
we were before with the simple words of the Bible? Is it easier
for us to understand a God who shall, 'for his own glory,' pick
and choose among his creatures, giving some a certainty of

salvation, and some not the smallest chance, than to understand that he loves us all with a love that ' passeth knowledge.' Is the puzzle of the universe, the ' riddle of the painful earth,' simplified when you have set up over it as your highest idea of the divine, the decree of an absolute will, instead of the love of an all-embracing heart? Does the mystery of the universal love of God to such as we are, the mystery of Christ's willing sacrifice for the sins of the whole world, survive such treatment as this? Does this explanation leave us with a love that 'passes our knowledge?' Is there any difficulty in comprehending a love so partial and so wayward as this would represent the love of God to be, a love of which any man with his own children round him would be ashamed, if he felt that to serve mere ends of his own, ends which they could not understand, and which he could never make them understand, he was deliberately doing some of them the greatest kindness, and dooming others of them, in secret, to the most hopeless misery? Would you not call such a man selfish, and such children unjustly used? Would that not be the verdict of the calmest, wisest, and justest minds, and rightly so? And what right has any man, or any set of men, to invest God with attributes which we condemn in man ; to ascribe to the Creator conduct which even in the creature we should say was unworthy and unjust? Is this ' giving God glory,' as it is professed to be? On the contrary, it is doing him dishonor. It is explaining in the coarsest way, and according to the harshest ideas, that which his word has told us is too vast and lofty for us to comprehend."

2. *The Calvinistic doctrine of predestination necessarily involves fatality*, and thereby sweeps away the basis of freedom of the will, of the moral quality of actions, and of what, in the usual acceptation of the term, is called moral government. According to this system, moral government can be as appropriately predicated of the world of matter as of the world of mind. In the physical world, as Chalmers says, every mile of a planet's

orbit, every gust of wind, every wave of the sea, every particle
of flying dust, every rivulet of flowing water, "receives a determinate character from the power of God," and, according to the
same author, the same power operating in the world of mind
gives birth to every purpose, impulse to every desire, shape and
color to every conception. If the power thus controlling "the
will, the fancy, the understanding, with all the countless variety
of their hidden and fugitive operations," be the power of an
omnipotent Creator who thus executes his decrees, man is, as to
all ideas of responsibility, as utterly destitute of freedom as is a
locomotive. One is run by the power of steam, the other by
the power of God—rather, as Chalmers would have it, both by
the power of God. So Thomas Aquinas taught, following
Augustine, "that, as God's providence extended itself to every
thing, it immediately concurred in the production of our
thoughts, motions, and actions, and by a physical influence."
Can we, with an open Bible, and with the views we must entertain of the moral deserts of human conduct, call it less than
blasphemy against Heaven, and treason against humanity, to
assert, as do these predestinarians, that the impulse which
causes the murderer to inflict the deadly blow, and the blow
itself, are suggested, concurred in, and necessitated by the
will of God? Yet, such extreme fatalistic views are not
only avowed by the more daring predestinarians, but are
logical sequences from which no possible explanations can
relieve the system. According to the Augustinian doctrine that
the will of God is the necessity of things, and that every man is
created and predestinated eternally and unchangeably, some to
life, some to death, it must be true that every human being is
tending to one of these destinies under a necessity from which
it is as impossible for him to escape as it is for a lifeless body to
burst the bands of death. If that is not fatality, there is no
such thing.

3. *That the doctrine of the universal, unconditional decree*, as

taught in the Westminster Confession, *if not pantheistic, is very nearly allied to that idea.* Pantheism is the doctrine that the universe is God, God the universe. If the number of ears of corn produced in a year, the number of rows on each ear, and of grains in each row, and every chirp of a bird, and flexure of a rivulet, and impulse of the human sensibility, and every dream of the imagination, and every volition, with every other phenomenon of mind and of matter, are to be ascribed to the direct agency of God, I feel myself bordering on the thought that the world is God.

It is by no means the writer's purpose to attempt a systematic discussion of the subject of decrees, or to attempt a refutation of the system of doctrine known as Calvinism. In the desultory collation of the ideas presented, it has been his purpose to indicate the line of thought pursued by Cumberland Presbyterians in their departure from that mixture of fatalistic philosophy and scriptural doctrine, as it has been justly designated, from which multitudes in the Presbyterian Church are to-day struggling to free their Standards.

Cumberland Presbyterians Wonderfully Vindicated.

Believing that in their departure from the Westminster system Cumberland Presbyterians made most important progress toward the true interpretation of the system of the Bible, we feel that if these pages shall, in any measure, contribute to our steadfastness in those great principles for the recognition of which our fathers struggled so nobly, a valuable service will have been rendered in the interest of precious truths. Men who are, in piety and learning, recognized lights in the Presbyterian Church are to-day fighting the very battles our fathers fought eighty years ago, and with this repetition of the struggle comes most grateful testimony to the wisdom and justice of the course pursued by those fathers. The following declarations by the pastor of Madison Square Presbyterian Church, New York, are the sentiments uttered, in language less severe, by Ewing, King, Donnell, and others, at the opening of the century: "The love of God stands out on the face of the gospel. In the Confession you have to hunt for it in order to find it. The center of gravity of the Confession does not coincide with the center of gravity of the gospel. If, now, we are going to retain this preterition idea in our Confession, then we must be true to it in our preaching as Presbyterian ministers, and on occasion declare it in all frankness. We shall be obliged to address our congregations somewhat after this manner: 'My friends, I am sorry to say it, but as a Calvinistic Presbyterian I am bound to say it, that Christ did not die for all. There is a certain amount of fatalism in the case. Some men are damned, and not only that, but congenitally damned—damned before they are born, hated of God even in the moment of conception.'"

Did a Cumberland Presbyterian ever make graver charges against the Westminster Confession than does this eminent divine occupying a metropolitan Presbyterian pulpit? And his presbytery did not prefer charges of heresy, but voted solid for revision.

Rev. Dr. S. M. Hamilton, of the Presbytery of New York, is reported as saying, during the two weeks' discussion on revision: "Preterition is a mere attempt of men to confine the ways of the Almighty by their petty syllogisms. To infer that God has for his own pleasure 'passed by' any living soul is impossible, except to a man who has never caught the first glimmer of the radiance from the Savior. . . . You may say that the Confession does not teach unconditional preterition, but at any rate it makes every body think it does." Similarly Dr. M. R. Vincent, of Union Theological Seminary, declared his belief that "the root of the difficulty lies in the Standards, not in the Church." "The Confession claims," he continued, "to represent the word of God. And this claim, as it respects certain statements of the Confession, is challenged. I am one of those who challenge it. . . . The third chapter declares that some men and angels are foreordained unto everlasting death, and that their number is so certain that it can not be either increased or diminished. As a teacher of the New Testament Scriptures in one of the Church's Theological schools *I declare my belief that that doctrine is not taught in the Holy Scriptures.* . . . I can not understand how it is possible for any man who declares his belief in the statements of the Confession to go into his pulpit and make a free offer of salvation to his congregation." Expressions of like character could be cited almost without limit. The foregoing, from men eminent for learning and occupying high positions in the Presbyterian Church, suffice to illustrate the clear and powerful vindication of the teachings and policy of Cumberland Presbyterians developed by the current discussion on revision.

In milder terms than these men have employed, Rev. Finis Ewing, one of the men who organized the Cumberland Presbyterian Church, said that "the great decree of God which concerns man's salvation is, 'He that believeth and is baptized shall be saved, and he that believeth not shall be damned.' . . . If words have any determinate meaning, these are conditions on which our salvation depends. Here, then, is a *revealed* decree. Men may talk or say what they please about secret decrees, purposes, predestination, election, etc., but we have just seen the decree of the Bible; the predestination, foreordination, and election of the Bible. . . . God is a mighty sovereign, possessing the right to work where, when, how, and on whom he will, yet it is nowhere definitely stated that God chose some to eternal salvation, except on the condition of faith and repentance."

Rev. Robert Donnell, D.D., an eloquent and powerful preacher of the gospel in its simplicity, and one of the ablest expounders and defenders of the doctrines of the Cumberland Presbyterian Church, fifty or more years ago enunciated in the subjoined little summary, the very statement of the Bible doctrine of salvation by grace for which the progressive party in the Presbyterian Church is to-day nobly contending:

"The plan of the Bible is grace and duty. God calls; the sinner must accept it. Then God justifies, adopts, renews, sanctifies, and glorifies. The scheme of salvation originates with God, and is carried out in man's agency. The system is gracious, and personal accountability is secured. Election in the first instance was sovereign, gracious, and free, choosing all men to a day of mercy. Personal election turns on the choice of the sinner elect through sanctification of the Spirit, and belief of the truth. And thus free moral agency is sustained. God receives all the glory of faith; and man all the damnation of unbelief."

NOTE.

EXPLANATORY AND APOLOGETIC.

"For we can do nothing against the truth, but for the truth."—*Paul.*

"We do not take possession of our ideas, but are possessed by them.
They master us, and force us into the arena,
Where, like gladiators, we must fight for them."—*Heine.*

To distinguish Cumberland Presbyterians doctrinally as a branch of the great Presbyterian family necessitates a clear and full statement of the teaching of the Cumberland Presbyterian Confession of Faith on the subject of the Decrees of God, in contrast with the teaching of the Westminster Confession. Such presentation of our views, however, whether through the press or from the pulpit, has not unfrequently been the occasion of complaint that we are unfair in our interpretation of the Westminster Confession, and that, as theological disputants, we are disturbers of the peace of the Church. It seems suitable, therefore, to ask our brethren of the other side, at this stage of the statement of our views, to consider what we regard the necessity that has been upon us to discuss this subject, both in view of our obligation to defend the truth, as we understand it, and in order to answer honest inquiry in regard to the doctrinal difference between Cumberland Presbyterians and other branches of the Presbyterian family.

Many times have members of the Presbyterian Church said to us, after our attempt at stating our doctrinal views on the controverted points, "Why, that is just what we believe." To all such we might justly say, "Then, certainly, if you are not in the wrong Church, your Church has the wrong confession of faith." It is with the writer a matter of recollection that the early Cumberland Presbyterian ministers in Pennsylvania frequently discussed from the pulpit the doctrines of decrees, election, freedom of the will, infant salvation, and other doctrines wherein by formal statement or logical sequence our standard differs from the Westminster. While those controversial discourses sometimes stirred up strife, and were the occasion of bitter charges of unfairness and even of bad motives as prompting them, it is our belief that they did good, and that, for the most part, they were prompted by sincere convictions of duty on the part of men seemingly endowed with wonderful power in the presentation of the great truths they felt themselves set to defend. Nor can it be doubted that many a good and faithful minister of the Cumberland Presbyterian Church has come to the discussion of the disputed doctrines with the sincere desire which pervades the writer's mind in this allusion to the controversy—namely, *that the controversy come to an end.* Yet, whatever the conditions it impose upon us, whether of peace or controversy, we must unwaveringly heed the divine command to "buy the truth, and sell it not."

As a last word upon the subject, the following points are submitted as affirming what the writer firmly believes to be the truth touching this controversy:

1. The difference between the teaching of the Cumberland Presbyterian Confession, and that of the Westminster Confession, is radical, and is widely related as a determining factor in

a theological system, necessarily affecting our views of the love of God, the extent and design of the atonement, the gospel call, of the sinner's ability to accept the gospel offer, of moral merit and demerit, of the very foundation of moral government.

2. That Cumberland Presbyterians have interpreted the Westminster Confession according to the obvious and literal meaning of its language, in its true historic sense, and as it is now usually interpreted in the Calvinistic theological schools.

3. That many pious and learned men in the Calvinistic branches of the Presbyterian Church now interpret the Westminster Confession exactly as Cumberland Presbyterians have interpreted it, and on that interpretation base their pleas for a revision of that Confession.

Of the truth of the last proposition, the present discussion which agitates the mother Church from center to circumference affords interesting and abundant proof; so that, were they in need of it, Cumberland Presbyterians could find in the pending discussion ample justification of their interpretation and rejection of the Westminster Confession. In illustration of the statement here made, from the vast number of pertinent declarations which have gone to the public we can not make a better selection than the brief, but most comprehensive, statement of the late Judge Alexander Wilson Acheson, of Washington, Pa. Judge Acheson, who died in July, 1890, at the advanced age of eighty years, was a man widely known for ability in his profession, for his general intelligence, and his deep interest in all movements for the good of society. He was esteemed indeed a just judge, who feared God, and regarded man in all that pertains to man's well-being. Himself a Presbyterian, a student of theology as well as of law, so correct an interpreter of the meaning of language that his judicial decisions covering many years in a busy court were seldom if ever reversed, Judge Acheson, prompted by his disappointment in the vote of the Washington Presbytery on the question of revision, penned, seemingly as a dying testimony, the following plea for revision, setting forth therein, as the reader will note, such an interpretation of the old standards as fully concedes all that Cumberland Presbyterians have claimed. It will be seen, too, that the learned jurist, whose "most prominent characteristic" a eulogist declared to be "his quick grasp of legal principles, joined with peculiar power in tracing the analogies of the law, and applying them to new questions at issue," did not desire only such a revision as would preserve the old doctrinal system intact, but clothe it in a more modern dress, but that the "iron collar" might be entirely broken, and his Church thus freed; which "iron collar," be it observed, is the very same "fatalism" which the fathers of the Cumberland Presbyterian Church cast off, which *they* believed to be taught under the mystery of Calvinistic predestination. Here is the truth as "grasped in the struggle of the great soul" of the advocate, judge, and Christian philanthropist, and uttered with a courage born of honest convictions, and with faith that his people would finally eliminate from their creed the vicious element "which obscures the infinite love of God in Christ Jesus for a lost world : "

"REVISION REVIEWED—VIEWS OF A LEARNED LAYMAN THAT
CAN NOT BE MISUNDERSTOOD.

"*Editor Journal :*—Allow an old Presbyterian to express his disappointment at the result of the revision question in our Washington Presbytery. I am not a scholastic theologian, and therefore may lack clear insight into mysteries difficult of comprehension; but I am a firm believer in a coming closer Church union and affiliation among Christians of all denominations. I see the signs now in the increase of fraternal intercourse and the softening of religious intolerance and bigotry.

"If John Calvin were living to-day I think he would be a sweeter tempered Christian, a less dogmatic theologian, and not so much of a fatalist, indisposed to consign infants to dam-

11

nation, or even Catholics, on the ground of their being infidels and outside the covenanted mercies of God.

"The famous old lawyers of the last century, Lord Eldon, Sir William Blackstone, and other legal celebrities, resisted to the death all changes in the English criminal law, for the reason that it had the sanction of antiquity, and any change would endanger the pillars of jurisprudence. True, it visited the murderer and the stealer of bread with equal and exact justice by hanging both of them by the neck, but what of that so long as the sacred standards sanctioned it?

"I believe in God's sovereignty over man's destiny for time and eternity, but I do not believe in the infallibility of the learned Westminster divines nor of the Pope. I believe in the inspiration of the great Apostle to the Gentiles, but to get clear insight into his mind, we must sit at the feet of the Master, and learn of him the mysteries of his kingdom. I should be puzzled touching the mission of womankind in his church if I stopped with Paul. I can understand what it is, however, when I listen to his gracious words of tenderness and love to women. So we must study Christ and Paul together. Christ before Paul always, to get at the harmony existing in the sacred word. I think the Westminster divines in their excessive admiration for Calvin forgot this. They lived in a stormy time; a fierce conflict was raging about dogmas; persecution reigned, and they were filled with the wrath of Sinai more than touched by the tender mercy of Calvary. If we are to understand that there is no salvation out of Christ, in the sense of our Confession of Faith—that in the councils of eternity, before time began, the damnation of the larger portion of mankind was predestined and decreed, the mercy of God becomes overclouded, his justice eclipsed, and the mission of our Savior shorn of its sweetest attraction.

"The old last century lawyers resisted all change of the criminal creed of their day, but were constrained by an enlightened public conscience to provide some outlet of escape from the horrible result of their creed, and this consisted in the interposition of executive clemency, staying the prescribed punishment. And so the rank and file of Presbyterian Church members are exempted from the rigors of the Confession, only ministers and Church officers being made amenable to strict discipline for their lack of faith. This speaks feebly for the outcry against revision on the ground of danger to the pillars of our faith.

" Nearly nineteen centuries have passed away since the crucifixion. The command to preach the gospel to every creature remains unfulfilled to this day. Have all the innumerable host of human souls brought into existence by the fiat of the Almighty through these centuries been sunk to endless perdition by the default of the Church to fulfill his dying command? 'How can they hear without a preacher?' Are they lost for not accepting Christ or for not living up to the light afforded by nature and natural instinct? Bad as unregenerate human nature is, what warrant have we for saying that no heathen soul during the past centuries has lifted itself by the light of nature to search after God, if peradventure it could find him?

" Is God still calling infants into existence to consign them to perdition by his electing grace? Regret as you may the agitation of revision, it is upon the Church, it will not down, there is too much moral force behind it. If it should rend the grand old Presbyterian body, where will the dreadful responsibility lie? It is in vain to say that there are wolves in sheep's clothing within the Church seeking to overthrow the fundamental doctrine of God's elective grace and sovereignty. The sincere advocates of revision seek not to lay sacrilegious hands on the ark of the covenant ; they aim to take off us a cruel iron collar burthensome to their consciences, which obscures the infinite love of God in Christ for a lost world.

"A. W. ACHESON."

These words of a Christian layman, brief, but wonderfully comprehensive, in no ambiguous manner reveal his position touching this controversy, clearly showing his belief (1) that the Westminster doctrine of decrees fairly interpreted means the " iron collar " of fatality about man's neck, or, in his own language, " that in the councils of eternity, before time began, the damnation of the larger portion of mankind was predestinated and decreed ; " (2) that according to the teaching of Christ, no one of the human race, whether of those who hear the gospel, of those who hear it not, or of those dying in infancy, is doomed to inevitable destruction by an eternal unconditional decree of God absolutely predestinating some men to life and others to death; (3) that a refusal to revise theological codes simply because they are " time-honored " does not comport with that true spirit of progress and of freedom of thought through which the human mind has achieved its great advancement in the interpretation of the word and the works of God.

With Judge Acheson, the writer of these lines is "a firm believer in a coming closer Church union and affiliation of Christians of all denominations," and whatever signs there may be, "in an increase of fraternal intercourse and the softening of religious intolerance," of this "coming closer Church union and affiliation," we too rejoice in those signs, as did the good and venerable man who now enjoys the full measure of the union and affiliation often, alas, but too feebly foreshadowed in the Church on earth. The reader is asked, however, not to construe the foregoing expression as any declaration of opinion on the part of the writer regarding the practicability or desirableness of organic union of Cumberland Presbyterians with the Calvinistic branches ; and equally does the writer desire that neither this note, nor the preceding presentation of the subject of decrees, nor any other section of this doctrinal statement shall be regarded as an effort to build a dyke against any tendency to union that is likely to come out of the pending movement for the revision of the old standards. On this question of very grave importance we are open to conviction, and willing, we trust, to walk, from time to time, in what Providence may indicate to be the path of duty. In passing it is not amiss to avow our conviction that if the two great branches of the Presbyterian Church whose chief difference seems to be that of geographical distribution, and the Cumberland Presbyterian Church, could unite on a brief doctrinal formula clearly stating the impartial love of God, a general atonement, the offer of salvation to all men, man's responsibility in view of the Spirit's quickening influences secured to all to whom the gospel comes, and that a godly life is the scriptural test of saving faith in Christ, and of right to membership in the body of Christ, the united Church, on such a doctrinal basis, and with such a baptism of the Spirit as would endow it with the zeal which characterized the Cumberland Presbyterian Church in the first half century of its existence, would prove such a power for good as the world has yet scarcely beheld. Not only is the door wide-open, in the providence of God, for the immediate publication of the gospel in all lands, and opportunity and the world's need thus challenging the mightiest energies of God's people of all names, but the gravest social, moral, and religious problems will tax the energies of the Church to the uttermost in order to the salvation of our own country, which, as one has said, must be held for Christianity, or all is lost. The Christianity of to-day is indeed doing much. It is potentially the light of the world, and such it may soon be in fact; but as it is nearly two thousand years since the Master gave command to preach his gospel to every creature, and so large a portion of the world has not yet heard that gospel, is there not serious ground for considering whether the multiplicity of Christian sects does not involve the expenditure of much means and energy which might otherwise be much more directly available for the world's conversion?

CHAPTER V.

CREATION.

It pleased God, for the manifestation of the glory of his eternal power, wisdom, and goodness, to create the world and all things therein, whether visible or invisible; and all very good. After God had made all other creatures, he created man in his own image; male and female created he them, enduing them with intelligence, sensibility, and will; they having the law of God written in their hearts, and power to fulfill it, being upright and free from all bias to evil.—*Confession of Faith.*

In the beginning God created the heaven and the earth.—*Genesis i. 1.*

" For the invisible things of him, even his eternal power and Godhead, since the creation of the world are clearly seen, being understood by the things that are made."—*Rom. i.* 20.

" What therefore ye worship in ignorance, this set I forth unto you. The God that *made the world and all things therein*, he, being Lord of heaven and earth, dwelleth not in temples made with hands, neither is he served by men's hands as though he needed any thing, seeing he himself giveth to all life, and breath, and all things; and he *made of one every nation of men* for to dwell on all the face of the earth, having determined their appointed seasons, and the bounds of their habitation; that they should seek God, if haply they might feel after him, and find him, though he is not far from each one of us: for in him we live, and move, and have our being; as certain even of your own poets have said, *For we are also his offspring.*"—*Acts xvii.* 23-28.

" By faith we understand that the worlds were produced by the command of God, so that the things which are seen were not made of things which did appear."—*Heb. xi.* 3.

ON the last cited passage, *Macknight*, whose translation has been followed, has this note : " By revelation we understand that the worlds, namely, the sun, moon, and stars, with their appurtenances, ' were brought into being by the word of God : So that the things which are seen (the worlds) were not made of things which did appear' before they were made;—that is, the worlds which we see were not made of matter which had existed from eternity, but of matter which God created and formed into the things which we see ; and having formed them, he placed them in the beautiful order which they now hold, and impressed on them the motion proper to each, which they have retained ever since."

"It is as easy to conceive that an Almighty Power might produce a thing out of nothing, and to make that exist *de novo*, which did not exist before, as to conceive the world to have had no beginning, but to have existed from all eternity."—*Dr. South.*

In its protracted effort for a satisfactory explanation of the universe of which itself is a part the human mind has exhibited its sublimest endeavor. What *is*, whence it came, how it came to be as it is, for what end it exists, and whither it is tending, are inquiries which in all ages have exercised the powers of the most gifted. The problem of *being* in its many phases has been indeed the problem of problems. Is it possible for man to know whence he came, for what purpose he exists, what his destiny, and the destiny of the universe mirrored to his soul? Or is he hopelessly shut in to an empty echo from barriers of impenetrable darkness which tauntingly hurl back his inquiries? The problem of our existence is " utterly inscrutable," says modern skepticism ; and the same skepticism hopelessly bewails the darkness of its own making. Late in life, the gifted David Hume, the prince of modern skeptics, said :

" I am appalled at the forlorn solitude in which I am placed by my philosophy ; and I begin to fancy myself in the most deplorable condition imaginable, environed in the deepest darkness ! "

According to the positive philosophy, as taught by its chief master August Comte, it is vain to inquire concerning the origin, the purpose, or the destiny of the universe. We can know only facts, it tells us, and to attempt to draw from them any conclusion as to an author of nature or its destination is foolish, as ut-

terly transcending man's powers to know. In the language of
one of its expounders: "When the natural philosopher is convinced that the essential nature of things,—the origin and destination of the universe, and the causes of phenomena,—are insol-
uble problems, positive science begins. Accepting only the
results of experiment and observation, the mind gives over the
vain search after absolute notions beyond the reach of either.
While positive science, thus freed from impediments, steadily
advances, carrying conviction to man's intellect, that same intellect turns away from metaphysical speculation ever agitating
questions to which there is no reply. Every thing is judged by
facts and results."

But man's desire to know whence he came, and why he is
here, and whither he goes will not down at any such bidding of
an arbitrary philosophy. The unquenchable desire for an explanation of the universe about him, and of its and his own origin and destiny, heeds no demands for silence, but asserts its
claim, as a most veritable and potent fact, to be heard by every
philosophy that claims to build with facts. While it would be
quite beyond the designed limits of these pages to enter upon a
discussion or even a statement of the various atheistic theories
of the world, it is well to note that Positivism, Materialism, Agnosticism, and all other theories which deny or ignore an intelligent First Cause, and thus leave man without a divine Father
whose love and guidance he may trust, do necessarily subvert
the foundation of our hope and well-being, and invest the future
with painful uncertainty or blank despair. Thomas Carlyle,
whose "grand, rough soul" "saw deep into the heart of things,"
well expressed, in his rough and vigorous style, the tendency of
every system of cosmology which attempts an explanation of
the universe without the factor of a superintending omnipotent
and all-wise Intelligence: "Ah, it is a sad and terrible thing to
see nigh a whole generation of men and women professing to be
cultivated, looking around in a purblind fashion, and finding no

God in this universe. I suppose it is a reaction from the reign of cant and hollow pretense, professing to believe what in fact they do not believe. And this is what we have got to. All things from frog spawn ; the gospel of dirt the order of the day. The older I grow—and I now stand upon the brink of eternity, —the more comes back to me the sentence in the catechism which I learned when a child, and the fuller and deeper its meaning becomes, 'What is the great end of man ?—To glorify God and enjoy him forever.' No gospel of dirt, teaching that men have descended from frogs through monkeys, can ever set that aside."

In this teaching of the catechism, so simple, and yet so comprehensive, implying a rational explanation of man's origin, and stating the rational end for which he exists, is laid the foundation of social and civil order, the basis of moral law, the stimulus to the highest endeavor for all that is true and noble and good, and the charter of all our hopes for the boundless future to which we go. Cut loose from this mooring, humanity drifts aimless, rudderless, hopeless. From this brief attempt to contrast the gloomy speculations of science falsely so called which professes to find a world without an intelligent author or ruler, with the cheerful faith that the worlds were framed by the word of God, and that

> " The hand which bears creation up
> Will guard his children well,"

let us seek to analyze the doctrine of *creation* as presented in the Confession, and supported by the texts cited therewith. We here have, then,

1. *A specific act of absolute creation.*

By "absolute creation" we mean the bringing into being what did not before exist. That is the scriptural account of the origin of the universe, or the biblical cosmology. As logically defined, "creation is the act by which God produced out of nothing all things that now exist." But when it is said that

God made all things out of nothing (*ex nihilo*), it is not meant that "nothing" is an entity, a material, a "stuff" out of which God made the things that exist. We are to understand there was literal creation in the most absolute sense. Once the universe was not, did not exist, as to the substance of which it is composed, and as to the form the universe now presents. Now it does exist, and creation is that act of divine will by which the universe now is. Of the idea of transition from not existing to existing, or from nothing to substance, we may form a clear conception ; but how the transition is effected by a fiat of Infinite Power, utterly transcends human understanding.

The doctrine of absolute creation as stated in the foregoing paragraph is clearly taught in numerous plain passages in the Scriptures, as in the passages heading this chapter. It is a doctrine both fundamental and peculiar in Christian cosmology. Heathen philosophy teaches the eternity of matter, and if it admits creation in any sense, as some of the ancient philosophers did, it is in the subordinate sense of arranging, or constructing, the cosmos out of eternally existent material. Likewise is the fact of absolute creation seemingly implied in the inspired representations of the independence and sovereignty of God. Says Dr. A. A. Hodge (*Commentary on the Confession*), "If God be not the creator of substance *ex nihilo*, as well as the former of worlds and things, he can not be absolutely sovereign in his decrees or in his works of creation, providence, or grace. On every hand he would be limited and conditioned by the self-existent qualities of pre-existent substances. But the Scriptures always represent God as the absolute sovereign and proprietor of all things." Rom. xi. 36; 1 Cor. viii. 6; Col. i. 16; Rev. iv. 11; Neh. ix. 6.

Again, it is argued, and seemingly with very great force, that the elementary substances we know as oxygen, carbon, nitrogen, and the rest, do, by their properties, their affinities, and other relations they sustain to the composition of the goodly material frame built out of their combinations in definite proportions, certainly compel us to believe that they are endowed with what Sir John Herschel denominated " the essential character of *a manufactured article*." If " the heavens declare the glory of God, and the firmament showeth his handiwork," then must the very atoms, which are so constituted and endowed as to rear the wonderful cosmos of forms animate and inanimate, have come from the hand of Him whose power and wisdom made the world as it is. Thus theologians distinguish what they call *creatio prima*, or the creation of the substances (whether material or non-material) of the universe, from the *creatio secunda*, or the distribution and combination of these substances in the harmonious system we call the universe.

That such has been in all ages the faith of the Church in regard to the doctrine of creation can not be doubted. The Apostles' Creed, as given in a preceding chapter, opens with the sublime expression, *I believe in God the Father Almighty, Maker of heaven and earth*. Pearson, in his admirable exposition of the Creed, tells us that the " first rules of faith " thus expressed the doctrine of creation, and that " the most ancient *creeds* had either instead of these words, or together with them, *the maker of all things visible and invisible*." So the Nicene Creed; and the Constantinopolitan says, " I believe in one God the Father Almighty, *Maker of heaven and earth, and of all things visible and invisible*." According to Pearson, who justly observes that " the work of creation properly followeth the attribute of omnipotence, the phrase, ' maker of heaven and earth,' was not at the first a part of the Apostles' Creed, and that it was probably not added until as late as the eighth century, when in the Western Confessions we read: *Credo in Deum Patrem Omnipotentem, Creatorem cœli et terræ*."

" The Hebrew word translated ' to create,' and used by Moses to reveal the fact that God created the world, is the very best afforded by any human language anterior to revelation to express the idea of absolute making. It is introduced at the beginning of an account of the genesis of the heavens and of the earth. In the beginning—in the absolute beginning—God created all things (heaven and earth). After that there was chaos, and subsequently the Spirit of God, brooding over the deep, brought the ordered world into being. The Creation came before chaos, as chaos came before the bringing of things into their present form. Therefore the substance of things must have had a beginning, as well as their present forms." So says Dr. Hodge, and other Hebrew scholars agree with him as to the significance of the word translated " to create."

The doctrine of creation, as held by theologians, admits the existence of only one eternal being, and that being a pure spirit, who is "at once substance and cause, intelligence and power, absolutely free, and infinitely good." As alternatives to the Christian idea of creation we have (1) *dualism*, which asserts the eternal existence of matter, while it admits God as creator in the secondary sense, as when it is said God formed man of the dust of the earth; and (2) *pantheism*, which in reality means that matter, or the substance of which all beings consist, is the sole necessary and self-existent eternal being. It identifies God and the universe; while the biblical doctrine clearly teaches that God and the universe are essentially distinct—the former a spirit self-existent, infinite, eternal, omnipotent; the latter dependent, finite, created being. If the reasons previously stated for rejecting the idea of *two* eternal beings are conclusive, there remains the idea of the eternity of the universe, as the sole alternative of the theological doctrine of creation by an Omnipotent Intelligence. Has the world always existed? If not, since it can not have been self-caused, and must have had some cause, it must have been created by a being other than itself.

Such, in its simplest and final form, is the point at issue between the *atheistic* and the *theistic* systems of philosophy—a problem of immense significance in its practical relation to the peace and order of society and to the highest hopes of humanity.

Manifestly, the demand upon philosophy is, to determine whether the universe, so far as man can know it, exhibits characteristics which prove that it must have had a beginning; or whether it presents the characteristics of that which is self-existent and, therefore, eternal. The great battle of to-day on the field of thought is between the Christian and the Materialistic philosophy. Though a very old, old philosophy, Materialism is none the less a dangerous foe in the nineteenth century. Its aim through all the ages has been, as it is to-day, to drive the Creator from his universe, and subject all the phenomena of mind to such necessitated causation as sweeps away all rational basis of responsibility, and so to open the flood-gates of vice. Never, perhaps, more than to-day, was there demand that Christian scholars wield their learning and talents to embank against the incoming tide of materialistic thought; for "if the foundations be destroyed, what can the righteous do?"

Over against the Christian philosophy, which interprets the universe as being in all its parts, both material and spiritual, the product of an Infinite and Absolute Intelligence, from whose fiat it has arisen through successive creative acts, Atheistic Materialism, certainly the most formidable adversary of our times, to every idea essential to religious orthodoxy, constructs the universe in this style:

"Hydrogen, carbon, oxygen, etc., are the elements at present recognized as constituting the earth, its products, its inhabitants, and its atmosphere. From the facts thus acquired, we draw a conclusion broad enough to comprehend all the partial modifications with which experience may make us acquainted. The things which in their totality are expressed by the word universe, are formed of *a certain number of known substances, beyond which there is nothing.* Simple bodies, combined in various proportions have received and will retain the generic name of mat-

ter." So says A. Lefevre, who has won the distinction of "one of the strongest advocates of materialism." The words italicized suffice to indicate the immeasurable assumption of which the atheistic philosophy is capable, which is, in fact, a necessary postulate of the whole system. It simply says, "What I perceive by the senses—that is all; in this universe stretching on all sides into unfathomed depths of space, there is, I am sure, nothing but this matter which I discern by sensation." Can the most dogmatic theological faith exceed such credulity? Far back in the time of Leucippus, its accredited founder, and as Democritus taught it, and as Lucretius later expounded it, this theory ascribed the universe to a fortuitous combination of an infinity of atoms eternally dashing about in infinite space, and coming finally to the juxtaposition which constitutes the world as it is. The universe had, in fact, no beginning, it assures us; and it will have no end, for what we now call the universe is but a phase of an eternal series of transformations. As formulated by another, the theory says:

"Matter is eternal. Matter consists ultimately of atoms, which were at first distributed through empty space. The atoms are homogeneous in quality, but heterogeneous in form; motion is the eternal and necessary consequence of the original variety of atoms in the vacuum; the atoms are impenetrable, and, therefore, offer resistance to one another. All existing forms—the stars, the planets, the earth, plants, animals, mind itself—evolved from these atoms. The process of evolution began by the atoms striking together, and the lateral motions and whirlings thus produced were the beginnings of the worlds; the varieties of things depend on the variety of their constituent atoms. The first cause of all existence is necessity, that is, the necessary succession of cause and effect."

So Strauss, distinguishing "world" in the relative sense, as meaning a body or system of related bodies, from world in the sense of the universe, or totality of what is, tells us that "though it is true that every world (in the former sense) has its limitation in space as it has its beginning and end in time, yet the universe spreads itself forth and maintains its continuity illimitably, alike through all space and all time." "Consequently," as he further explains, "not only our earth, but our solar system also, and every other part of the totality of the universe, has at one period been what it no longer is (in this sort did not exist at all), and will one day cease to be as it now is." But of the "universe" he affirms "there never was a time when it was not, a time when there was in it no distinction of celestial bodies, no life, no reason. All this, if it was not in one part, was in another part, and had ceased to be in a third part; here it was coming into being, there it was in full subsistence, in a third place it was passing away; the universe is an infinite complex of worlds in all the *stadia* of origin and transition, and because of this eternal revolution and alternation preserves itself in eternal, absolute fullness of life." Into the eternally self-existent universe, Strauss finds an easy method of introducing life at such stages of the ever-shifting cosmos as favor it, declaring that its appearance "does not involve the creation of something new, but only the bringing of existent forms of matter and forces into another species of combination and movement, for which a sufficient occasion may be found in the conditions of primeval time so totally diverse from those of the present, the wholly different temperature, and of atmospheric composition, and similar causes."

We propose no analysis or refutation of this theory of the universe which dispenses with Intelligent Creative Power, our aim being only to contrast the atheistic with the theistic conception of the universe. It is in place to note that modern atheistic theories have little or nothing new to offer. The Roman poet Lucretius, assuming "matter ample" and endowed with "causal force," constructed the universe as readily as the materialists of the present day:

" If then you 'll understand, you 'll plainly see
How the vast mass of matter, Nature free
From the proud care of the meddling Deity,
Doth work by her own private strength, and move
Without the trouble of the powers above.
For, matter given, space and causal force,
Formation follows as a thing of course."

As noticed by Cocker in his admirable work, *Christianity and Greek Philosophy*, Lucretius felt the necessity of something more than the "space and matter" admitted by the Epicurean system, in order to construct the universe. To obtain this " something " he admits freedom of action in the human will, and then argues that since man, who is only an aggregate of atoms, exhibits spontaneous movement, such movement must be an attribute of the atoms of which he is composed. The atoms being liberated, by this begging of the question, from the necessity of moving eternally in straight lines, the universe arises thus : By a slight voluntary deflection from the straight line atoms (distributed through infinite space) are now brought into contact with each other; "they strike against each other, and by the percussion new movements and new complications arise "—" movements from high to low, from low to high, and horizontal movements to and fro." The atoms "jostling about *of their own accord*, in infinite modes, were often brought together confusedly, irregularly, and to no purpose, but at length they successfully coalesced ; at least such of them as were thrown together suddenly became, in succession, the beginnings of great things—as earth, and air, and sea, and heaven."—(*Cocker's Christianity and Greek Philosophy, pp.* 436-7.)

Philosophers of the Epicurean sect encountered Paul at Athens. The practical side of the Epicurean creed is expressed in 1 Cor. xv. 22—" Let us eat and drink, for to-morrow we die." The founder of the sect, born B.C. 432, was a practical atheist, admitting the existence of gods to save himself from public censure, but relegating them to a sphere beyond all concern about human affairs. Hence, the Epicureans denied Providence, accountability, and the possibility of any life beyond the present mortal state; and so held that the part of wisdom is to enjoy to the greatest possible extent whatever pleasure this world may afford, seeing there is for man no other. Modern materialistic writers have advanced nothing in support of their theory beyond what Epicurus presented; and the tendency of the system is to-day what it was two thousand years ago. Though somewhat aside from the main line of discussion, the following excellent paragraph (from Cocker's work) is cited as justly characterizing the tendency of materialistic philosophy, and illustrative of the fact that a theory of the universe must take a most important bearing on man's practical life in all that pertains to his well-being:

" The system of Epicurus is thus a system of pure materialism. . . . . His openly avowed design is to deliver men from the fear of death, and rid them of all apprehension of a future retribution. ' Did men but know that there was a fixed limit to their woes, they would be able, in some measure, to defy the religious fictions and menaces of the poets; but now, since we must fear eternal punishment at death, there is no mode, no means of resisting them.' To emancipate men from ' these terrors of the mind,' they must be taught that the soul is mortal, and dissolves with the body—that ' death is nothing to us, for that which is dissolved is devoid of sensation, and that which is devoid of sensation is nothing to us.' "

" It is evident that such a system of philosophy outrages the purest and noblest sentiments of humanity, and in fact condemns itself. It was born of selfishness and social degeneracy, and could perpetuate itself only in an age of corruption, because it inculcated the lawfulness of sensuality and the impunity of justice. Its existence at this precise period in Grecian history forcibly illustrates the truth that atheism is a disease of the heart rather than of the head. It seeks to set man free to follow

12

his own inclinations, by ridding him of all faith in a Divinity and in an immortal life, and thus exonerating him from all accountability and all future retribution. But it failed to perceive that, in the most effectual manner, it annihilated all real liberty, and all true nobleness, and made of man an abject slave."

The more fully and carefully we reflect upon the subject, the more clearly must we see that in the theistic conception of the universe must be found the basis of any system of morals adequate to the regulation of man's behavior, and to his progress in what elevates, refines, and happifies. To believe, as atheistic materialism teaches, that man is matter only, and that after a few fleeting years he is destined to inevitable return to unconsciousness as but a drop of the eternal uncaused ocean of matter on whose surface he was cast for a moment, is to believe that we are in a world that has no moral governor, which exists without a purpose, and into which we ourselves, as ephemeral creatures, have come under conditions that utterly exclude the conception of any moral end for which we exist. It is no less a necessity in the nature of the case, than a fact practically demonstrated again and again, that the tendency of the atheistic conception of the world is to the regression, the degradation, the destruction of the race. It destroys incentive to self-improvement, leaves no stimulus to effort for the common weal, and excludes all hope of a better day through the subjection of ﾠhuman wills to a divine will that orders all things for harmony, righteousness, and well-being.

Over against the Epicurean atheism, we have the Stoic philosophy acknowledging God, asserting creation (but in a sense that practically indentifies the Creator and the universe), and placing man's well-being in conformity to the will of his Creator. The Stoic taught, as Diogenes Laertius tells us in his *Lives of the Philosophers*, that "God is a living being, immortal, rational, perfect, and intellectual in his happiness, unsusceptible of any kind of evil; having a foreknowledge of the world, and of all that is in the world." As Aurelius asserts, "God made men to this end that they might be happy; as becomes his fatherly care of 'us, he placed our good and our evil in those things which are in our own power." As Laertius asserts, "God is a being of a certain quality, having for his peculiar manifestations universal substance. He is a being imperishable, who never had any generation, being the maker of the arrangement and the order we see; who at certain periods of time *absorbs all substance into himself, and then reproduces it from himself.*"

The foregoing doctrines of the Stoics are an attempt at combining the idea of creation with that of the eternity of the substance of the universe, the doctrine of Laertius seeming to identify the substance of the universe with that of the Creator. The idea of the eternity of matter is discernible as the one line of thought holding unbroken through the almost endless jarring systems of heathen philosophy regarding the nature and origin of the visible universe. The fundamental assumptions of the heathen philosophy is that out of nothing nothing can come, and that whatever is can not return to nothing, or must continue to exist. So the Brahmins teach to-day: "The ignorant assert that the universe, in the beginning, did not exist in its author, and that it was created out of nothing. O ye, whose hearts are pure, how could something arise out of nothing?" This conception of the existence of the universe in its author, and of a subsequent production from his substance, seems to indicate an Indian origin of the Stoic philosophy, which, like that of India, is essentially pantheistic. From Greek philosophy Jewish theologians and Christian fathers borrowed the same ideas of the impossibility of creation out of nothing, and of the necessary eternity of the substance of things. Accordingly the Book of Wisdom (chap. xi. 17) asserts that "*the almighty hand of the Lord* created the world out of unfashioned matter." Justin Martyr affirms that such was the general belief of his day, "For," says he, "that the word of God *formed the world*

out of unfashioned matter, Moses distinctly asserts, Plato and his
adherents maintain, and ourselves have been taught to believe."

A profound thinker of the early part of the current century,
distinguished alike as a scientist and a biblical critic, speaking
of the attempt of the Christian fathers to harmonize Platonism
and the doctrine of creation as taught in Genesis, declares that
"the text of Moses, when accurately examined, will be found to
lead us to a very different conclusion," as asserting in the first
and second verses, "first, an absolute creation of the heaven and
the earth, which, we are expressly told, took place foremost, or in
the beginning; next, the condition of the earth, when it was
thus primarily created, was amorphous and waste, or in the
words of the text, 'without form and void;' and, thirdly, the
earliest creative effort to reduce it from this shapeless and void
or waste condition into a state of order and productiveness—the
Spirit of God moved upon the face of the waters." The same
critic observes that while the word rendered "created," in the
opening of Genesis, is frequently used in the Scriptures to
denote the production of something out of material already
existing, "we have sufficient proof that it was also understood
of old to import emphatically, like our own word 'create,' an
absolute formation out of nothing." "Maimonides, expressly
tells us," he affirms, "that it was thus understood in the passage
before us (Gen. i. 1) as well as in all others that have a reference
to it, by the ancient Hebrews; while Origen affirms that such
was its import among many of the Christian fathers, whatever
might be the opinion of the rest, and forcibly objects to the
passage quoted from the Book of Wisdom, as a book not
admitted into the established canon of Scripture."

To the theory of the eternity of matter as unproduced self-
existent substance of the universe, which substance the atheistic
materialist declares the sole substance known to us; and the
theory of the emanation of the universe from the substance of
the Creator, which, in its boldest and baldest form teaches that

"the universe is the Creator, proceeds from the Creator, exists in him, and returns into him, " we may add that of idealism, which holds to the non-existence of a material world, or, in other words, that pure spirit is the only entity, the ideas of which spirit have no outward and material entities corresponding to them. Of this school in modern times were Bishop Berkeley, characterized as "a man in whom every virtue dwelt," and David Hume, worthy of his designation of "his prince of skeptics." Berkeley's fundamental assumption is that "the various sensations, or ideas, imprinted on the sense, can not exist otherwise than in the mind perceiving them." All our sensations can be accounted for, Berkeley held, as rationally on the supposition of some kind of force operating from without upon the mind, as on the supposition of the existence of an entity that we call matter, and so referred all our modifications of consciousness to the will of God as the source of the force producing them. Hume advanced a step farther, arguing that if it be unnecessary to suppose an external material entity as the basis of the phenomena of sensation, it is equally unnecessary to infer the existence of a hidden entity called mind, since all we can know by inward experience are the fleeting states of the consciousness. And so, Hume argued, of the nature of things we know absolutely nothing at all, thus carrying idealism to the extreme of a complete agnosticism. It might on first thought be supposed that a theory so remote from and contradictory to the common sense of mankind, as is the idealistic philosophy, could exert but little influence upon the public mind, but, wielded by so acute a reasoner as Hume, it was the means of destroying confidence in the ordinary grounds of belief to such a degree as to threaten the foundations of social and civil order; and Frederick Schlegel, a German student of philosophical questions, declared that "since the time of Hume, nothing more has been attempted in England than to erect all sorts of bulwarks against the practical influence of his destructive skepticism, and to maintain, by various substitutes and aids, the pile of moral principle uncorrupted and entire."

Without design of explaining or even of naming the varied philosophical theories which attempt a solution of the problem of the origin of the universe, a few references have been made rather to suggest and to insist that, of all the theories proposed, not one can satisfy the demands of reason as to this fundamental question of philosophy. Modern systems are practically but repetitions of those known thousands of years ago. Æschylus, who declared that "Zeus is earth, air, heaven, and altogether all," was as intelligent a pantheist as Spinoza,* according to whom there is one infinite substance, and only one, and as infinite is divine, while man and other finite beings are parts of this one infinite substance. The materialism of the nineteenth century, as an explanation of the universe, is no more satisfactory than that of the old Epicureans. For the most part these multitudinous systems, as did the kine of the vision of Egypt's king, devour one another, so that we may well take up the inquiry of the author of a *Comparative History of Philosophical Systems:* "About what, then, are philosophers agreed? What single point have they placed beyond dispute?" Of many of these systems we may say what a critic has said of Kant's *Critique of Pure Reason:* "Announced with pomp, received with fanaticism, disputed about with fury, after having overthrown

---

* Strictly speaking, pantheism is, as A. M. Fairbairne observes, a modern theory, as the word also is modern. Spinoza did not regard the universe as God, but, rather, "construed the world through God," and hence his system was "most ethical in character, and sublimed by the most exalted religious ideas." His system is manifestly the product of an effort, as is the Leibnitzian idea of "pre-established harmony," to get rid of the seemingly irreconcilable contradictions of duality as recognized in the common conceptions of mind and matter, the finite and the infinite, Creator and creature. But the author of the article, *Spinoza*, in the Library of Universal Knowledge, declares Spinozism to teach that "there is no real difference between mind, as represented by God, and matter, as represented by nature," and that "God neither thinks nor creates."

antagonistic systems, it could no longer support itself upon its own foundations, and has produced no permanent result." From these fruitless and discordant efforts at the solution of a problem which must forever, it would seem, baffle and transcend the powers of unaided reason, it is restful to faith and to reason to turn to the sublime declaration of the word which proclaims that, "IN THE BEGINNING GOD CREATED THE HEAVEN AND THE EARTH."

Notwithstanding the multiplicity of theories of the nature and origin of the universe, the great body of Christian thought of to-day maintains that the universe is finite, dependent, created, and that its Author is a Supreme Intelligence, independent of the creation planned for a benevolent end by his infinite wisdom and goodness, and realized through his omnipotence; while over against the Christian doctrine stands the atheistic conception of the eternity of the substance of the universe, and of an endless series of phenomena attributable solely to the nature of that substance and its inherent forces. On the one side it may be said that there are no known properties of matter, no facts apparent in the universe, no laws of human reason that can be assumed as valid premises for concluding that the world is eternal. Herbert Spencer is credited with saying that "the eternity, or self-existence, of matter is unthinkable," and in his *First Principles* he justly observes that "the assertion that the universe is self-existent does not really carry us a step beyond the cognition of its present existence; and so leaves us with a mere re-statement of the mystery." On the other hand, no principles of reason, no fact in the world about us, no properties of matter, no truths of science require us to reject the theory of creation in the biblical sense, as being absurd or self-contradictory. As great intellects as the world has known have accepted the Scriptural idea of creation as the most plausible explanation of the universe. "So far, indeed, from intimating any absurdity in the idea that matter may be created out of nothing by the interposition of an Almighty Intelligence," says a profound thinker, "reason seems, on the contrary, rather to point out to us the possibility of an equal creation out of nothing of ten thousand other substances, of which each may be the medium of life and happiness to infinite orders of being, while every one may, at the same time, be as distinct from every other, as the whole may be from matter, or as matter is from what, without knowing any thing further of, we commonly denominate spirit."

So far as it lies open to our knowledge, the universe is full of what we must regard the products of intelligence, which fact necessitates the admission of a Creator and of creation in some sense of the term. From the wonderfully endowed invisible atoms, with their affinities in definite and multiple proportions, up to vast globes swinging around vaster centers of heat and light by virtue of which they are abodes of life and activity, in all parts the universe plainly exhibits itself to us as a plan executed in view of a foreseen end. Between the all-pervading ether and the eye, between the air and the ear, and in thousands of other instances there are correlations that can not be rationally interpreted except as they are referred to creative intelligence that designed the human body as an instrument by which the mind of man is to know, enjoy, and use the world about him. Professor Pritchard, a naturalist of the highest reputation, declares: "From what I know through my own specialty, both from geometry and experiment, of the structure of the lenses of the human eye, I do not believe that any amount of evolution extending through any amount of time, could have issued in the production of that most beautiful and complicated instrument, the human eye. The most perfect, and at the same time the most difficult, optical contrivance known is the powerful achromatic object-glass of a microscope; its structure is the long unhoped-for result of the ingenuity of many powerful minds, yet in complexity and in perfection it falls infinitely below the structure of the eye. Disarrange any one of the curvatures of the many surfaces, or distances, or densities of the latter; or worse, disarrange its incomprehensible self-adaptive powers, the like of which is possessed by the handiwork of nothing human, and all the opticians in the world could not tell you what is the correlative alteration necessary to repair it, and, still less, to improve it as a natural selection is presumed to imply." But if it be granted that "evolution" did issue in the production of the eye, and that "natural selection" is a force under which the evolution went forward, it still seems impossible to evade the conviction that through the method and the force an intelligence was working out an ideal designed to enable man to look upon the universe that spreads around him. In the argument for creative wisdom and power, method of formations is nothing, design is every thing. It is not more impossible to believe that human hands and tools and mechanical principles and forces could have produced a steamship without mind having conceived the ideal, and guided the hands in the use of the tools, than it is to believe that the world about us, filled on all sides with admirable adaptations, could have resulted from any unintelligent and unconscious forces, without mind which planned the wondrous whole and guided the forces which worked it out in this goodly frame.

Scarcely less perplexing than the problem of the origin and the nature of the universe is that of the Creator's relation to the universe, those who admit a Creator differing widely in their views in respect to the latter point. One school of ancient philosophers excluded their gods from participation in the production and the management of the visible universe, leaving them to undisturbed blessedness in their empyrean abode. Thus, Lucretius, in his marvelous poem, depicts an atheistic world, though declared to have been himself " perhaps more profoundly religious in spirit than any other Roman that ever lived, save Augustine." This error of theism in conceiving God as outside of a universe under the sway of unconscious material forces, is the source, as Mr. Fiske asserts in his monogram on *The Idea of God as Affected by Modern Knowledge*, of ancient atheism; and "we shall find the cause of modern atheism," the same author asserts, "to be quite similar." Plato, regarding the world as essentially vile, "separates the Creator from his creation by the whole breadth of infinitude," and the Gnostics, adopting Plato's doctrine of the vileness of the world, accounted for the action of the spiritual God on the material universe by calling in mediating æons partly material and partly spiritual, or else supposed the world to be a product of the principle of evil. This error of Augustine, as charged by Mr. Fiske, has fastened upon modern thought, "his intense feeling of man's wickedness dragging him irresistibly" to extreme views in this direction. The following passage from Mr. Fiske's *Idea of God*, though containing sentiments we can not adopt, is nevertheless suggestive of the sources of difficulties that have perplexed candid inquirers for the truth on these great questions:

"In his (Augustine's) views of original sin he represents humanity as cut off from all relationship with God, who is depicted as a crudely anthropomorphic Being far removed from the universe and accessible only through the mediating offices of an organized Church. Compared with the thoughts of the Greek fathers this was a barbaric conception, but it was suited alike to the lower grade of culture in western Europe, and to the Latin political genius, which in the decline of the Empire was already occupying itself with its great and beneficent work of constructing an imperial church. For these reasons the Augustinian theology prevailed, and in the Dark Ages it became so deeply inwrought into the innermost fibers of Latin Christianity that it remains dominant to-day alike in Catholic and Protestant Churches. With few exceptions every child born of Christian parents in Europe or in America grows up with an idea of God, the outlines of which were engraven upon men's minds by Augustine fifteen centuries ago. Nay, more, it is hardly too much to say that three fourths of the body of doctrine currently known as Christianity, unwarranted by Scripture, and never dreamed of by Christ or his apostles, first took coherent shape in the writings of this mighty Roman, who was separated from the apostolic age by an interval of time like that which separates us from the invention of printing and the discovery of America. The idea of God upon which all this Augustinian doctrine is based is the idea of a Being actuated by human passions and purposes, localizable in space, and utterly remote from that machine, the universe in which we live, and upon which he acts intermittently by the suspension of what are called natural laws. So deeply has this conception penetrated the thought of Christendom that we continually find it at the bottom of the speculations and arguments of men who would warmly repudiate it as thus stated in its naked outline. It dominates the reasonings alike of believers and skeptics, of theists and atheists; it underlies at once the objections raised by orthodoxy against each new step in science, and the assaults made by materialism upon every religious conception of the world; and thus it is chiefly responsible for that complicated misunderstanding which, by a lamentable confusion of thought, is commonly called ' the conflict between science and religion.' "

Over against the Augustinian conception of God's relation to the universe, as depicted in the foregoing, Mr. Fiske thus presents what he designates as Cosmic Theism: " We are now prepared to see that the theological objection urged against the Newtonian and Darwinian theories has its roots in that imperfect kind of theism which Augustine did so much to fasten upon the Western World. Obviously if Leibnitz and Agassiz had been educated in that higher theism shared by Clement and Athanasius in ancient times with Spinoza and Goethe in later days—if they had been accustomed to conceive of God as immanent in the universe and eternally creative—then the argument which

they urged with so much feeling would never have occurred to
them. To conceive of 'physical forces' as powers of which the
action could in any wise be 'substituted' for the action of Deity
would in such case have been absolutely impossible. . . . The
higher or Athanasian theism knows nothing of secondary
causes in a world where every event flows directly from the
eternal First Cause. It knows nothing of physical forces save
as immediate manifestations of the omnipresent creative power
of God. . . . Once really admit the conception of an ever-present
God, without whom not a sparrow falls to the ground, and it
becomes self-evident that the law of gravitation is but an expression of a particular mode of divine action. And what is
thus true of one law is true of all laws. The thinker in whose
mind divine action is thus identified with orderly action, and to
whom a really irregular phenomenon would seem like a manifestation of sheer diabolism, foresees in every possible extension
of knowledge a fresh confirmation of his faith in God. To him,
no part of the universe is godless ; . . . . and each act of scientific explanation but reveals an opening through which shines
the glory of the eternal Majesty."

In his efforts to look beyond mere phenomena and secondary
causes, and to know the essence underlying phenomena, and to
find that first cause through which all phenomena may be interpreted as a unity, man is influenced, and must be influenced, by
the received philosophy of each particular age. In this age of
special studies there are "terrific dangers," as Joseph Cook
observes, "of a fragmentary view of God." Error upon a
question so fundamental as that of the relation of the Creator to
the universe, and especially of his relation to man as a creature
dependent, rational, and a subject of moral law, must be far-
reaching in its influence as a vitiating element. While Mr.
Fiske, in accordance with the best thought of the age, discovers
that Mind is the ultimate fact, the primal cause which affords a
rational explanation of the universe, he seems to us to so dis-

pense with secondary causes as to identify God and nature, and thus to have gone so far from Augustine as to land, with Spinoza and Goethe, in absolute pantheism. His theory of the divine *immanence* implies a universe without God, or God without a universe. The personal living God is taken away, and a deified universe is substituted. In gravitation and other impersonal forces eternally operating, he finds the only thing to be recognized as the will of God. According to his theory, "Matter is but the generalized name we give to those modifications which we refer immediately to an unknown something outside of ourselves," while "the eternal source of phenomena," ever active, "eternally creating," is the "Force," the "Reality," the "infinite and eternal Power," the "Universal Life," of which universal life all living things are but "specialized forms," and these "specialized forms" the products of an "evolution" necessitated by the persistence of force, and operating eternally and everywhere, through which evolution man, "the crown and glory of the universe and the chief object of divine care, yet still the lame and halting creature, loaded with a brute inheritance of original sin," is to experience ultimate salvation "through ages of moral discipline."

While the theory of creation, and of the Creator's relation to the world, thus briefly sketched seems to us open to very grave objections, especially as identifying the life of the universe with the life of God, and thereby making all creatures, and all actions whether good or bad, but phenomena of the one divine sea of infinite existence, and, seemingly at least, necessarily excluding the idea of human responsibility, Mr. Fiske is certainly to be credited with having produced a most thoughtful discussion of "the idea of God, as it is affected by modern knowledge;" and the following paragraph from his work is herein quoted, alike for its intrinsic excellence and from a desire to be just to its author:

"The infinite and eternal Power that is manifested in every

pulsation of the universe is none other than the living God.
We may exhaust the resources of metaphysics in debating how
far his nature may fitly be expressed in terms applicable to the
psychical nature of Man; such vain attempts will only serve to
show we are dealing with a theme that must ever transcend our
finite powers of conception. But of some things we may feel
sure. Humanity is not a mere local incident in an endless and
aimless series of cosmical changes. The events of the universe
are not the work of chance, neither are they the outcome of
blind necessity. Practically there is a purpose in the world
whereof it is our highest duty to learn the lesson, however well
or ill we may fare in rendering a scientific account of it. When
from the dawn of life we see all things working together toward
the evolution of the highest spiritual attributes of Man, we
know, however the words may stumble in which we try to say
it, that God is in the deepest sense a moral Being. The everlasting source of phenomena is none other than the infinite
Power that makes for righteousness. Thou canst not by
searching find him out; yet put thy trust in him, and
against thee the gates of hell shall not prevail; for there is
neither wisdom nor understanding nor counsel against the
Eternal."

We have dwelt upon this phase of our subject because of the
tendency of the day, notably with writers of one scientific
school, toward such a conception of *divine immanence* as unavoidably leads to the identification of God and nature, and thus
utterly takes away the God of our fathers and of the Bible. If
the universe be but an "evolution of the substance of God,"
and the "cosmical forces" are all the "will of God" of which
we can have any knowledge, then indeed have we no God whom
we can rationally worship, nor is there a divine compassion that
cares for men. Poets, novelists, and mystics have tinged our
literature with the pernicious sentiment which identifies the
human soul with what they choose to call the general soul of

the universe or, with mystic pietism, the Infinite Spirit, the outcome of which is

> " That each, who seems a separate whole,
>   Should move his rounds, and, fusing all
>   The skirts of self again, should fall
>   *Remerging in the general soul.*"

The thoughtful scientist sees that this visible universe, as
transient and dependent in all its parts, must rest upon a power
back of itself, not less really and certainly than the steamer
rests upon the ocean's bosom. "We are ever," says Herbert
Spencer, "in the presence of an infinite and eternal energy,
from which all things proceed, manifested within and without
us." What is this eternal energy of the philosopher but the
power of the living God whose is the " hand which bears creation up?" The conception of the absolute *immanence* of the
Creator in the universe, as it is taught by philosophers of the
school of Mr. Fiske, is but a step, on one side, from rigid pantheism, and, on the other, from blank materialistic atheism.
We have elsewhere called attention to the fact that the doctrine
of universal, unconditional divine decree of whatsoever comes
to pass is essentially pantheistic, and as utterly excludes the
ideas of freedom of will, human responsibility, and moral government, as does absolute atheistic necessity. We must not
exclude God from his universe, nor confound him with the
universe. He indeed made the world and all that is therein,
impressing matter and the finite mind, alike products of his
power, with the attributes now immanent in them. These forces
of matter and attributes of mind are as God willed them to be;
but to confound these forces and attributes with the will of God,
is virtually to substitute for the God of the Bible an impersonal
unconscious intelligence working in the universe. God indeed
notes the fall of the sparrow, but a sparrow is not a "specialized
form " of the divine substance, nor is the force which controls
its fall a specific and immediate volition of God. "We must

not," says Dr. Valentine, " fall into the mistake of some theistic writers, who have attributed each individual and separate event in nature to a direct act of the divine will or energy. This error annihilates the reality of secondary causation. It is not only plain contradiction to all we know of the constitution of nature, but it vacates the very postulate on which the theistic argumentation is based. Natural forces are real, and the laws of their action are made immanent in the nature of the elements or organism in which they show themselves. But they are the real products and ordinations of the Deity who gave them their reality or appointed them their modes or laws. . . . They are the sequences according to which God ordinarily acts, yet their results come, not as direct, but as mediate products of the divine power. . . . God is above nature and below it, without it and within it, yet never a part of it. He is not nature, but nature is from him, and subsists by him."

Finally, it is in place to repeat that the " idea of God as affected by modern knowledge " is not the idea of a power identical with the forces of nature, nor of a power absolutely and eternally immanent in the universe; but of an infinite Being who is omnipotent and all-wise, the Source of all finite being, Cause of causes, the absolute Mind, in which only can be found an explanation of the wisdom and unity of the universe, who is Creator, Presever, Benefactor, God over all, blessed for evermore!

CHAPTER VI.

CREATION—CONTINUED.

"It pleased God, for the manifestation of the glory of his eternal power, wisdom, and goodness, to create the world and all things therein, whether visible or invisible; and all very good.

"After God had made all other creatures, he created man in his own image; male and female created he them, enduing them with intelligence, sensibility, and will; they having the law of God written in their hearts, and power to fulfill it, being upright and free from all bias to evil."—*Confession of Faith.*

"And God said, Let there be light; and there was light."—Gen. i. 3.

> "Happy is he that hath the God of Jacob for his help,
> Whose hope is in the Lord his God:
> Which made heaven and earth,
> The sea, and all that in them is."—Psalm cxlvi. 5, 6.

"For from him, and by him, and to him are all things: To him be the glory forever."—Rom. xi. 36.

"It is clearly delivered in the teachings of the apostles that there is one God who created and arranged all things, and who, when nothing existed, called all things into being—God from the first creation and foundation of the world . . . . But that we may believe on the authority of the Holy Scriptures that such is the case, hear how in the Maccabees, where the mother of seven martyrs exhorts her son to endure torture, this truth is confirmed; for she says, 'I ask of thee, my son, to look at the heaven and the earth, and at all things which are in them, and, beholding these, to know that God made all these things when they did not exist.' In the book of the Shepherd also, in the first commandment, he speaks as follows: 'First of all believe there is one God, who created and arranged all things, and made all things to come into existence, and out of a state of nothingness.'"—*Origen.*

IT is nothing to our purpose in these chapters to advocate a *theory* of creation. As Dr. Briggs says of the Presbyterian Church, of the Cumberland Presbyterian it may be as truthfully said, that "it has no *consensus* of opinion on the doctrine of creation." The *fact* of a creation, as a theory of the origin of

13

the universe, we hold in common with all Christians, as of fundamental importance. Moses was a profound philosopher in rearing his great system of theistic teaching on the cornerstone, "God created the heaven and the earth." If Creator, then is God the sovereign ruler of the world.

It is a blessed thing to so look upon the universe as to bring God near to us, and thus to rise to the comforting assurance that

> "The voice which rolls the stars along
> Spake all the promises."

But the only adequate foundation for such assurance is the doctrine that we live in a real world, a world everywhere exhibiting plan and purpose, "the work of an Almighty hand."

Upon the Christian doctrine of creation, as held under all dispensations and through all the centuries of the Church, infidelity has made its most bitter assaults. The doctrine is to-day a battle-ground thick strewn with the weapons of agnosticism, positivism, materialism, and every other species of atheistic philosophy. Astronomy, geology, biology and other sciences have been claimed by the enemy, each being in its turn paraded upon the field as a Goliath about to utterly demolish the scriptural idea of there having been a beginning and a creation of the world. But Christian students have pushed their observations as far out into the heavens and as deep into the strata of the earth as any other class of men, and they return from their investigations to assure us that rocks and stars alike, viewed in all the light of recent scientific progress, show unmistakably the footprints of a Creator. Marvelous, indeed, both in extent and richness, is the literature the recent discussion of this subject has produced. Even since the last preceding chapter was written the press has announced several valuable new works, one of which essays the arduous task of an explanation, as implied in its title, of *The Genesis of the Universe*. Did space permit, we would gladly enrich these pages with suitable paragraphs from some of the most instructive of recent works

relating to this discussion. But it is well for us continually to
bear in mind that though we may know that the theory of creation by an Omnipotent Intelligence, as an explanation of the
universe, is the most rational explanation of what lies open to
our very limited knowledge, the subject necessarily and infinitely transcends the powers of the most gifted of human minds;
so that beyond very narrow limits all our endeavors at explaining the "genesis of the universe" find just rebuke in those
remarkable words, as applicable to any Tyndall or Huxley of
to-day, as to Job, whose arraignment of Providence was
answered out of the whirlwind: "Who is this that darkeneth
counsel by words without knowledge? Gird up now thy loins
like a man; for I will demand of thee, and answer thou me.
Where wast thou when I laid the foundations of the earth?
declare, if thou hast understanding. Who determined the
measures thereof, if thou knowest? or who hath stretched the
line upon it? Whereupon are the foundations thereof fastened?
or who laid the corner-stone thereof; when the morning stars
sang together, and all the sons of God shouted for joy? . . . .
Hast thou commanded the morning since thy days, and caused
the dayspring to know his place? . . . . Knowest thou the
ordinance of heaven? canst thou set the dominion thereof in
the earth? . . . . Wilt thou also disannul my judgment?"

Lotze, the German philosopher, well says that "the two
hostile parties should return to modesty—namely, that theological learning on the one side, and irreligious natural science on
the other, should not assert that they have exact knowledge
about so much which they neither do know nor can know."
The theories possible respecting *creation* are comprised, as
Lotze maintains, in these three—namely, (1) a "consistent development of the nature of God," (2) a product of his will, (3)
the product of a creative act. Excluding the first, which "appears in all the emanation theories of ancient and modern
times," Lotze makes the following judicious and most valuable

remarks touching the religious bearing of the theory which, claiming science as its basis, would displace a Creator by what it terms evolution :

" So far as this view endeavors to exclude a God who rules without principle in blind arbitrariness, it is correct; and in this respect corresponds also to our religious need. But we must resist with the greatest possible decisiveness the further apotheosis of the notion of ' development' consequent upon this view, which it is customary just now to express and to extol with such great emphasis, as though it were identical, as a matter of course, with all that is great and sublime and holy.

" If it were only a question concerning a theoretical explanation of the course of the world, then such a conception would be satisfactory. But it is wholly useless from the religious point of view, because it leads consistently to nothing but a thorough-going determinism, according to which not only is every thing that must happen, in case certain conditions occur, appointed in pursuance of general laws; but according to which even the successive occurrence of these conditions, and consequently the whole of history with all its details, is predetermined.

" In such a mechanical contrivance there is no place whatever for any ' freedom' or ' activity,' or for an effort that shall produce aught which does not originate from the mechanism itself. Religious opinion assumes rather that, while there are universal laws, without whose efficacy no ' design' whatever would be able by definite means to attain to a definite goal, there is however at the same time, on the basis and in the domain of this reign of law, a free, voluntary activity, which, by the use and combination of the given elements acting in accordance with law, produces that even which would have no existence without such activity.

" The above-mentioned assumption has its difficulties. Until, however, it is shown decisively to be impossible, the religious

feeling will never return to the thought of an 'undesigned, inevitable development' of the world from the nature of God, but
will derive it from an act of the divine will, *without* which it
would not have existed."

So, as it seems to us, every phase of materialism, as a theory
of the world, involves principles utterly subversive of all ideas
of freedom and responsibility in any and every sense in which
these are essential to religion. Materialism is fatalistic determinism. Though neither blind " inevitable development " nor
materialism is necessarily exclusive of the idea of God, they are
alike exclusive of the idea of religion ; for, as Sir William
Hamilton declares, "the assertion of absolute necessity, is
virtually the negation of a moral universe, and consequently of
the Moral Governor of a moral universe."

So, as the subject is pursued, will it appear that any false
system of philosophy relating to the fundamental principles of
morals and religion will of necessity vitiate the whole stream
flowing therefrom, and entail upon society the most direful
calamities. False philosophy is a powerful agency for evil,
working unrest in the public mind, wresting thought and feeling from safe moorings, slackening the moral bands which hold
men in peaceable and helpful relations, and paving the way for
stormy revolution. One's life may indeed be better than his
theory, but his theory, if false, must nevertheless work evil in
the world of thought and action. Hence, we have insisted
again and again on the Christian idea of a divine origin of the
world, in which theory only is it possible to find an enduring
basis for the idea of moral government. This foundation destroyed, humanity's prospect is pessimistic indeed.   " Once
thoroughly established," says de Pressense, " this conclusion
(the possibility of a divine and moral world) suffices to secure to
humanity its most precious possession—that higher life, apart
from which man misses all that distinguishes him from the
brute, and is without any light beyond the grave, without any

compass on his voyage through life, without morality, without law, without liberty, given up to the chances of brute force, a helpless and degraded thing."

Christian teaching, then, is that the world in which we live is a real one, that our cognitive faculties, within limits required by our well-being, are reliable, and not imposed on us to deceive; that, as dependent and finite, the world must have had a cause; that, as exhibiting order, adaptation, and design, it must have had an intelligent cause, which cause is an Omnipotent Intelligence, "who spake and it was done, who commanded and it stood fast." And what is the attitude of this doctrine in relation to the wonderful progress in science, which, along so many lines of investigation, has so notably distinguished the last half a century? The following propositions will, it seems to us, fairly and substantially express the truth upon this point:

1. Science has illustrated and confirmed the position that the world must have had a beginning, in other words, that it is not eternal, and, therefore, that it must have had a cause.

The universe, as we know it, exhibits only that which is finite, dependent, transient. Every phenomenon is dependent on a cause, and that cause on an antecedent cause. It is no more true, as science views the world, that insects and flowers are ephemeral, that man fleeth as a shadow and continueth not, and that the human race can not have been always in existence, than it is that the earth itself once was not, that the great solar system once was not, that the parent orb dispensing light and heat is, as the poet declares, but "a transient meteor in the sky." Astronomy has opened up to us almost infinite depths of the astral universe, to show us that "even now, at this very time, there exist in the depths of space all orders of suns—suns still growing; suns ruling over schemes already formed; and, lastly, dead and used up suns, waiting, as it were, for some future change, by which they will be restored to activity and usefulness."

In like manner, geology, reading the earth's history in its own records in the rock, tells us there was a time when man was not, a time when the present plants and animals were not, a time when an unbroken sea covered the globe, a time when life had not yet dawned, and when the conditions were such that life would have been impossible. Thus has science powerfully and most thoroughly refuted the scoffers of St. Peter's time, who, arguing from what they supposed the changeless stability of all parts of the universe, ridiculed the idea of the destruction of the earth, and of the formation of new heavens and a new earth. And so in many points science has risen to vindicate the Bible, to silence scoffers. Understood in the light of science, the notable passage in Hebrews (i. 10–12) puts on transcendent beauty and significance: "And thou, Lord, in the beginning hast laid the foundation of the earth; and the heavens are the works of thine hands. They shall perish, but thou continuest; and they shall wax old as doth a garment. And as a vesture shalt thou fold them up, and they shall be changed; but thou are the same, and thy years shall not fail." It is reason's demand and the Bible's assertion, that back of this ceaselessly shifting panorama we call the universe there is, not something only, but a some One, who is the same yesterday, to-day, and forever, who reveals himself to his rational creation through these garments changed, laid aside, and renewed as may serve the purpose of his sovereign will.

2. Science proposes no adequate or plausible theory of the origin of the universe.

Agnosticism denies that we can know any thing about God or any other cause of the universe. Positivism says we can know facts only, and that to inquire about causes is foolish. But science says there was a beginning, and reason postulates the necessity of a cause. Evolution comes forward to explain the mode in which and the forces by which great changes from lower to higher have been effected in the organic life of the globe;

but even in this little domain of nature's vast field it can not make a beginning without God, for its most intelligent expounders confess that they meet with numerous chasms, a dozen or more, which evolution is utterly unable to bridge. Here the advocates of the theory may themselves be allowed to testify. Darwin says: " In what manner the mental powers were first developed in the lowest organisms is as hopeless an inquiry as how life first originated. These are problems for the distant future, if they are ever to be solved by man." Similarly he speaks of " the great break in the organic chain between man and his nearest allies, which can not be bridged over by any extinct or living species." Darwin believed, however, that, with the start of one or a few primordial forms into which God had breathed life, evolution has worked out the manifold and wondrous varieties of life, from the monad up to man.

Science has thrown no bridge across the chasm during the few years which have transpired since Tyndall, in a lecture on " The Origin of Life," gave utterance to the following:

" This discourse is but a summing up of eight months of incessant labor. From the beginning to the end of the inquiry, there is not, as you have seen, a shadow of evidence in favor of spontaneous generation. There is, on the contrary, overwhelming evidence against it; but do not carry away with you the notion, sometimes erroneously ascribed to me, that I deem spontaneous generation impossible, or that I wish to limit the power of matter in relation to life. My views on this subject ought to be well known. But possibility is one thing, and proof is another; and when in our day I seek for experimental evidence of the transformation of the non-living into the living, I am led inexorably to the conclusion that no such evidence exists, and that, in the lowest as well as the highest of organized creatures, the method of nature is, that life shall be the issue of antecedent life."

Professor Huxley has conceded that " of the causes which

have led to the origination of living matter it may be said that we know absolutely nothing. . . . The present state of knowledge furnishes us with no link between the living and the not-living."

To the foregoing utterances of men whose authority as scientists will not be questioned, we may add the remarkable language of Sir William Thompson in his inaugural address when assuming the presidential chair of the British Association, at a meeting in Edinburgh, but a few years ago:

"A very ancient speculation, still clung to by many naturalists (so much so, that I have a choice of modern terms to quote in expressing it), supposes that, under meteorological conditions very different from the present, dead matter may have run together or crystallized or fermented into 'germs of life,' or 'organic cells,' or 'protoplasm.' But science brings a vast mass of inductive evidence against this hypothesis of spontaneous generation, as you have heard from my predecessor in the presidential chair. Careful enough scrutiny has, in every case up to the present day, discovered life as antecedent to life. Dead matter can not become living without coming under the influence of matter previously alive. This seems to me as sure a teaching of science as the law of gravitation."

Since, then, it is absurd to regard the universe, which is dependent and ever changing, as an eternal series of progression and regression; since the phenomena of life and intelligence upon our globe exhibit gaps which can not be bridged by any laws or forces known to science; and since if evolution can be shown to account satisfactorily, by forces working in nature, for the origin of life and the vast and varied expansion of the organic kingdoms, such an endowment of matter would necessitate an intelligent endowing cause, science teaches nothing that invalidates, but much that fortifies the scriptural testimony that, "In the beginning *God created* the heaven and the earth." Nor need the doctrine of the divine creation of man and his world

fear any startling surprises that yet await the progress of
science; for if it turn out that there is truth in the dogmatic assumption of Huxley that "the whole existing world once lay
potentially in the cosmic vapor, and that from a knowledge of
the properties of its molecules it would have been possible to
predict the present state of the British flora and fauna as easily
as one might tell what would happen to the vapor of the breath
on a winter's day," yet would reason insist that it required infinite wisdom and infinite power to endow "cosmic vapor" with
potency to work out a scheme so stupendous in its proportions
and rational in its ends.

But science has most certainly taught us:

3. That the creation, in the sense in which it has usually been
conceived, occurred at a period vastly longer ago than biblical
scholars have been accustomed to assign.

So late as the beginning of the seventeenth century, the
English Parliament directed Archbishop Usher to settle the
question as to the exact date of the creation, whereupon that
eminent ecclesiastic and biblical scholar assigned the event to
October 25, B.C. 4004. The Westminster divines held the creative days to be literal days of twenty-four hours each, and
almost countless have been the well-meant but fruitless efforts
to reconcile that interpretation of Genesis with the now unquestioned teachings of geology. It would require many pages to
even state intelligently all the geological proofs of the earth's
high antiquity. In its own rocky strata it chronicles a history
which can not be questioned, embracing vast cycles of time
during which—

> " Many a change both wild and strange
> Reversed the sea and land."

In the earth's records of its vast and varied life-periods we
encounter facts innumerable which demand for their production
periods of time beyond our comprehension. During a half day
spent in the British Museum, London, it was the writer's privi-

lege and never-to-be-forgotten satisfaction to stroll through a long series of apartments in a great room allotted to a fossilliferous representation of the life-history of the globe. Turning from the azoic rocks in one end, we find, on the right and on the left, rocks containing the rudimentary forms of the earliest life period; a few steps brings us to the limestones literally packed with the fossils of the molluscs which flourished in warm and widespread seas; and now the rocks on either hand tell us of the wonderful dynasty of the fishes; passing on, we are amid the records of the great plant period of the earth, during which the vast coal measures were stored away for man's use; and now there gleam upon us the huge, weird forms of the age of the reptiles; beyond these we are amid the great beasts of a by-gone age—the megatherium, the dinotherium, and other gigantic creatures who have now no like upon the earth; and now we have the progenitors of the beasts of to-day, and last of all, with his associated animals on either hand, there is in the center of the end of the hall, directly facing us as he stares out of his rocky tomb, the famous fossil man from Guadaloupe. Of all the interesting impressions associated with this panoramic view of perhaps millions of years of earth's history, no one was more vivid than that of the palpable and startling confirmation it affords of the truth of the biblical declaration that man was the last and crowning work of the creation. How came Moses to anticipate by thousands of years the teachings of the science of to-day?

If, now, we turn our attention from the earth beneath us to the heavens above us, on all sides we find manifold proofs of great antiquity. According to the nebular hypothesis, our Solar System has been evolved, by cosmic forces now in operation in the heavens, from an original nebula, or cloud of intensely heated gas, which extended beyond the orbit of the now outermost planet. If the present system has resulted from cooling and contraction in the parent mass at rates for which present facts furnish any reliable data, the process has required, astronomers tell us, from fifteen millions to twenty millions of years. We need not be startled at this demand for time—and astronomy could be allowed a few millions more still, for in the calendar of the Eternal a thousand years are but as one day. Time in his creative processes can not put the Creator far away from us. It seems equally true that the heavens have been of old, and that processes now known to be going on in the heavens "can have," as Professor Young declares, "but one ultimate result—that of absolute stagnation." "That in some way this end of things will result in a 'new heaven and a new earth' is, of course, very probable," says the same writer, adding, "but science can yet present no explanation of the method."

In concluding this part of our subject it may both suitably and truthfully be said that, if science has required great modification in our interpretation of the Mosaic account of creation, and has raised some difficulties which may not yet have been fully explained, the general effect of the fuller light of science thrown upon this ancient record is to reveal its almost infinite superiority to other cosmogonies of its time, and its incalculable and imperishable value to the race. The narrative of the creation is to be interpreted by the purpose for which it was given, on which point Geike's *Hours with the Bible* has these judicious words:

"It is clear from this abstract that it could not have been the design of God to give in the few opening lines of Genesis an exact scientific statement of the stages observed in creation. The sublime truth that nature was prepared step by step for the appearance of man, is the great lesson intended, and science corroborates it throughout. . . . . Man is recognized by the highest authorities of modern science as beyond question the ideal being toward whose appearance 'nature had been working for the earliest ages; a being, therefore, whose existence had been foreordained.'"

So Professor Owen, the eminent naturalist, alluding to the manifold orders of life which have existed upon the globe, says: "The link by which they are connected is of a higher and immaterial nature; and their connection is to be sought in the view of the Creator himself, whose aim in forming the earth, in allowing it to undergo the successive changes which geology has pointed out, and in creating, successively, all the different types of animals which have passed away, was *to introduce man upon the surface of our globe. Man is the end* toward which all the animal creation has tended."

The following sentences from Dr. Foster's *Old Testament Studies*, a work fresh from the press, are very pertinent and suggestive:

"The Mosaic doctrine of creation places itself far above all heathen and non-biblical theories, by the sublime declaration, 'In the beginning God created the heaven and the earth;' though it is evident that the first chapter of Genesis and the subsequent inspired commentaries upon it are, so far as their *form* is concerned, addressed to the religious faith of the people, rather than to the scientific curiosity. It stands in direct contradiction to the atheistic theory of chance. The world was not produced by any process of self-generation, nor by the unintelligent action of impersonal forces, nor by many agents like the good and evil principles of the Persian theory, with which the Israelites may have become acquainted during the Babylonish captivity. It implies, and it implied to the Israelitish mind, the eternity of the God whose existence it assumes, for, having created all things, he must be before all things; it implied his omnipotence, for he who created the heavens and the earth could do any thing that was conceivable; it implied his absolute freedom, for it represented him not only as beginning a new course of action, but as doing it by the free exercise of his own will; it also implied to them his infinite wisdom, for such an orderly heaven and earth as was known even to the Israelites could be the product only of a mind of absolute intelligence."

Perhaps from no other point of view are we so clearly and profoundly impressed with the majesty, grandeur, and divine origin of the Scriptures, as when we compare their teachings respecting the origin and nature of the world with the puerilities and ludicrous absurdities found in the very best of heathen cosmogonies. Thus, the Hindu idea of the universe is fitly expressed in this paragraph: "Millions upon millions of cycles ago, this world came to be. It was made a flat triangular plain with high hills and mountains and great waters. It exists in several stories, and the whole mass is held up on the heads of elephants with their tails turned out, and their feet rest on the shell of an immense tortoise, and the tortoise on the coil of a great snake, and when those elephants shake themselves, that makes the earth quake."

From the Babylonian doctrine of the origin of things we have this: "In the beginning all was darkness and water, and therein were generated monstrous animals of strange and peculiar form. There were men with two wings, and some even with four and with two faces; and others with two heads—a man's and a woman's—on the same body; and there were men with the heads and horns of goats, and men with hoofs like horses, and some with the upper parts of a man joined to the lower parts of a horse, like centaurs; and there were bulls with human heads, dogs with four bodies and with the tails of fishes; men and horses with dogs' heads; creatures with the heads and bodies of horses, but with fishes' tails, mixing the forms of various beasts."

It is asserted by those competent to give a reliable judgment in the premises, that, in like manner, the teachings of the wisest uninspired men of antiquity, not excepting even those of Seneca, Socrates and Plato, Pythagoras or Aristotle, contain absurdities which are not only utterly disproved by well ascertained scientific facts, but are sheer nonsense in the judgment of enlightened reason. In view of this solitary exception exhibited by the Bible, a recent writer inquires: "Who guarded this most ancient volume from the superstitions which corrupted chemistry into alchemy, and astronomy into astrology? Who taught the writer of the 104th Psalm to compose that grand poem on the wonders of the created world, and yet introduce not one of the scientific errors current in those days? so that even von Humboldt was compelled to confess that 'in a lyrical poem of such limited compass, we find the whole universe, the heavens and the earth, sketched with a few bold touches?'"

If any are perplexed over seeming discrepancies between the teachings of science and the teachings of Genesis, let them remember that almost innumerable scientific theories, regarded for a time as about to otherthrow the Bible, have, one after another, been abandoned. At the opening of the century the French Institute of Science counted, it is said, eighty theories "hostile to the Bible," of which theories every one has been abandoned by scientists. And so, while man's progress in knowledge—for he does progress—consists largely in casting aside theories that were but "science falsely so called," the Christian may with unshaken confidence rest in that record whose Author declares "Heaven and earth shall pass away, but my word shall not pass away."

As relating to the adjustment between the Bible doctrine of creation, and the teachings of modern science, these words of Dr. A. A. Hodge (Commentary on the Confession) are judicious and comprehensive: "(1) The record in Genesis has been given by divine revelation, and therefore is infallibly true. (2) The book of nature and the book of revelation are both from God, and will be found, when both are adequately interpreted, to coincide perfectly. (3) The facts upon which the science of geology is based are yet very imperfectly collected and much more imperfectly understood. The time has not come yet, in which a profitable comparison and adjustment of the two records can be effected. (4) The record in Genesis, brief and general as it is, was designed and is admirably adapted to lay the foundation of an intelligent faith in Jehovah as the absolute creator and the immediate former and ruler of all things. But it was not designed either to prevent or to take the place of a scientific interpretation of all existing phenomena, and of all traces of the past history of the world God allows men to discover. Apparent discrepancies in establishing truths can have their ground only in imperfect knowledge. God requires us both to believe and to learn. He imposes on us at present the necessity of humility and patience."

It is knowledge superficial and one-sided, as a rule, which prates of "discrepancies" between God's word and his works. On this point the observation of Bacon has most pertinent application: "A little learning inclineth men's minds to skepticism; but much learning bringeth them back again to religion."

In the further analysis of the doctrine of the Confession we note:

2. *The content of the creation*, namely, "the world and all things therein, whether visible or invisible."

This statement implies that only God is uncaused and eternal, and that whatever is, besides him, owes its existence to the divine creative agency. If we hold the doctrine of the creation of any thing, in its substance and in its form as a creature, we will consistently hold the creation of all things. " By him were created all things which are in the heavens and which are upon the earth, things visible and things invisible, whether thrones or lordships, or governments or powers; all things were created through him and for him."—Col. i. 16. In this Pauline statement of the heirship of Christ to all things, because all were made through and for him, the "things visible" are thought to be the material fabric and all material objects therein, and the "things invisible" are thought to be the various orders of angels, further represented as principalities, powers, etc. While the sacred writer doubtless meant to ascribe to Christ the creation of all things, we are not to suppose his enumeration of things created was at all designed to be a complete inventory of the orders of being or of the elementary substances making up the universe.

While some philosophers have held that mind is the sole entity, and others have held that matter is the sole entity, the majority of thinkers have held that mind and matter are distinct entities, and that *dualism* is therefore the true theory of the universe. No necessary laws of thought require the acceptance of any one of these theories. If God has created substance, he may have created many species of substance. Why not? It may be that what we call matter exists in species, although all forms of it known to us possess some properties in common. We can not know substance. We know phenomena, and believe there must be a substance, an entity that *knows*, and also a something that is known as existing and acting on the percipient being. Thus we arrive at a *dualism* embracing (1) that which is extended, called matter, and that which thinks, or mind. Some claim that we have knowledge of four species of non-material substance: (1) The eternal Creator, (2) the soul of man, (3) the brute mind, (4) the principle of vegetable life. Origen says that "God created two general natures—a visible, that is, a corporeal nature, and an invisible nature, which is incorporeal." According to Rosmini, an Italian philosopher, cosmology has for its scope the study of (1) pure spirits, (2) souls, (3) bodies. "Since the body is the proximate cause of our sensations," says Rosmini, "and these are facts which happen in us without our agency, while we are merely passive subjects, it follows of necessity that *we* are not body. And since that which the word WE expresses is the feeling and thinking subject, therefore this subject is a substance entirely different from corporeal subtance." Through phenomena we know there is a something we call matter, and for a like reason we know there is a something which exhibits the experienced phenomena of thinking, feeling,

14

willing, which something we call mind. There is a material
world, and there is a world of mind. The former exists for the
latter. God is the creator of both. What matter is, what mind
is, and how God caused either to be, are things that absolutely
transcend our power to know.

We must not, however, in referring all things visible and invisible to the creative power of God as the efficient cause of
their existence think of them as simultaneous products of a
single creative act or "work," nor that they were all called into
being, as was formerly thought, within the space of six literal
days. Long had the earth existed as the abode of multitudinous life ere "dust was fashioned into man." Perhaps we may
rightly believe, with some, that God is ever-creating, and all
about us, though we have known it not; or with others, as
Lotze, that "the will to create is an absolutely eternal predicate
of God, and ought not to be used to designate a *deed* of his, so
much as the absolute dependence of the world upon his *will.*"

3. *That man was last created.*—In the statement of Genesis on
this point there is, as already remarked, a complete correspondence with a fact thoroughly and independently established by
science—a correspondence it would be almost impossible for us
to believe a mere coincidence! When the abode, long in preparation, was ready for man, the divine creative agency introduced man to his abode ; and thus was consummated a purpose
which worked ceaselessly through the geological transformations preceding man's appearance. In man the long series, ever
working to an end, finds a rational interpretation—a world fitted
for the abode of one capable of knowing it, using it, enjoying it,
and of seeing therein the glory of the wisdom, power, and goodness of its and his Creator.

Of man's creation the Confession states specifically :

(*a*) He was created in God's image. There has been much
dispute among theologians as to what is to be understood by the
" image of God " as predicated of man in his original endow-

ment. The Westminster Confession uses language that seems to define the meaning to be, "with reasonable and immortal souls, endued with knowledge, righteousness, and true holiness," adding, "after his (God's) own image."

The sacred record not only positively asserts, but reduplicates the astounding assertion: "So God created man in his own image; in the image of God created he him." Wonderful kinship of nature is man's! Made in the image of his Creator! Endowed to know and to enjoy; to plan and to be a worker together with God; to discern good and evil; to be a subject of the vast moral empire of Jehovah, and an heir to the eternal blessedness of virtue! "If we would see God's conception of man," says Joseph Parker, "we must look upon the face of his Son—him of whom he said, 'This is my beloved Son, in whom I am well pleased.' . . . . Let us steadfastly gaze on Christ, marking the perfectness of his lineaments, the harmony of his attributes, the sublimity of his purpose, and then pointing to him in his solitude of beauty and holiness, we may exclaim, 'Behold the image of God.'" To restore to man that image, Christ came; and if transformed by his power we shall in very truth "be like him," and "shall see him as he is."

(b) "Male and female created he them." From a pair was the race to come, the world to be peopled. Of one blood God hath made all men, to dwell upon the face of the earth. Related thus in his bodily nature, by the wonderful law of sex, with the creatures about him, man's soul is endowed with capacity to rise immeasurably above the brute, in thought to wing its way to God and immortality.

(c) Man was endued with intelligence, sensibility, and will.

Intelligence, sensibility, and will are terms used to designate the soul's power to put forth three generically different kinds of phenomena. The soul *thinks, feels, wills.* Intelligence designates the soul's power to think and to know; sensibility, its power to feel; will, its power of choosing, and putting forth volitions. It is *man*, thus endowed, "the one indivisible, intelligent, self-conscious, free agent that thinks, and feels, and chooses, and acts from choice."

Thus endowed, man is conscious of his mental states and activities, and conscious of their relation to himself as their source, and conscious of freedom in relation to the volitions he puts forth. Thus man is constituted a person, "a being," says Mark Hopkins, "who knows himself as the subject of phenomena, and so can say I." "This," adds the same writer, "no being below man can do. No animal can do it, nor the sun, nor the stars; and the power to do it places man above them all. . . . . Finding such a being, we find, not an act, but its source." Thus does man's natural endowment render him necessarily a subject of moral law—that is, a being capable of experiencing good, of discerning like capacity in others, and the means of its attainment for himself and others, and of choosing, and acting from choice, with reference to this chief end. The infinitely wise Creator, being also infinitely good, endowed man with capability of good, wills that man shall seek and realize the good of which he is capable, and commands him so to do; for he "willeth not the death of any." And so the moral law, as issuing from man's own nature, and as expressed in the revealed will of his Creator, is the law prescribing and commanding that course of action which issues in man's own highest good, and the highest good of all other sentient creatures affected by his actions.

(*d*) The law of God was written in man's heart. The passage cited by the Confession, in proof of this assertion, is Rom. ii. 14, 15: "For when the Gentiles, which have not the law, do by nature the things contained in the law, these, having not the law, are a law unto themselves: which show the work of the law written in their hearts, their conscience also bearing witness, and their thoughts the meanwhile accusing or else excusing one another."

Perhaps it has been justly observed "that there is scarcely in the whole New Testament any greater difficulty than the ascertaining the various meanings of νόμος (*law*) in the Epistles of St. Paul," and the passage cited is one on which expositors differ widely. Perhaps the passage is rightly interpreted to mean that "*the voice of conscience*, which proceeds from a moral feeling of dislike or approbation, and the judgment of the mind, when it examines the nature of actions, unite in testifying that what the moral law of God requires, is impressed, in some good measure, even on the hearts of the heathen." Of Adam it may be said (1) that his Creator endowed him to be a subject of moral law, and, (2) that out of the nature thus bestowed arose the law of his behavior. The law of God was thus written in his heart, in the very constitution of his mental being. In the absence of experience and of the knowledge that would come only by the study of his powers, it was all the more necessary that Adam should at once receive a revelation of the will of his Maker in the form of positive instruction and command.

(*e*) Endowed with power to fulfill the law. A law they could not have fulfilled, could not have been to them a moral law. Man is accountable for what he hath. Our first parents had power to choose, and to act from choice, among the several ends within their knowledge, and discriminated by them as right or wrong. They had power to do the right, to turn away from the wrong, to obey the commands of God. Nothing within them, nothing from without, acting upon them, necessitated the disobedience that brought their and our woe; for—

(*f*) They were made upright and free from all bias to evil.

This view of man's original endowment vindicates the ways of God as man's Creator and Lawgiver, and affords a rational explanation of the actual condition of the race. Sin is a fact. Freedom of will is an experienced fact. Neither by force of their constitution, nor by purpose of their God, secret or ex-

pressed, nor by their environment were our foreparents necessitated to disobey. Of choices possible to them, they made a
sinful choice ; and so sin entered the world, and death by sin.

4. That the final cause, or purpose, of the creation is "*the
manifestation of the eternal power, wisdom, and goodness*" *of the
Creator.*

If we regard the world as a product of creative wisdom and
goodness, we of necessity believe that the world was created
for an end, or purpose, good and wise. What we believe this
end to be is, as Dr. Hodge observes, a question of the highest
importance. "Since the chief end of every system of means
and agencies must govern and give character to the whole system, so our view of the chief end of God in his works must
give character to all our views as to his creative, providential,
and gracious dispensation. Our Confession (Westminster) very
explicitly takes the position that the chief end of God in his
eternal purposes, and in their temporal execution in creation
and providence is the manifestation of his own glory."

"The Scriptures explicitly assert," Dr. Hodge continues,
"that this is the chief end of God in creation," citing in proof
Col. i. 16 and Prov. xvi. 4, neither of which texts, however, is
conclusive proof of the doctrine in its Calvinistic sense. By
other theologians it is maintained that "God proposed for himself, as his ultimate end, the promotion of the happiness of his
creatures." The two conceptions of the divine purpose in the
creation, taken in their relation to theological systems, lead to
widely different views of the attributes of God and of the nature and design of the gospel provision of mercy. According to
the former view, God's decrees have, likewise, his own glory as
their end, and so his providence in the government of the
world, and so the provision of salvation. If to this scheme of
thought we add that God decrees whatsoever comes to pass, we
land at once in the most rigid fatalism, and are hopelessly be-
reft of all premises from which to predicate freedom of will,

man's responsibility, the distinction between virtue and wickedness, and the impartial goodness of God.

Surely if the mind of God is at all opened up to his creatures,
it is in the gracious provision for man's salvation, and it is explicitly declared that "God so loved the world that he gave his
only begotten Son that whosoever believeth in him should not
perish, but have everlasting life." Could language more positively or plainly assert that God's purpose in sending his Son is
the promotion of the happiness of his rational creature man?
So, we must believe, God's purpose in creation was to bring
about the happiness that would come through a universe of
creatures rational and sentient. Goodness delights in happiness, and seeks to multiply it. A good ruler will desire and
promote the happiness of his subjects, and the more he desires
it and promotes it, the more will he glorify his own wisdom and
goodness; but if he seeks the happiness of his subjects solely
or chiefly to manifest his own glory, then does he not love goodness and happiness, but is selfish and himself not good. In
places and phrases almost numberless the Bible asserts the
goodness of God, and that he delighteth not in the suffering or
unhappiness of his creatures. It is Cumberland Presbyterian
doctrine, that God loves all his rational creatures, made all to be
happy, and provides a way for the redemption of all who had
through sin forfeited happiness. This doctrine glorifies God as
he is seen through his infinite goodness. Calvinism glorifies his
infinite sovereignty.

According to the Calvinistic system, "whatsoever comes to
pass" is not only as God decreed it, but he decreed it to be as it
is, solely to promote his own glory; and that this divine purpose holds every thing in absolute bondage to an omnipotent decree reaching from the inception of creation to man's changeless
state in heaven or hell. Such a theological system is not characterized unjustly in the following words of Rev. John Miller, of
Princeton, New Jersey, in his commentary on Romans ix. 14, 15:

"The sovereignty of God, which even infidels are inclining to under the modern naturalism, has been frightfully marred by two additions, which men otherwise good have rashly made to it. One is, that God is sovereign over the actions of my mind, which he undoubtedly must be to be any God at all, and *shapes the choices of his sovereignty for the display of his perfections;* a gospel that is simply horrible. Hell must measure its depth of mischief. Atheists have attacked it with zeal, and then pretended they were attacking Christianity. We are indeed taught that God does every thing for display (Psalm viii. 1 ; xxix. 9), but always as a gracious instrument. We are taught that this display is vital for our Good (Psalm lxiii. 2). We are taught, therefore, that it is an intermediate end. But that God damns a creature for display, and that such is his final, and therefore only and in itself all-sufficient and absolutely positive and necessary end, must sink any conceivable system. And sadly enough, the same men who teach this wickedness, teach another —namely, that this self-adulating conduct of the universe is sovereign in the sense of naked, stark, and absolute pleasure of the governing will." To view the creation as prompted by the display-motive, and such display as having no basis but the mere-good-pleasure of the Creator, is to overlook the righteousness of God revealed in the creation and the gospel, and, as the author last quoted remarks, "really to throw away the beauty that converts, and to put in its place a horror which repels the perishing."

It is the writer's clear conviction that the great majority of theologians in the Cumberland Presbyterian Church heartily agree in rejecting the Calvinistic interpretation of the words in which our book expresses the final end of God in the creation. We concur in the sentiment of the Rev. John Miller, that "God's chief end, therefore, in creation and providence, is his own infinite holiness" (not the display of holiness), and that "holiness demands the highest results of benevolence, and the highest diffusion of holiness, all over the world that he shall have brought into being."

After all, the parties to this controversy as to what is the chief end, or final cause, in creation, providence and grace, may not differ so widely, when once all are fully understood. We can quite agree with Dr. Hodge that "the highest attainment of this supreme end"—the manifestation of God's own glory—"carries with it the largest possible measure of good to the creature."

We hold, however, that God creates, and governs, and saves, to promote happiness in the universe he creates; and thereby all the glory accrues to God: while the Calvinistic system teaches that God creates, and governs, and saves some and passes by others, to manifest his own glory; and that "the largest possible measure of good to the creature," as Dr. Hodge puts it, accrues only because that is the best way of displaying the glory, and not as an end in either creation or salvation.

But to show how an eternal unconditional decree to "pass by" some of the human race, reprobating them, and carrying them inevitably to destruction, can "carry with it" what Dr. Hodge calls "the largest possible measure of good to the creature" (to these creatures, at least), is an undertaking which no system of theology or metaphysics has yet achieved.

If, however, in accordance with what is called the law of the conditioning and the conditioned, we look upon the inanimate creation as existing for the display of the sentient life of which it is a grand theater; and the inanimate and the lower orders of animated nature alike as existing for man; and man as endowed with intelligence, sensibility, will, and a moral nature in view of happiness as the chief end of his creation, and the happiness which arises from the practice of virtue as the crowning and supreme good for which he was made, then are we prepared to see in the creation, and to the fullest extent, the manifestation of the power, wisdom, and goodness of God; and thus are we enabled to give a rational explanation of the last point in our analysis, namely:

5. *That the creation is all very good.*

That which is good is good for something, or because it serves some valuable end. The well-being of a sentient creature, or its happiness, is intrinsically good; and the happiness which accrues to a moral being from the practice of virtue is the crowning intrinsic good. Whatever promotes intrinsic good is a relative good. In view of the end for which man was made, the world in which he lives is very good. In man it finds its explanation. Alike in body and mind man himself displays the workmanship of a Creator infinitely wise, infinitely good. As ministering to his wants, the world in which he lives manifests the same wisdom and goodness. Without man as an end toward which all the lower stages of the creation worked, and for which they existed or now exist, the world can not be called " good " in any rational or moral sense. In view of their ministration to man's well-being the iron in the mountains, the marble in the quarry, the vast magazines of coal stored up thousands of ages ago are all very good. This earth its Maker has given to man. Man's physical organization brings him into relation to his material abode, enabling him to know, to use, to enjoy it. His spiritual nature allies him to God, and makes him the favored one of all earth's creatures, for whose weal " Heaven husbands all events." For man, air, water, light and heat, fruit on the boughs of the trees, fields of grain ripened by summer suns, and ten thousand other things are " good; " and it is because man is made in the image of God that he can be a worker-together-with-God, planting, sowing, improving nature's products, opening up its vast store-houses of mineral treasures, spanning continents with iron rails and traversing all seas with ships, in order to gratify his desires and promote his well-being. Marvelous indeed, it seems to us, is it that any one with intelligence can look upon this creation crowded with adaptations, and fail to see that it is full of mind, full of good, full of God.

If now we remember that man has sinned, and so has brought evil upon himself; that in consequence of this moral defection we "see through a glass darkly" in our efforts to understand the creation of God; that this present state is a state of probation and discipline, and that a great scheme of redemptive regeneration, running through the age, is to issue in a restoration typified by "new heavens and a new earth" with purified and glorified man subject to his glorified Redeemer and King, we behold, even in this humble province of God's vast empire, a creation truly good, over which morning stars may sing together and the sons of God shout for joy.

Creation, no less than redemption, proclaims the dignity and worth of man: "Thou madest him but a little lower than the angels. Thou hast crowned him with glory and honor. Thou hast made him to have dominion over the works of thy hands. Thou hast put all things in subjection under his feet." Only man was made in the image of God. "Nothing on earth is great," said a philosopher, "but man; and in man, nothing is great but the soul."

> "Knowest thou the worth of a soul immortal?
> Behold the midnight glory! worlds on worlds!
> Amazing pomp! Redouble this amaze;
> Ten thousand add; add twice ten thousand more;
> Then weigh the whole: ONE SOUL outweighs them all,
> And calls the astonishing magnificence
> Of unintelligent creation, poor."

CHAPTER VII.

PROVIDENCE.

"God the Creator upholds and governs all creatures and things by his most wise and holy providence.

"God, in his providence, ordinarily works through the instrumentality of laws or means, yet is free to work with and above them, at his pleasure.

"God never leaves nor forsakes his people; yet when they fall into sin he chastises them in various ways, and makes even their own sin the occasion of discovering unto them their weakness and their need of greater watchfulness and dependence upon him for supporting grace.

"God's providence over the wicked is not designed to lead them to destruction, but to a knowledge of his goodness and of his sovereign power over them, and thus to become a means of their repentance and reformation, or to be a warning to others; and if the wicked make it an occasion of hardening their hearts, it is because of their perversity, and not from necessity.

"While the providence of God, in general, embraces all creatures, it does, in a special manner, extend to his church."—*Confession of Faith.*

"What are God's works of providence?

"God's works of providence are his preserving and so governing his creatures, and overruling their actions, as to manifest his wisdom, power, and goodness in promoting their welfare."—*Catechism.*

PERHAPS no other idea so generally and thoroughly pervades man's thinking as that of a power above himself by which, in some manner, and to some extent, he is affected as to his surroundings, his conduct, and his destiny. This sentiment is common to the peasant and the philosopher. History and poetry and literature are full of it. Everywhere and in all time it has threaded the creeds, the instructions, the worship of the wisest and best. Our hymns and prayers and sermons are full of it, and our ordinary conversation and friendly greetings and farewells bear testimony to its remarkable hold upon the mind and heart of the masses. If, from his own finite and dependent nature, the contingent and transitory world in which he lives, and the persistent tendency of the progress of human affairs toward ends rational and moral, man's reason necessarily asserts a Supreme Intelligence as a cause of the universe, in like manner does man's reason assert that this harmonious progress of the universe depends on *guiding* and *governing* intelligence and power out of and above himself. And this is the substance of the doctrine of PROVIDENCE.

If now we propose an inquiry into the extent and the means of God's providential guidance and government of the world, we shall find an almost endless diversity of view. It is doubtful, indeed, whether any theologian of to-day can formulate a half a score of propositions defining the doctrine of providence, which any half score of theologians would unqualifiedly indorse. Nor should we wonder or be troubled on that account, for its very nature is such that the subject must transcend the limits of human knowledge and human reason. No doctrine is taught more certainly, however, in the sacred Scriptures, nor by a greater number of passages, than that of God's providential care and guidance of the world, and especially of his people, as witness the following texts:

"The eyes of all wait upon thee, and thou givest them their meat in due season." Ps. cxlv. 15.

"His kingdom ruleth over all." Ps. ciii. 19.

"But if God so clothe the grass of the field, which to-day is, and to-morrow is cast into the oven, shall he not much more clothe you, O ye of little faith?" Matt. vi. 30.

"These wait all upon thee, that thou mayest give them their meat in due season.

"That thou givest them they gather; thou openest thine hand, they are filled with good.

"Thou hidest thy face, they are troubled: thou takest away their breath, they die, and return to their dust.

"Thou sendest forth thy spirit, they are created; and thou renewest the face of the earth." Ps. civ. 27–30.

"Thy kingdom is an everlasting kingdom, and thy dominion endureth throughout all generations.

"The Lord upholdeth all that fall, and raiseth up all those that be bowed down.

"Thou openest thine hand and satisfiest the desire of every living thing." Ps. cxlv. 13–16.

"Are not two sparrows sold for a farthing? and not one of them shall fall on the ground without your Father.

"But the very hairs of your head are all numbered.

"Fear ye not, therefore; ye are of more value than many sparrows." Matt. x. 29–31.

An orthodox theological writer, citing numerous passages as authority for his views, thus summarizes what he regards the teaching of the Bible on the subject of providence: "(a) The preservation of the existence of all things depends on God alone. (b) God is the ruler and proprietor of the universe, his title in it being founded on his having created it. (c) The state and circumstance of all created things are determined by God; he needs nothing, but his creatures receive from him the supply of all their wants. (d) Nothing is so insignificant as to be unworthy of his notice; his providence extends even to the smallest object. (e) Through his watchful care all his creatures, in their several kinds, enjoy as much good as from their nature they are susceptible of. (f) But his providence is most conspicuous in reference to the human race, both as a whole and as composed of individual men. He preserves their lives, provides them with food, clothing, and every thing which they need. Their actions and their destinies are under his guidance and at his disposal; and their race is preserved from generation to generation through his care. The whole is comprised in the words of Paul, Acts xvii. 28, 'In him we live, and move, and have our being.'"

The foregoing scheme, while stating in a general way the main drift of the popular idea as to the relation of the divine providence to the world, is not wholly free from objectionable statements. The author of it, speaking of the practical uses of these representations, says that " they furnish us with the means of forming just notions of God, and with motives to induce us to reverence and serve him. . . . Indeed, the whole object and tendency of this doctrine, as exhibited in the sacred writings, is to excite and cherish pious dispositions in our minds. It leads us to think with every passing event that *God knows it;* to feel that it is exactly as he willed, and in it to see his agency." Now, that God knows every event, the Scriptures plainly teach; but that every event is " exactly as he willed " is what many do not believe, and what, in the judgment of many, the Scriptures nowhere teach. When the writer quoted goes on to say that if we were duly affected by the doctrine of providence "our constant maxim would be *nothing without God,*" he is guilty of sheer inconsistency, for the assertion implies that we do many things without God, whereas he had just asserted that every event is just as God willed it. Such contradictions defy all logical juxtaposition of moral ideas, and subject the whole doctrine of providence to doubt in the minds of those who think coherently, but have not for themselves studied thoroughly what the Scriptures teach.

In its relation to providence, as in its relation to grace, the Calvinistic unconditional decree of absolute divine predetermination of whatsoever comes to pass, must forever and hopelessly embarrass any and every rational idea of a moral government of the world. Materialistic fatality no more certainly annihilates the possibility of moral agency, responsibility, and the distinction of actions as virtuous or sinful, than does this vicious theological fatality which Augustine imported from heathen philosophy. If to the declaration that every event occurs just as God had willed it we add the comment of an accepted expositor of the Westminster Confession, that "God not only efficaciously concurs in producing the action, as to the matter of it, but likewise predetermines the creature to such or such an action, and not to another, shutting up all other ways of acting, and leaving that only open which he had determined to be done;" and that "God not only preserves and supports the faculties with which a man sins, but likewise previously, immediately, and efficaciously concurs to the substance, matter, or entity of the action;" and that "the sole reason why any thing comes to pass is because God has decreed it," we have a scheme of providence fatalistic to the extreme of divesting the infinite Jehovah of all moral attributes as a governor of a universe, and leaving him without any moral universe to govern. And since, according to this scheme of providence, no event could fall out otherwise than as it does, it is apparent that it can be of no possible concern to man whether the necessity which determines his thoughts, behavior, and destiny lie in an eternal, unconditional decree of God, or in a "material necessity of all things without a Deity," according to which latter view, as the materialistic philosophy now puts it, our thoughts and feelings were in the fire-mist millions of years ago, out of which they have been evolved by the operation of blind cosmic forces. We turn with disgust from the vices ascribed by Greek and Roman mythologies to their long list of

> " Gods, partial, changeful, and unjust,
> Whose attributes are rage, revenge and lust,"

but by this false scheme of providence we charge the Christian's God, the God we adore, with direct agency in all the vices and crimes of men.

The rejection of that scheme of providence which in its relation to man is fatalistic, is not the rejection of the doctrine of providence. The fact that God created the world justifies the assumption that he governs the world. There is abundant proof that both creation and providence look to ends rational and good, and from these ends, as seen in the works and providence of God, we infer his wisdom and goodness. We believe that the world exhibits a Creator who formed the creature man to be a rational and moral agent, who endowed him with the power of freedom of action in view of ends in themselves worthy, and thus to be a subject of moral law, and that the providence of God respecting man has made man's history, as it has unfolded through the sweep of centuries, an "increasing expression and illustration and demonstration of a moral purpose." Equally manifest is it that a unity of purpose, ever expanding and rising, holds through all the lower stages of creation up to man, and that one great moral purpose is now carrying humanity through a moral progress to a possible goal whose glories and grandeur are yet but dimly foreshadowed. On this ground most of all it is that the idea of a Creator and Ruler of the universe most powerfully appeals to man's reason and his sense of need. It is undeniable, also, that Christian belief in the existence of God, and in his providence over the world is the most potent of all causes operating to direct, sustain, and augment the grand progress along the line of ethical transformation into the spiritual and the heavenly. That faith gone, a thousand good influences sustained by it must likewise go, and man again relapses to the lower plane of the carnal, doomed to a fruitless search among the beggarly elements for that which is truly good and satisfying.

In this grand moral transformation, generated and sustained and directed and prophesied by Christian faith in the providence of God, the Christian religion manifests a most wonderful contrast to all other systems of religion or philosophy known to the world; and this contrast finds its highest expression and significance when we take into account the mighty transformation of humanity, past, present, and prospective, through the redemptive agency peculiar to Christianity. If one will impartially and sufficiently reflect upon that PROGRESS

15

through the centuries, which began with the call of Abraham, and has reached our day, with millions of subjects—that for ages in a remarkable manner kept a people separate from all other nations—that in the fullness of time utterly abrogated a great typical system burdened with rites and ceremonies, to usher in and establish one never to be shaken—that is to-day sustained by agencies and potencies vastly superior to what it ever knew in the past, he will assuredly conclude that such a progress can no more be accounted for without a moral cause above and back of it all than that, without a cause, the great Mississippi, dividing our continent by its majestic stretch, flows continually southward, ever widening until it pours its silver flood into the Gulf. As Christianity is a fact, divine providence must be a fact. "Here," says Dr. Hitchcock, "we find a key of the history of other ages and nations—a thread that will lead us out of every labyrinth of the present and the future. Toward Calvary, for thousands of years, all the lines of history converged. And now for other thousands of years, to the end of time, from Calvary will the lines diverge, till 'the kingdoms of this world have become the kingdoms of our Lord, and he shall reign for ever and ever.'"

Turning to a volume of the sermons of a minister of the Protestant Episcopal Church who, more than half a century ago, was of the class called powerful preachers, we read: "There is in all of us, perhaps, a tendency to the substituting second causes for the first, to the so dwelling on the laws of matter, and the operations of nature, as to forget, if not deny, the continued agency of God. If our creed were to be gathered from our common forms of speech it might be concluded that we regarded nature as some agent quite distinct from Deity, having its own sphere, and its own powers, in and with which to work. We are wont to draw a line between what we call natural and what supernatural; assigning the latter to an infinite power, but ascribing the former to ordinary causes, unconnected with the immediate interference of God. . . . We do not indeed suppose that God exerts any such agency as to supersede the laws or nullify the properties of matter; but we believe that he is continually acting by and through these laws and properties, as his instruments, and not that these laws and properties are themselves effecting the various occurrences in the material world. What is that nature of which we rashly speak but the Almighty perpetually at work? What are those laws of matter, to which we confidently appeal, and by which we explain certain phenomena, but so many manifestations of infinite power and intelligence?" And so, he proceeds, "I reckon that the hand of the Almighty perpetually guides our planet, and that it is through his energies, momentarily applied, the ponderous mass effects its rotations"—that "Deity is busy with every seed that is cast into the ground, and that it is through his immediate agency that every leaf opens, and every flower blooms, . . . that pulse succeeds to pulse and breath follows breath."

According to views expressed in the last cited paragraph, the forces of nature are but the divine energy manifesting itself in the physical world, and the laws of nature but the modes and limitations under which that divine energy therein manifests itself. In the sense in which any thing is providential, all things are, and there is no justification for the distinction of some events as being natural, and others supernatural; for all are supernatural, as products of a power transcending every thing inherent in matter.

From the view which regards the forces operating in nature, to bring about its varied phenomena, as the immediate operation of the will of God, whether propelling a planet or unfolding a flower, it is but a step to the doctrine, held by Melanchthon and others of his day, and not wanting in current theology, that providence, so far as it relates to the preservation of the world, is a *continual creation;* since, as it is alleged, if the divine support were for a moment withdrawn, the world would revert to nothing, or cease to exist. It is certainly not a long step from such a theory of providence to the "all-God," a kosmic philosophy of Spinoza, according to which there is no universe but God, no God but the universe; which asserts that "God alone is mover and worker of all things; all creatures do their work not actively, but passively. The creature acts not, but is acted on; as God works through each, so it works; the creature only holds still, and is passive to God. . . . For the bird really does not sing and fly, but is besung and borne up into the air; it is *God* that *lives*, *sings*, *moves*, and *flies* in the bird. He is the essence of all essences, so that all creatures are full of him, and do and are nothing but what God tells and wills." And this is the idea of divine *immanence* carried to its extremest limit, the identification of God and nature, the resolution of all phenomena into immediate and direct exertion of the divine energy.

"And nature, what is it," said Zwingle, "but God's unceasing and perpetual working and disposing of all things?" And so Melanchthon: "Human infirmity, although it thinks God to be a Creator, yet it imagines that afterward, as a builder goes away from the ship he has constructed, and commits it to the sailors, so God goes away from his work, and leaves his creatures to self-guidance. In opposition to these errors, our minds should be steadfast in the true idea of the creation, namely, that not only were things made by God, but also that the substances of things are by God perpetually kept and sustained. God is present to his creature, not as the God of the Stoics is present, but as acting most freely, sustaining the creature, and guiding it in his boundless compassion, bestowing gifts, furthering or restraining secondary causes." Like sentiments were held by many of the fathers of the Greek Church, notably by Origen, Athanasius, and Clement of Alexandria, who, as Mr. Fiske in his *Idea of God* asserts, "regarded Deity as immanent in the universe, and eternally operating through natural laws." "In their view," Mr. Fiske adds, "God is not a localizable personality, remote from the world, and acting upon it only by means of occasional portent and prodigy; nor is the world a lifeless machine blindly working after some preordained method, and only feeling the presence of God in so far as he now and then sees fit to interfere with its normal course of procedure. On the contrary, God is the ever present life of the world; it is through him that all things exist from moment to moment, and the natural sequence of events is a perpetual revelation of the divine wisdom and goodness." As shown by Professor Allen in his *Continuity of Christian Thought*, Athanasius pushed his views much beyond those of Clement and Origen, viewing the universe through the scriptural idea of a divine Trinity, the eternal Son as revealing the Father immanent in nature, while through the Holy Spirit is revealed the spiritual and ethical character of the manifested Deity, in contradistinction to the idea of the pantheistic confusion of God with his works, and as revealing himself in humanity, in the highest form, "only in so far as humanity recognized its calling, and through the Spirit entered into communion with the Father and the Son."

It is claimed, moreover, by those who interpret the doctrine of providence in accordance with such a theory of God's *immanence* in the universe as "binds the creation to God in the closest organic relationship," that the popular idea of "physical forces" as inherent in matter and controlling its phenomena is a substitution for "the direct action of the Deity," of that which does not exist and, in the nature of the case, can not exist. Thus, speaking of gravitation, which is imagined only, as he alleges, to be a kind of "pull," Professor Fiske says: "It explains that in the presence of each other two bodies are observed to change their positions in a certain specified way, and this is all that it means. This is all that a strictly scientific hypothesis can possibly allege, and this is all that observation can possibly prove. . . . An atheistic metaphysics may imagine such a 'pull,' and may interpret it as the action of something that is not Deity, but such a conclusion can find no support in the scientific theorem, which is simply a generalized description of phenomena. . . . And what is thus obvious in this simple, astronomical example is equally true in principle in every case whatever, in which one set of phenomena is interpreted by another set."

And still further, it is urged that in the doctrine of evolution as a mode of creation is to be found the strongest of all proofs of an immanent God as the working force in nature. After reference to the fact that Leibnitz rejected Newton's theory of gravitation on the ground that it seemed to him to substitute material forces for the power of Deity, Professor Fiske goes on to say: "The theological objection urged by Leibnitz against Newton was repeated word for word by Agassiz in his comments upon Darwin. He regarded it as a fatal objection to the Darwinian theory that it appeared to substitute the action of physical forces for the creative action of Deity. The fallacy here is precisely the same as in Leibnitz's argument. Mr. Darwin has convinced us that the existence of highly complicated organisms is the result of an infinitely diversified aggregate of circumstances so minute as severally to seem trivial or accidental; yet the consistent theist will always occupy an impregnable position in maintaining that *the entire series in each and every one of its incidents is an immediate manifestation of the creative act of God.*"

To some of our readers it will doubtless seem that we have dwelt too long in this attempt to explain theories quite remote from the ordinary conception of the doctrine of divine providence. These, however, are questions of profound interest to those willing to reflect upon this subject of greatest possible concern to man. It will be remembered that the sacred writers, as a rule, refer all physical phenomena immediately to the divine agency, according to whom God sends the rain, causes the sun to shine, clothes the fields with pastures; stars and constellations of stars perform their revolutions through his immediate agency, and he opens his hand to satisfy the needs of all living things. This absence of reference to "secondary causes" has been attributed to their ignorance of such causes—and they certainly were in a large measure ignorant of secondary causes as modern science conceives them—but now it turns out that many of the profoundest thinkers of to-day, including not a few scientists, tell us that between the phenomena about us, and the "direct action of Deity," they can find nothing that corresponds to the ordinary conception of an efficient secondary cause. If this theory be correct, the Bible receives amazing confirmation in the fact that while it gives to the world a system of ethical teaching incomparably superior to that derived from any other source, its writers, who make no claims to scientific knowledge, and have been supposed to have had little or none, yet spoke in complete accord with a theory now gaining wide acceptance as a rational explanation of the universe. The doctrine of the existence of God, of creation, of providence, receives profound significance and illustration in the most advanced scientific disclosures of to-day.

But quite a different theory of the nature of the universe and of the Creator's relation to the universe claims our attention, as furnishing a basis for a different interpretation of the doctrine of providence, and, on the part of some, to a total denial of the doctrine. This theory asserts that the Creator endowed his creation with such attributes that it is not only self-sustained, but that all its phenomena come about through the operation of the secondary causes now operative in the universe, and inherent in it as impressed by the Creator. It tells us, in fact, in its most mechanical aspect, that for the last million of years all things— miracles aside, if such things ever occurred—the course of nature would have been precisely what it has been, had the Creator been asleep. It will be seen that this is complete opposition to the theory that makes the continuance of the universe a continual creation, and all its phenomena dependent on the immediate agency of an immanent Creator. To such a structure of the universe the atheist indeed holds, but admits no cause outside of eternally existent matter and its inherent potencies. Deism admits the creation of the world, but denies a conserving and governing providence. Christian theists admit the uniform operation of natural causes, some affirming that only through these God exercises his providence over the world, while others believe that some events come about through a suspension of the operation of natural causes, and by the immediate interposition of divine agency.

Such, it is claimed, is the conception of the universe, as shown in a preceding chapter, which the genius of Augustine fastened upon the Western world, in opposition to the teachings of the Greek fathers—Clement, his pupil Origen, and Athanasius. "Obviously," says Prof. Fiske, "if Leibnitz and Agassiz had been educated in that higher theism phased by Clement and Athanasius in ancient times, if they had been accustomed to think of God as immanent in the universe and eternally creative, ... to conceive of 'physical forces' as powers of which the action could in anywise be 'substituted' for the action of Deity would in such case have been absolutely impossible. The higher, or Athanasian, theism knows nothing of secondary causes in a world where every event flows directly from the eternal First Cause. It knows nothing of physical forces save as immediate manifestations of the omnipresent creative power of God. In the personification of physical forces, and the implied contrast between their action and that of Deity, there is something very like the survival of the habits of thought which characterized ancient polytheism."

The reader, anxious to come at the truth, will thank us for the following additional citation from Prof. Fiske, as further illustrating the widely different conceptions of the universe, and the not less widely different views of divine providence to which they severally lead: "The subject is of such immense importance that I must illustrate it from yet another point of view. We must observe the manner in which, along with the progress of scientific discovery, theological arguments have come to be permeated by the strange assumption that the greater part of the universe is godless. Here again we must go back for a moment to the primeval world and observe how behind every physical phenomenon there were supposed to be quasi-human passion and quasi-human will. . . . . After many ages of culture, men ceased to regard the familiar and regularly recurring phenomena of nature as immediate results of volition, and reserved this primeval explanation for unusual or terrible phenomena, such as comets and eclipses, or famines and plagues. As the result of these habits of thought, in course of time, Nature seemed to be divided into two antithetical provinces. On the one hand, there were the phenonena that occurred with a simple regularity which seemed to exclude the idea of capricious volition; and these were supposed to constitute the realm of natural law. On the other hand, there were the complex and irregular phenomena in which the presence of law could not be so easily detected, and these were supposed to constitute the realm of immediate, divine action. This antithesis has forever haunted the minds of men imbued with the lower, or Augustinian, theism; and such have made up the larger part of the Christian world. It has tended to make the theologians hostile to science, and the men of science hostile to theology. For as scientific generalization has steadily extended the region of natural law, the region which theology has assigned to divine action has steadily diminished. . . . . Still, as of old, the ordinary theologian rests his case upon the assumption of disorder, caprice, and miraculous interference with the course of nature. A desperate fight it has been for some centuries, in which science has won every disputed position, while theology, untaught by perennial defeat, still valiantly defends the little corner that is left it. . . . . It is not science that is responsible for the mischievous distinction between divine action and natural law. That distinction is historically derived from a loose habit of philosophizing characteristic of ignorant ages, and was bequeathed to modern times by the theology of the Latin Church. Small blame to the atheist who, starting upon such a basis, thinks he can interpret the universe without the idea of God! He is but doing the best he knows how, with the materials given him. One has, however, but to adopt the higher theism of Clement and Athanasius, and this alleged antagonism between science and theology, by which so many hearts have been saddened, so many minds darkened, vanishes at once and forever. 'Once really adopt the conception of an ever-present God, without whom not a sparrow falls to the ground, and it becomes self-evident that the law of gravitation is but an expression of a particular mode of divine action. And what is thus true of one law is true of all laws.' The thinker in whose mind divine action is thus identified with orderly action . . . . foresees in every possible extension of knowledge a fresh confirmation of his faith in God; . . . . and each act of scientific explanation but reveals an opening through which shines the glory of the Eternal Majesty."

These are important ideas expressed in Prof. Fiske's clear and energetic style; but he seems to us to carry his theory much beyond the teaching of the Greek fathers he esteems orthodox, and to be more nearly at one with Goethe and Spinoza. Origen expressly declares that when we say "the providence of God regulates all things," we utter a great truth if we attribute to that providence nothing but what is just and right. But if we *ascribe to the providence of God all things whatsoever, however unjust they may be, then it is no longer true* that the providence of God regulates all things, unless we refer directly to God's providence things which flow as results from his arrangements. And this he said in refutation of Celsus, who had asserted that

"since every event falls out (as Prof. Fiske teaches) by the agency
of God, and demons and heroes were therefore but powerful
agents doing the commands of the Most High, it is right to worship those heroes and demons."

The discussion of the subject has brought us to a point where
it is not unsuitable to state formally three theories of the universe which render it utterly and hopelessly fatalistic:

1. The atheistic theory, which teaches that the sole substance
of the universe is matter, and that all phenomena, including our
sensations, thoughts, feelings, and volitions, as well as the fall
of a rain drop or the revolution of a planet, are but an endless
series of combinations and movements transpiring by the operation of blind, unconscious forces inherent in matter.

2. The theory which refers every event, including our
thoughts and volitions, as does Prof. Fiske, to the direct and
immediate agency of God as their efficient cause.

3. The theory which makes the universe indeed a product of
creative power, but so constituted and endowed that every event
falls out through the operation of forces divinely impressed
upon its several substances, while every event falls out also necessarily, and necessarily just as it is, because of an eternal,
divine decree determining whatsoever comes to pass.

Among the advocates of the third scheme is to be found Dr.
McCosh, a leading theologian and philosopher in current discussions of religious problems, who says:

"As entertaining this view of the perfection of the original
constitution of all things, we see no advantage in callingin special interpositions of God acting without physical causes—always
excepting the miracles employed to attest divine revelation.
Speaking of the ordinary providences of God, we believe that
the fitting of the various parts of the machinery is so nice that
there is no need of any interference with it. We believe in an
original disposition of all things; we believe that in this disposition there is provided an interposition of one thing in refer-

ence to another, so as to produce the individual effects which God contemplates; but we are not required by philosophy nor religion to acknowledge that there is subsequent interposition by God with the original dispositions and interpositions which he has substituted. 'This is, in fact, the great miracle of providence, that no miracles are needed to accomplish its purposes.'"

This passage Dr. McCosh follows with a quotation from Leibnitz, who says:

"God has provided every thing, he has remedied every thing beforehand. There is in his works a harmony, a beauty, already pre-established. This opinion does not at all exclude the providence or the government of God. A true providence on the part of God demands a perfect foreknowledge; but it demands not only that he has foreseen every thing, but also that he has provided for every thing—otherwise he is deficient either of the wisdom to foresee or the power to provide."

"We see no advantage," says Dr. McCosh, "to be gained to religion by insisting that the ordinary events in the common providence of God can have no second cause," following his statement with this passage from Bacon:

"For certain it is that God worketh nothing in nature but by second causes; and if they would have it otherwise believed, it is mere imposture, as it were, in favor toward God, and nothing else but to offer to the Author of truth the unclean sacrifice of a lie. But farther, it is an assured truth that a little or superficial knowledge of philosophy may incline the mind to atheism, but a farther proceeding therein doth bring the mind back to religion; for in the entrance of philosophy when the second causes which are next unto the senses do offer themselves to the mind of man, if it dwell and stay there, it may induce some oblivion of the highest cause; but when a man passeth on farther, and seeth the dependence of causes and the works of providence, then, according to the allegory of the poets, he will easily believe that the highest link of nature's chain must needs be tied to the foot of Jupiter's chair."

But, so far as relates to the quoted paragraphs, neither Bacon nor Leibnitz nor McCosh gives us any information as to how God guides and governs the world through the uniform operation of invariable secondary causes, in any sense corresponding to the popular Christian doctrine of providence. The "original disposition of all things," of which Dr. McCosh speaks, to be realized in the unfolding of earth's history solely by the operation of natural causes—the miracles in attestation of divine inspiration excepted—is the same predetermination of all things asserted in the theological dogma, that "God from all eternity did by the most wise and holy counsel of his own will, freely and unchangeably ordain whatsoever comes to pass," by which "decree of God, for the manifestation of his glory, some men and angels are predestined unto everlasting life, and others foreordained to everlasting death." Every thing, thus, is indeed "providential," or predetermined, by the absolute decree—the exact number of human beings to exist upon the earth and the destiny of every one; the number of sermons to be preached, prayers to be said, songs to be sung, and curses to be uttered; the number of thefts, suicides, and murders; the exact number of drops of water to be in each particular ocean, of leaves to be on each individual tree, of times that each individual human being is to draw his breath—all was predetermined eternally and unchangeably, in view of which the Creator so constituted the universe, that through the action and interaction of natural forces, or secondary causes, it would work out the stupendous scheme of necessity. Did Leibnitz or any other of the necessitarians or fatalists of his day ever dream of a world from top to bottom more fatalistic than that embraced in this scheme of providence?

The scheme of Dr. McCosh teaches that God did not by direct agency raise the storm which wrecked the Spanish Armada when it threatened the liberty and the religion of England, nor calm the wind to the favoring breezes which enabled William of Orange to escape the hostile fleet about to seize him, but rather that God had so prearranged the operation of natural causes as to bring about the beneficent and pre-determined results. But God's providence has respect, he tells us, to the most minute event, as well as to the greatest. These references sufficiently define his views, to which we have taken exception because, as it seems to us, they bind human volitions and actions by divine necessity, or decree of providence, and hence, leave no basis for any rational scheme of moral government—the very end for which all lower providential arrangements exist, and from which they derive their chief glory. Perhaps no living writer has rendered the cause of evangelical truth more valuable service than has the venerable author whom we have quoted, but his views on this subject are, to say the least, far from satisfying. While every event comes about through the operation of proximate natural causes, as Dr. McCosh tells us, he finds a sphere for providential control in those events it is not in man's power to foresee, or what he calls the "complications and fortuities of nature." But it is only because of man's inability to calculate these fortuities that they stand in a relation to him at all different from that sustained by events dependent on conditions he can readily understand. "As we come closer to man," says Dr. McCosh, "the elements of uncertainty increase. How uncertain are all the events on which man's bodily and external welfare depends! . . . . A change takes place in the atmosphere which the individual breathes, and quickens into life a malady which wastes the lungs and frame till it ends in dissolution. A particular vital vessel bursts, and instant death follows. A derangement takes place in the nerves or the brain, and henceforth the mind itself reels and staggers. It appears that the uncertainty increases the nearer we come to man, and there is nothing so uncertain as bodily health and human destiny." Thus, according to this theory, the world is more largely providential with respect to human life and destiny, than in any other respect. Providence is thus made dependent on uncertainty, and uncertainty is wholly relative to man's limited knowledge, for events seemingly the most fortuitous are but the necessary results of natural causes, and, not only so, but were eternally decreed to fall out as they do, when they do, where they do. This theory seems to us quite a last shift to save the doctrine of a divine providence. Besides, man's welfare is dependent, to a very large extent, upon conditions it is in his power to control; and man's bodily health and destiny, instead of being the most uncertain of all things, are, with all the sanitary science now possible, and man's own willful vices and follies aside, among the things most nearly certain.

To the thoughtful reader we shall need to offer no apology for further illustrating the view last presented, and enriching these pages, by the following lengthy passage from *The Natural History of Enthusiasm*, by Rev. Isaac Taylor, a writer of rare excellence of spirit and of unusual metaphysical acumen. Having referred to the "substantial if not immovable *substratum* of causes and effects, upon which, for the important and practical purposes of life, calculations of futurity may be formed," Taylor says:

"The second, and the less numerous, class of events that make up the course of human life are those which no sagacity could have anticipated; for though in themselves they were only the natural consequences of common causes, yet those causes were either concealed or remote, and were, therefore, to us and our agency the same as if they had been absolutely fortuitous. By far the larger proportion of these accidents arises from the intricate connections of the social system. The thread of every life is entangled with other threads beyond all reach of calculation, the weal and woe of each depends, by innumerable correspondences, upon the will, and caprices, and fortune, not merely of the individuals of his immediate circle, but those of myriads of whom he knows nothing. Or, strictly speaking, the tie of mutual influence passes without a break, from hand to hand, through the human family. There is no independence, no insulation in the lot of man; and therefore there can be no absolute calculation of fortunes; for he whose caprice or will is to govern that lot, stands, perhaps, at the distance of a thousand removes from the subject of it, and the attenuated influence winds its way in a thousand meanders before it reaches the point of its destined operation.

" It is by the admirable combination of the two principles of order and disorder, of uniformity and variety, of certainty and of chance, that the faculties and desires are wrought up to their full play of energy and vivacity, of reason and feeling. But it is especially in connection with the doctrine of providence that we have at present to consider these two elements of human life; and as to the first of them, it is evident that the settled order of causes and effects, so far as it may be ascertained by observation and experience, claims the respect and obedience of every intelligent agent; since it is nothing less than the will of the Author of nature, legibly written upon the constitution of the world. This will is sanctioned by immediate rewards and punishments; health, wealth, prosperity, are the usual consequents of obedience; while sickness, poverty, degradation, are the almost certain inflictions that attend a negligent interpretation, or a presumptuous disregard of it. The dictates of prudence are in truth the commands of God; and his benevolence is vindicated by the fact that the miseries of life are, to a very great extent, attributable to a contempt of those commands.

" But there is a higher government of men, as moral and religious beings, which is carried on chiefly by the fortuities of life. Those unforeseen accidents, which so often control the lot of men, constitute a *superstratum* in the system of human affairs, wherein, peculiarly, the divine providence holds empire

for the accomplishment of its special purposes. It is from this
hidden and inexhaustible mine of chances—chances, as we must
call them—that the Governor of the world draws, with unfath-
omable skill, the materials of his dispensation toward each individual of mankind. The world of nature affords no instances
of complicated and exact contrivance comparable to that which
so arranges the vast chaos of contingencies as to produce, with
unerring precision, a special order of events adapted to the
character of every individual of the human family. Amid the
whirl of myriads of fortuities, the means are selected and combined for constructing as many independent machineries of
moral discipline as there are moral agents in the world; and
each apparatus is at once complete in itself and complete as part
of a universal movement.

"If the special intentions of Providence toward individuals
were effected by the aid of supernatural interpositions, the
power and presence of the Supreme Disposer might indeed be
more strikingly displayed than it is; but his skill much less.
And herein especially is manifested the perfection of the divine
wisdom, that the most surprising conjunctions of events are
brought about by the simplest means, and in a manner so perfectly in harmony with the ordinary course of human affairs that
the hand of the Mover is ever hidden beneath second causes,
and is descried only by the eye of pious affection. This is, in
fact, the great miracle of Providence—that no miracles are
needed to accomplish its purposes. Countless series of events
are traveling on from remote quarters toward the same point;
and each series moves in the beaten track of natural occurrences; but their intersection at the very moment in which they
meet shall serve, perhaps, to give a new direction to the affairs
of an empire. The materials of the machinery of Providence
are all of common quality; but their combination displays nothing less than infinite skill."

The entertaining writer of the quoted paragraph tells us that
16

every Christian should entertain "a strong and consoling belief of the doctrine of a Particular Providence, which cares for the welfare of each;" and that "in the divine management of the fortuities of life there may also be very plainly perceived a dispensation of moral exercise specifically adapted to the temper and powers of the individual. . . . Whoever is quite unconscious of this sort of *overruling* of his affairs by means of apparent accidents must be very little addicted to habits of intelligent reflection. . . . By such strong and nicely fitted movements of the machine of Providence is it that the tasks of life are distributed where best they may be performed, and its burdens apportioned where best they may be sustained."

Even Taylor's clear and beautiful presentation of this theory which identifies God's providence and the course of events produced solely by natural agencies working always and everywhere invariably in the same order—and no one could present it in a clearer or more interesting light than did Isaac Taylor—is far from satisfying the demands of reason and Christian faith. True, it links this chain of necessarily related causes and effects evolved by the operation of unconscious forces, somewhere in the infinite past, to a creative decree of Infinite Wisdom, thus marrying *naturalism* and *theism.* As every thing comes about in "the settled order of causes and effects," why should those events which come about by the concurrence and interaction of forces so numerous and remote as utterly to baffle human foresight, and to be rightly considered a "vast chaos of contingencies," be yet, for the purposes of well-being and moral discipline, and "with unerring precision," a "*special order of events adapted to the character of every individual of the human family?*" The difficulty is greatly increased if we allow the play of that freedom of the human will which is the sole basis of any rational theory of a moral government of mankind; for many men are not what they should be, not doing what they should be doing, and are where and what they should not be.

How, then, can an invariable order of natural sequence bring at every moment to every man, "with unerring precision," that particular combination of events exactly suited to his moral need? Moreover, it is a matter of fact that men of widely differing moral needs are subject to the same or like combinations of events, and that men of apparently like moral needs are environed by widely differing combinations of events. So this naturalistic theory of a divine providence seems untenable, as being utterly inconsistent with all conceivable theories of free agency, and not harmonizing well even with the doctrine of necessity, unless, indeed, we affirm that a combination of events adapted to cultivate the spiritual in one man is in another adapted to develop the carnal, and that God decreed it thus. It teaches that every man's character, occupation, and environment are what Providence appointed, since, as Mr. Taylor puts it, an " exact contrivance" of Providence " so arranges the vast chaos of contingencies as to produce, with unerring precision, a special order of events adapted to every individual of the human family." As an explanation of the moral condition of society, upon any principles compatible with the idea of merit and demerit, it is a bald and hopeless failure, for it makes Providence stand in the same relation to the minister proclaiming to men free salvation for all who will receive it and to the wretch dealing out damning drink, as the " machine of Providence," by its "strong and nicely fitting movements," brings to every man the divinely allotted work he was divinely fitted to perform.

In his " *Nature and the Supernatural, as Together Constituting the One System of God,*" Horace Bushnell thus enters his protest to the *naturalistic* theory of the method of Providence: "God is (according to this theory) only a great mechanic, who has made a great machine for the sake of the machine, having his work all done long ages ago. Moral government is out of the question—there is no government but the predestined rolling of the machine. If a man sins, the sin is only the play of cause and effect—that is, of the machine. If he repents, the same is true—sin, repentance, hope, love, joy are all developments of cause and effect—that is, of the machine. If a soul gives itself to God, in love, the love is but a grind-out of some wheel he has set turning, or ĥ may be turns, in the scheme of nature. If I look up to him, and call him Father, he can only pity the conceit of my filial feeling, knowing that it is attributable to nothing but the run of mere necessary cause and effect. If I look up to him for help, he can only hand me over to cause and effect, of which I am a link myself, and bid me stay in my place to be what I am made to be. . . . If there is nothing but God and nature, and God himself has no relations to nature, save just to fill it and keep it on its way, then, being ourselves a part of nature, we are only a link, each one, in a chain let down into a well, where nothing else can ever touch us but the link next above! O it is horrible. Our soul freezes at the thought. We want, we must have something better."

To satisfy the demands of reason and our moral and spiritual cravings, a theory of the providence of God must harmonize with—

1. The sovereignty, holiness, and goodness of God.

2. The freedom of man's will as freedom is asserted in his consciousness, and demanded by reason as the condition of moral government.

3. The observed facts in man's life and in the world about him.

Turning now to the doctrinal standard of our Church, we find that it declares:

1. That God, in his providence, ordinarily works through the instrumentality of laws or means; yet is free to work with and *above* them.

2. God's providence over the wicked is not designed to lead them to destruction, but to a knowledge of his goodness, and his sovereign power over them, and thus to become a *means of*

their repentance and reformation, or to be a warning to others; and if the wicked make it an occasion of hardening their hearts, *it is because of their perversity*, and *not from necessity*.

3. God's providence, though embracing all creatures in a general way, extends in a special manner to his Church.

On the important doctrine of the providence of God, therefore, as in relation to other fundamental doctrines of Christianity, Cumberland Presbyterian theology is a protest against the Calvinistic idea of necessity which attributes every event to the decree and the efficient agency of God. While our early theological writers have left us but little upon this subject, the *Lectures* of Rev. Reuben Burrow, D.D., who was for some time a professor of theology in a college of the denomination, contains a lecture that is clear and vigorous in thought, and valuable as an exposition of our view of "Divine Providence," from which we extract the following characteristic passages:

"It may be assumed and fairly maintained that, as there is no eternal evil in the universe, and Providence could not produce it in harmony with his will and attributes, it could only come into existence by disobedience and a violation of the supreme will and law by creatures. Moral evil is a transgression of the moral law; it is an act against the whole Godhead—decrees, laws, will, and nature, all. Such a thing as moral evil can not possibly be willed by the Holy One."

"Was it possible for any that were doomed to sin and death to escape, or for such as were ordained to life to be lost? There can be no change. But who did all this? We are told that the most wise and holy Providence did it all. He ordered and governed all the sins of all men and angels, and then punished some of them in hell for their sins. Then we are told that he who did all this is neither the author or approver of at least a part of his providential doings. As to the authorship, there need be no dispute when we are told that Providence did it all. This is the point, any way, against which I enter my protest."

"There is no necessity for running into such extremes by ascribing every thing which transpires in the universe to Providence. The position is wrong and contradicts itself, and never can result in any good whatever. . . . Permissive decrees and permissive providences must be associated together, and, if they mean any thing different from what is meant by absolute decrees and providences, must signify free agency and accountability, and, as a matter of course, freedom from the reign and rule of absolute decrees and providences, . . . that freedom of volition which the Creator granted to his accountable creatures."

" But it is said that Providence has not bestowed his gifts alike upon all this world; that he has bestowed more of his munificence upon some than upon others, and cast their lots in this world under circumstances widely different. . . . Much of the difference, however, which our eyes behold in earthly things is owing to the providence or improvidence of earth's children, and not attributable to our heavenly Father. *We do much ourselves to make our lots easy or hard in life, by our improvement or misimprovement of the gifts of Providence.*"

The late Rev. Richard Beard, D.D., eminent as a scholar, as an instructor in theology, and as endowed with all the loveliness of eminent piety, in his First Series of *Lectures on Theology*, discusses Divine Providence, in a clear and forcible exposition, a few extracts from which will sufficiently indicate his views:

"The subject is vaguely understood. We associate in our minds the idea of a particular providence with the idea of necessity, and become confused. We can not distinguish God's overruling whatever is done, and his doing, or causing to be done, whatever is done. Yet the two are as different as any two facts can be."

Again: "God foresees, overrules, and controls all events. He is not, however, the intentional author of all events. . . . If God were the only mind in the universe, it would be true that every action and every event must proceed from him, since mind is necessary to action. But there are subordinate minds endowed with the power of action. These minds become sources of action."

The inquiry, *In what way does God exercise his providence?* Dr. Beard thus answers:

" 1. In providing for the wants of men, especially of good men." Matt. v. 45.

" 2. In leaving sometimes his own children in darkness and doubt for purposes of discipline." Job is an example.

" 3. In afflicting good men for the purpose of promoting their sanctification. I allude more particularly to bodily afflictions, and to trouble in our circumstances." Ps. cxix. 67, 71, 75.

" 4. In afflicting good men, that they may serve as examples of faith and patience to others." Job is instanced.

" 5. In afflicting wicked men for the purpose of bringing them to repentance." Manasseh, king of Judah, an instance.

" 6. God exercises his providences in overruling the outbreaks of the selfish and lawless passions of men for the promotion of his own glory." Pharaoh and the king of Assyria.

" 7. In withholding his Spirit and grace from some wicked men, whereby they are judicially given over to hardness of heart and blindess of mind, in consequence of their former wickedness and rebellion." 2 Thess. ii. 11, 12.

The extracts here given from two authors who were leading theological teachers of the body may be regarded as a correct expression of the current views of Cumberland Presbyterians touching the doctrine of God's providence, and as substantially interpreting the doctrinal symbol of the Church. It is to be noted that, in addition to the points previously specified, this scheme of God's providence over mankind fully recognizes and emphasizes that rational freedom which is a part of man's original endowment, and indispensable to the idea of his moral responsibility. Thus our medium and safe theology conserves, in the doctrine of providence, as in the other great fundamental principles of Christianity, such consistency of parts as clearly harmonizes the moral government of the world and the moral endowments of the subjects of that government, and thereby justifies the ways of the moral Governor in his dealings with the children of men.

"Religious sentiment has always insisted," says Lotze, "at the outset very obscurely, though vigorously, that something new must happen in the world—something that is not a mere consequence of what has gone before—and there must exist in individual spirits just this capacity to initiate a new series of events; and therefore, in brief, a freedom of acting or primarily of willing;" . . . and that "in this way has the problem originated which leads to the conception of a government." . . . Moreover, this freedom of action—this wonderful power in man to be himself a cause, the author of moral sequences which else would not have been, is demanded "because we regard it," says Lotze, "as the *conditio sine qua non* of the fulfillment of ethical commands."

"It seems therefore," says Lotze in concluding his attempt at a *philosophy* of the Divine Government of the world, "that it is not at all nature directly, but primarily the inner life of the world of spirits only, that forms the object to which immediate interventions in the government of the world could have relation; and this in such manner that the interventions would not make use of the individual spirits merely as passive points of transition, but would supply their own activity with inducements and incentives, which the external course of nature can not offer them." By this means there would be introduced "into the world new beginnings of spiritual movements that are in conformity with the plan of the world;" and the new events we are to regard, according to Lotze, "as products of the reciprocal action of God with individual spirits, by means of which there is brought to pass in them an ideal appearance, of a truly valid content." As a final summary of the results of his effort at a philosophical view of the world, Lotze formulates in three propositions what he regards as "the characteristic convictions of every religious apprehension, in contradistinction to a merely intellectual view of the world:"

" (1) Ethical laws we designate as the will of God.

" (2) Individual finite spirits we designate, not as products of nature, but as children of God.

" (3) Actuality we designate, not as a mere course of the world, but as a kingdom of God."

Lotze's scheme of the world as a totality makes all other parts subordinate to man's well-being, and man's glory and highest bliss to consist in those ethical and religious relations which bring him into favor and fellowship with God. The supreme end of the creation and of the government of the world is the kingdom of God, for the establishment, progress, and final triumph of which kingdom God's providence, by the direct action of his supreme will on finite minds, is so shaping the issues of time as to culminate in the fulfillment of his purpose and prophecy concerning the incoming glorious dispensation which is to be everlasting.

CHAPTER VIII.

THE FALL OF MAN—EFFECTS ON THE ORIGINAL TRANS-GRESSORS—EFFECTS ON THE RACE—THE COVE-NANT OF GRACE, ETC.

FALL OF MAN.

" 17. Our first parents, being seduced by the subtlety and temptation of Satan, sinned in eating the forbidden fruit ; whereupon God was pleased, for his own glory and the good of mankind, to reveal the Covenant of Grace in Christ, by which a gracious probation was established for all men.

" 18. By this sin they fell from their original uprightness, lost their communion with God, and so became dead in sin, and defiled in all the faculties of their moral being. They being the root of all mankind, sin entered into the world through their act, and death by sin, and so death passed upon all men.

" 19. From this original corruption also proceeds actual transgression.

" 20. The remains of this corrupt nature are felt by those who are regenerated, nor will they altogether cease to operate and disturb during the present life.

" 21. Sin, being a transgression of the law of God, brings guilt upon the transgressor, and subjects him to the wrath of God and to endless torment, unless pardoned through the mediation of Christ."

GOD'S COVENANT WITH MAN.

" 22. The first covenant made with man was a Covenant of Works, wherein life was promised to Adam upon condition of perfect and personal obedience.

" 23. Man by his fall having made himself incapable of life by that covenant, the Lord was pleased to make the second, commonly called the Covenant of Grace, wherein he freely offers unto sinners life and salvation by Jesus Christ, requiring of them faith in him, that they may be saved. This covenant is frequently set forth in the Scriptures by the name of a testament, in reference to the death of Jesus Christ, the testator, and to the everlasting inheritance, with all things belonging to it, therein bequeathed.

" 24. Under the Old Testament dispensation the Covenant of Grace was administered by promises, prophecies, sacrifices, circumcision, the paschal

lamb, and other types and ordinances delivered to the Jews—all foresigni-
fying Christ to come—which were sufficient, through the operation of the
Holy Spirit, to instruct them savingly in the knowledge of God, and build
them up in the faith of the Messiah.

"25. Under the New Testament dispensation, wherein Christ, the substance, is set forth, the ordinances in which the Covenant of Grace is dis-
pensed are the preaching of the word and the administration of the sacraments of Baptism and the Lord's Supper, which are administered with
more simplicity, yet in them it is held forth in more fullness and spiritual
efficacy to all nations, Jews and Gentiles.

"26. As children were included with their parents in the Covenant of
Grace under the Old Testament dispensation, so are they included in it
under the new, and should, as under the old, receive the appropriate sign
and seal thereof."

IN these sections of the Confession, and in the few that immediately follow them, are contained doctrines of transcendent
importance on account of their practical relation to man's duty
and accountability, his moral career upon the earth, and his everlasting destiny: man as endowed with the intelligence and freedom which make him a subject of moral law; man as involved
in sin and condemnation because of the violation of that law;
man as the subject of a merciful scheme of redemption through
divine mediation and expiation; man as the author of his own
destiny by his power to accept or to reject the offered salvation
—these and allied subjects are as important and interesting as
any that can challenge attention or absorb reason's profoundest
meditation. On these great and cardinal themes is Cumberland
Presbyterian theology in harmony with the facts of man's nature and condition, the dictates of enlightened judgment, and the
plain teaching of the word of God? If discordant to any of
these tests, so far must that system be rejected; if accordant
with all, then must it stand approved by the highest tribunals
by which moral and religious systems can be judged.

Next to the Bible itself a plain, logical doctrinal formula
which embodies substantially the teachings of the Bible on these
great themes must be esteemed of inestimable value. When we
consider how numerous, varied, and even antagonistic have been

the interpretations given to the Bible in some of its most important parts, and how absurd, hurtful, and demoralizing have been
many practices growing out of these false interpretations, we
should be ready to see in this brief, rational statement of belief
touching the great facts of man's moral freedom, sin, and
supernatural grace and redemption, a "confession" for which
Cumberland Presbyterians may with justice earnestly contend
as embodying "the faith (concerning the common salvation) formerly delivered to the saints."

Departing from the order of the topics in the sections of the
Confession, as far as seems necessary in order to a logical
arrangement of the doctrinal points, we notice:

1. *Man was created in a state of holiness.*

As it is expressed in the section (11) on "creation:" "God
created man in his own image, . . . they having the law of God
written in their hearts, and power to fulfill it, being upright and
free from all bias to evil." In section 18 it is declared that the
foreparents fell from "their original uprightness," and so "lost
their communion with God." The passage cited in section 11,
to prove that man's original state was one of uprightness, is
Eccl. vii. 29, "Lo, this only have I found, that God hath made
man upright; but they have sought out many inventions." The
same passage is cited under section 18, to prove man's fall from
the original uprightness. It is doubtful, however, whether this
passage, so often quoted in the connections named, has primary
reference to either an original state of holiness or a lapse from
such a state.

The declaration that man was made "in the image of God"
seems to furnish unquestionable ground for the belief that
uprightness, or holiness, is the moral condition in which the first
parents of the race came from the Creator's hand, to begin their
moral career upon the earth. In what does that "image of
God" consist? "So God created man in his own image; in the
image of God created he him." Certainly this image would

embrace the communicable moral attributes of God, a distinction which would separate man from the brute creatures by what a philosopher calls "the greatest difference in the universe." There is great value in the suggestion of Dr. Joseph Parker, who exhorts us "not to mock one another, and tauntingly ask if we are made in the image and likeness of God, but to steadfastly gaze on Christ, marking the perfectness of his lineaments, the harmony of his attributes, the sublimity of his purpose, and then, pointing to him in his solitude of beauty and holiness, we may exclaim, ' Behold the image of God.'"

As to the metaphysical distinction that holiness is not an endowment, and that, therefore, before Adam had put forth moral action he was destitute of moral character, it is enough to answer, with Dr. Richard Beard, that before man acted, after God had breathed into his nostrils the breath of life, man was "so endowed that all the tendencies of his nature were then toward knowledge, righteousness, and holiness."

Rev. Joseph Miller, B.D., in his admirable treatise on Hamartiology, puts all the features into "one picture" as follows: "(1) Intimate and unbroken communion of the created spirit with God; (2) love to him with the faith and obedience which spring from love; (3) holy conformity with the divine will, which raises man above the world and confers supremacy above all other creatures; (4) the 'real' freedom, distinguished from 'formal,' though growing from it, which comes from divine sonship and holy love; (5) a clear and salutary knowledge of God himself; (6) a goodness, purity, and truth, as yet unmixed with evil."

Lordship over all creatures, righteousness, and true holiness, with immortality, constitute, according to another symbol, the elements of that "divine image" expressive of man's original state. Had man continued in this state of original uprightness, freely and constantly choosing the will of God as the rule of his behavior, he would have been completely happy, and, by some provision of divine Wisdom, would have become heir of immortality without the pain and humiliation of death and corruption, but

2. *Man fell from original uprightness.*

Satan's subtlety tempted to disobedience of God's command, and our first parents, freely choosing evil, sinned; sinning, they fell. Such is the brief account of that moral lapse which, occurring at the fountain head of humanity, subjected the race to death and all the moral woes attendant on sin.

Why did not God, some one will ask, seeing that he is infinitely wise to foresee what would come to pass, and infinitely good to choose the happiness of his creatures, make man incapable of sinning? It was morally impossible for God to make man a subject of moral law, and yet *not* a subject of moral law. Without power to disobey, there could not be freedom; without freedom, there could not be virtue; without virtue, there could not be the happiness which the infinite Benevolence chooses as the end of his vast moral empire.

"There is, doubtless, a higher necessity," says the Rev. Joseph Miller, "to love God and conform in all things to his holy will, wherein consists the real liberty of humanity, but such love and conformity is really valueless if it be not the voluntary and deliberate outcome of the will, or if it be impossible for the creature to do otherwise. But sin, though possible in the very conception of created personality, is not necessary, since it was in the power of the first man to resist and overcome all seductions to evil, just as Christ did, just as the regenerate are expected to do increasingly as the principle of grace and spiritual life grows stronger in them."

"Our first parents, being left to the freedom of their own will, fell from the estate wherein they were created by sinning against God," says our Catechism; and it adds that the specific "sin whereby our first parents fell from the estate wherein they were created was their disobeying God's command in eating the forbidden fruit."

in their view of the nature of man and the introduction of sin into the world, Cumberland Presbyterians emphasize the doctrine of man's freedom, which freedom they hold to be inseparable from the idea of sin, and the ground of the just vindication of the providence of God respecting the fall. Without freedom virtue is an illusion, and what we have been accustomed to think of as God's vast empire of rational and virtuous creatures, the crowning glory of his creation, is but a dream of the imagination. Any scheme of *necessity* as an interpretation of the fall must dishonor both man and God, making man incapable of virtue, making God to choose evil for its own sake. Nor was Adam free to disobey the divine command, with power of contrary choice, in any other sense than that in which the man who now lies or steals knows himself to be free in putting forth the volition so to do, and as having power to abstain from so willing and doing. Not in mockery, but in sincerity and with deepest solicitude for human weal, God said to the first parents, and evermore is saying to humanity, " Behold, I set before you good and evil, blessing and cursing, life and death; now, therefore, *choose life*, that ye may live."

3. *The state into which their sin brought the first parents.*

The Confession says (section 18) " they fell from their original uprightness, lost their communion with God, and so became dead in sin and defiled in all the faculties of their moral being; " and the Catechism says that "Adam's sin corrupted his moral nature and alienated him from God." Now, it may be noted in passing that all the things here affirmed to be effects coming directly upon the transgressors themselves are not only effects that could come, but results that must come under the conditions supposed. The Bible account and the Confession accord with the facts of human nature and the requirements of enlightened reason.

The Council of Trent declared: " If any one shall not confess that the first man, Adam, when the command of God had been transgressed in paradise, lost holiness and justice, and by that offense incurred the wrath of God, and that the whole man in soul and body had been thereby thoroughly deteriorated, let him be accursed."

"Sin, being a transgression of the law of God, brings guilt upon the transgressor, and subjects him to the wrath of God and to endless torment, unless pardoned through the mediation of Christ."—*Confession, section* 21.

The change which came to Adam as a subject of moral law, in consequence of his fall, embraces these points:

1. The loss of the original uprightness, or righteousness, of character. Righteousness is the state of a free moral agent so long as he chooses in accordance with the will of God, or in accordance with what is essentially right.

2. He incurred guilt, falling under the condemnation of the holy law ordained for his government, in consequence of choosing to disobey a positive and clearly revealed divine command.

3. He became obnoxious to the penalty of the violated law. Before the transgression obedience entitled him to the rewards stipulated in the covenant of works; after the transgression he was justly liable to all the penalties set over against disobedience.

4. Corruption of his moral faculties. Retaining all his faculties, the transgressor experiences a depraved operation of these. Intelligence is blinded, sensibility blunted, will perverted. In the language of the Confession, man became "dead in sin."

5. Loss of communion with God. "His thoughts no longer revolved around God as their common center. His thoughts no longer entwined around Jehovah, as the vine twines around the oak. He began to cherish enmity against him whom formerly he supremely loved. He became terrified for that God whom formerly he delighted to meet. He sought his happiness no more in communing with, but in fleeing from, God." (Frame, on Original Sin.)

6. Internally he experienced consciousness of unworthiness, depravity, guilt, remorse, and the pangs of mental anguish incident to the apprehension of evil in consequence of sin.

7. The death of the body. The Confession declares (Sec. 18) that sin entered the world through the act of the first parents, "and death by sin," which clearly implies that aside from man's fall death would not have been in the world. If Adam's sin brought death into the world, it must have brought death upon him, and hence, death is to be included in the effects of the fall, upon the original transgressors. Such seems to have been the view of the leading theologians in the first Christian centuries. "Death was the punishment which Jehovah had threatened to inflict on the transgressors of his law. Nevertheless the act of transgression was not immediately succeeded by death, but by a train of evils which came upon both the man and the woman, introductory to death, and testifying that man had become mortal. Accordingly both death and physical evils were considered the effects of Adam's sin, as by Iræneus and others." (Hagenbach's Hist. of Doct.)

When God laid upon Adam the prohibition—that of the tree of the knowledge of good and evil he should not eat—the command was accompanied (Gen. ii. 17) with the explicit warning, "For in the day thou eatest thereof thou shalt surely die," which passage, as well as numerous New Testament passages, seems unmistakably to teach that our first parents were made liable to bodily death as a consequence of their sin.

Since man's body was doubtless essentially the same in the Edenic state as it is now, and since sin is a moral act involving the exercise of free will, and has no necessary direct effect upon the body, we must suppose that death, as the penalty of transgression, came about, not by divine infliction of mortality upon an organism essentially immortal, but by Adam's forfeiture of the provisions by which exemption from death would have followed as the reward of obedience. As to his body, man is

17

essentially a part of and of a piece with the animal world about him, in the very constitution of which are inseparably involved the facts of change, decline, and death, "dust thou art, and unto dust thou shalt return," being as truly a law of man's physical being as it is of the worm he treads upon.

It is not out of place in this connection to call special attention to the reasonableness and the simplicity of Cumberland Presbyterian theology on the subject of the introduction of sin into the world, a view which admits to the fullest man's freedom and responsibility, while it justifies to the fullest the goodness and righteousness of God. Man is in fact a subject of moral government, giving account at the bar of his own conscience and before the law of a God whom his moral nature postulates. If we receive the biblical account at all, and believe man's natural powers of head and heart obscured through sin's blight, we must not invest Adam with the weakness of a moral infant, but with the endowment of intelligence, sensibility, and will in such a measure as to render him a fit subject for the probation through which he was called to pass, and in which probation, though encompassed by transcendent motives to stand, yet, endowed with power of self-determination to either the right or the wrong, he fell and involved himself and posterity in sin and death.

"How the wrong volition originated in a perfectly holy mind," says a thoughtful writer, "has been the *crux crucis* of speculative theologians from that day to the present, while it is likely to remain such in all subsequent periods. With its origin, I have at present, however, no concern except to deny that it was kindled by divine power. To imagine this were not merely to represent God as the cause of sin, but as being himself the sinner."

In like manner Howe insists: "Man's defection from his primitive state was merely voluntary, and from the unconstrained choice of his own mutable and self-determining will.

The pure and holy nature of God could never be the original of man's sin. This is evident in itself. God disclaims it; nor can any affirm it of him without denying his very being. He could not be the cause of unholiness but by ceasing to be holy, which would suppose him mutably holy; and if either God or man must be confessed mutable, it is no difficulty where to lay it: whatever God is, he is essentially; and necessity of existence, of being always what he is, remains everlastingly the fundamental attribute of his being."

The following excellent note we transfer from Dr. A. A. Hodge's Commentary on the Westminster Confession: "God did neither cause nor approve Adam's sin. He forbade it, and presented motives which should have deterred from it. He created Adam holy and fully capable of obedience, and with sufficient knowledge of his duty, and then left him alone to his trial. If it be asked why God, who abhors sin, and who benevolently desires the excellence and happiness of his creatures, should sovereignly determine to permit such a fountain of pollution, degradation, and misery to be opened, we can only say, with profound reverence, 'Even so, Father, for so it seemed good in thy sight.'"

As Dr. Hodge observes, the two great questions which have perplexed men's minds, in regard to the fall, are (1) how sin could originate in the soul of a being created holy, and (2) why a holy God should permit sin. Upon the latter point it is in place to observe that God did not permit the fall of man for its own sake, but because of a purpose to make this world the theater of happiness through an economy of free moral agents, to which economy liability to rebellion against the divine government would be an inseparable attendant. Furthermore, as Hodge observes, "it appears to be God's general plan, and one eminently wise and righteous, to introduce all new created subjects of moral government into a state of probation for a time, in which he makes their permanent character and destiny depend upon their own action. He creates them holy, yet capable of falling." The motives which swayed the minds of the first parents to evil, despite the divine prohibition and warning, Dr. Hodge thus enumerates: "(1) Natural appetite for the attractive fruit. (2) Natural desire for knowledge. (3) The persuasive power of the superior mind and will of Satan. In this last fact—that they were seduced thereto by the subtlety of Satan—much of the solution of this mystery lies."

We must now examine the doctrine of the Confession in relation to—

4. *The effects Adam's sin brought upon the human race.*

Herein Cumberland Presbyterian teaching takes a wide and radical departure from the Westminster symbol, and from all hyper-Calvinistic standards. While it is impossible for us to enter upon a general discussion of the important and very interesting subject now before us, it is appropriate that enough be said to show the doctrinal attitude of the Church, and the extent of the divergence from the theological system against which the Church was in its very organization an earnest and explicit doctrinal protest.

In answer to the question (16), "What effect did Adam's sin have upon his posterity?" our Catechism says:

"Adam's sin corrupted his moral nature and alienated him from God; and all mankind, descending from him by ordinary generation, inherit his corrupt nature, and become subject to sin and death."

And in reply to the 17th question, "Into what estate did the fall bring mankind?" similarly, and with seeming repetition of idea, the answer is, "The fall brought mankind into a state of alienation from God, which is spiritual death."

Further, in reply to question 21st, "What are the evils of that estate into which mankind fell?" the reply is:

"Mankind, in consequence of the fall, have no communion with God, discern not spiritual things, prefer sin to holiness, suffer from the fear of death and remorse of conscience, and from the apprehension of future punishment."

In harmony with these answers, the language of the Confession is: "They (the first parents) being the root of all mankind, sin entered into the world through their act, and death by sin, and so death passed upon all men."

A comparison and analysis of these statements of the Catechism and the Confession seem to justify the following propositions as representing the Cumberland Presbyterian view of the effects which Adam's sin has entailed upon his posterity:

1. Adam's posterity, because of his fall, as the Catechism affirms, "inherit his corrupt nature." As a result of this corruption of nature, men "have no communion with God," "discern not spiritual things," "prefer sin to holiness," "suffer from fear of death and from remorse of conscience," etc. Thus the race, through its relation to its first parents, has "become subject to sin," in the sense that the inherited moral corruption is the source of so great a tendency to sin as to make it certain that, grace aside, all the individuals of the race will sin and continue to sin. It is because all mankind "descend from Adam by ordinary generation," that they "inherit his corruption of nature." There is no intimation in the Confession or the Catechism that it is because of any positive divine appointment, or even that it is in accordance with the divine will that Adam's posterity "inherit his corruption of nature," but that it results simply from the natural relationship of Adam to his posterity, which relationship involves that law of heredity by which offspring inherit the characteristics of the parents.

Our standards are silent as to the *degree* of this corruption of man's nature, unless the expressions "dead in sin" and "defiled in all the faculties of their moral being," are to be interpreted to mean that the depravity not only extends to all the functions of man's moral nature, but also that it is complete. "This innate hereditary depravity," says Dr. Hodge, "is total, for by it we are utterly indisposed, disabled, and made opposite to all good, and wholly inclined to evil;" and this "moral corruption which results from the penal withdrawing of God's Holy Spirit in the case of our first parents," he further asserts, "is necessarily conveyed to all those of their descendants who are produced by ordinary generation." It is not improbable—it is quite certain, indeed—that among Cumberland Presbyterian divines will be found quite numerous shades of opinion upon this point. If, as Dr. Hodge asserts, man is so depraved in his moral faculties as to be "disabled and opposite to all good, and wholly inclined to evil," we must expect to find among men, aside from the renewing grace of God, not a single virtuous act. Bad as the world is, and it is certainly very bad, it does not seem so bad as that theory makes it. Even where gospel light has never shone, there have been beautiful illustrations of the domestic and philanthropic virtues and of even piety itself. We may, indeed, with Augustine, call the "virtues" of the pagans only "splendid vices," but that is an extremely pessimistic view, and opposed by numberless facts that seem to show unregenerate and even heathen sinners capable of benevolent affections, volitions, and actions.

Touching the extent of man's inherited depravity, the following paragraph from Dr. Blake's valuable little compend of theology is cited, not with approval only, but as believed to be in harmony with the views of the majority of the best thinkers in our body:

"Before answering the question (whether the soul is *totally* depraved) we should know just what is meant by the term *total depravity*. If it means that the soul is just as corrupt as it is possible for it to be, then we answer in the negative. But if it means that every faculty of it is corrupt—that it is, without regeneration, unfit for heaven—then we unhesitatingly answer in the affirmative. There are, certainly, *degrees*, so to speak, in wickedness. Some souls are more debased and corrupt than others, owing to surrounding influences; but, as stated previously, all are defiled and *wholly* defiled. To illustrate: A glass of water containing a few grains of arsenic is a poison; but twice the amount of the deadly drug will make that water a still greater poison. Just so with the human soul."

2. All mankind have become subject to death. In other words, because of the act of the original transgressors they were made mortal, and thus, "through their act," "they being the root of all mankind," "death passed upon all men."

Whatever other signification the word may in some instances have, it is unquestionable that in many passages of Scripture the term "death," as expressive of an effect that came upon the race in consequence of its relation to the original transgressor, is used most literally in the sense of the dissolution of the body. For instance, 1 Cor. xv. 21, 22, can not, without ignoring alike the laws of language and all logical juxtaposition of ideas, be made to yield any other meaning of the terms "death" and "die," than that which they usually have as applied to bodily dissolution: "For since by man came death, by man came also the resurrection of the dead. For as in Adam all die, even so in Christ shall all be made alive." That is to say, As in consequence of his sin, all the natural descendants of Adam are partakers of natural death, so through Christ shall all men be made alive by a resurrection of the dead.

In Romans v. 12, we are taught, not only that by man came death, but why it is so: "Wherefore as by one man sin entered into the world, and death by sin; and so death passed upon all men, for that all have sinned."

As Calvinists rely upon this text for proof of the doctrine of the *imputation* of Adam's sin to his posterity, it is well that it be briefly considered in this connection. And how is the text made to teach imputation? Simply by reading "imputation" into it, thus: "And so death passed upon all men, for that all have sinned" (*in Adam*).

If we assign to the word "impute" the theological meaning given to it by Dr. Hodge (Commentary on the Confession, p. 156), namely, "*to lay to the charge or credit* of any one as a ground of judicial punishment or justification," we are constrained to say that we fail to find the doctrine in the Bible, and that it contravenes the fundamental principles of moral government and moral rectitude as they are taught by the word of God.

If we sinned in Adam, we should repent of Adam's sin; but that were a moral impossibility. We may disapprove, regret, deplore Adam's sin, but to *repent* of it, or of our having "sinned in him," is a moral and psychological impossibility.

The argument runs thus: Death comes through sin. Infants die. But infants have committed no actual sin: and therefore, the sins of another must be imputed to them—that is, laid to their charge as a ground of judicial punishment.

If because of the vices of its parents a child inherits the seeds of disease, and early passes to the tomb, shall we say that its weakness, sufferings, and death are a judicial punishment inflicted on it by divine retribution because its parents' guilt is imputed to the child? The thought is abhorrent to reason and to our ideas of the Judge of all, who is good and righteous in all his ways. Nor is the case in any degree mended, if we say that God's retributive justice punishes the child with death because the *guilt of Adam's sin is imputed* to it. A child may die, indeed, *because* of the sins of its parents, but not because guilty of them; and thousands do annually pass in infancy to the grave because of the vices of parents. And so it is true that, in the divinely appointed economy of this world, sin and death are inseparably linked; and as Adam sinned, death came to him; and since through (this) "one man sin entered the world," death entered by sin, for all have sinned, and must, by the very constitution of human nature, entail sin and mortality upon all born of them as parents sinful and mortal."

As the passage in the fifth chapter of Romans is cited by all imputationists in support of their position, we ask the reader's careful attention to the following remarks of Dr. Forbes, himself an imputationist, in his most valuable *Analytical Commentary on Romans*, pp. 208–9:

"The restriction of the words, 'For that all have sinned,' to mere imputation is contrary to the context. The verb 'sinned' must take its meaning from what precedes and follows. 'Sin' in the words of verse 12, 'By one man sin entered into the world,' can not, as has been shown, refer to mere guilt only, or *imputed* sin. In the words again that follow in verse 13, 'For until the law sin was in the world,' the reference manifestly is to the historical existence of sin in the world, as evidenced by the murder of Abel by Cain, by the general violence which had filled the earth before the flood, and which called forth that awful judgment from the Lord, because 'all flesh had corrupted his way upon the earth,' by the sins of the Sodomites, etc., in all which cases sin was 'imputed' by God to the perpetrators *personally*, proving therefore that the sin for which they suffered was not *imputed* sin (in the sense of the transgression of another being reckoned to them), but their own personal sin."

In theological views, no less than in other respects, it is often true that one extreme leads to another. In controverting the views of Pelagius, who taught that Adam's sin injured only himself, and that infants come into the world as pure as Adam was before the fall, his great contemporary Augustine was led to look upon the human race as a "compact mass, a collective body, responsible in its unity and solidarity," and formally promulgated the doctrine of imputation, in these words: *"As all men have sinned in Adam, they are justly subject to the condemnation of God on account of this hereditary sin and the guilt thereof."*

And so the Westminster Confession: "They being the root of all mankind, the guilt of this sin was imputed, and the same

death in sin and corrupted nature conveyed to all their posterity, descending from them by ordinary generation."

And so the Westminster Catechism, in the answer to the
sixteenth question : " The covenant being made with Adam, not
only for himself but for his posterity ; all mankind, descending
from him by ordinary generation, *sinned in him*, and fell with
him, in his original transgression."

The Rev. Mr. Miller, in his chapter on " original or birth sin,"
in the work hitherto noticed, says that " the Westminster Confession is characteristically severe," and admits that some of the
strong phrases of the Calvinistic standards may, on a superficial
view, be justly liable to the charge of teaching fatality, and, for
defending them from the charge of fatality, proposes an illogical
and novel device. " Does not the pronounced imputation of
guilt," he asks, " in these reformed standards preclude the
charge of Manichæism, since human nature is no longer *essentially* a mass of corruption and perdition, but only *imputa-
tively ?* " But this expedient for getting rid of the " utterly indisposed, disabled, and made opposite to all good, and wholly
inclined to all evil " (which Calvinism not only declares to be
man's state, but to render him utterly incapable of freedom
toward good until unconditionally regenerated by divine influence), is inadequate, for it ignores the obvious fact that corruption is not " imputed," and in the nature of the case can not
be. Guilt can be imputed. The Westminster Confession
rightly says that " death in sin and corrupted nature " the first
parents " *conveyed* to all their posterity." Neither personal guilt
nor imputed guilt necessarily impairs the freedom of the will.

"Among the Arminians or Remonstrants," says Mr. Miller,
" the tenet of the universality of redemption is held side by side
with that of the human will to co-operate with divine grace,
both positions being firmly taken by distinguished Anglicans
like Jeremy Taylor and Isaac Barrow. Richard Baxter himself,
strict Puritan in other respects, has strong leanings this way."

On this broad, solid, and, as we must believe it, scriptural "medium ground" in theology, in company with Taylor and Barrow and Baxter, of England, stand Donnell and Bird and Beard and other men of cherished memory in the Cumberland Presbyterian Church.

We have dwelt upon the subject of man's present moral and spiritual state as affected by the original transgression, not only because it is a subject of interest and of vital relations in a theological system, but also because much of the public teaching on the subject is not accordant with human experience and is, therefore, unsatisfying to the minds of the thoughtful. No other than a rational theology can be a true theology, for all truth is harmonious.*

We will be greatly helped in our endeavor for clear and satisfying views on this subject if we keep in mind two obvious facts:

1. Man is subject to much evil that is in no proper sense a direct result of sin. To suppose that all evil or suffering implies sin as its cause, is an old, old error. "Who did sin, this

---

* We can not overestimate the value of the declaration of Mark Hopkins, that "Nothing that can be shown to be really in opposition either to the reason or the moral nature of man can be from God." And so, as he further asserts: "If Christianity be not fundamentally in accord with our original constitution, and will not restore man to a true manhood, and the highest manhood, we can not accept it."

In the following paragraph we must recognize not only a just distinction made between the relation of Adam and that of his posterity, to temporal death, but also a just and needful warning as to the pernicious effects of propagating theological dogmas at war with man's reason, or those moral ideas fundamental to the conception of moral government: "All the criminality belongs to Adam, and we are no more guilty of his sin," says Frame, "than Christ was guilty of ours. Temporal death was punishment to Adam, but it is only suffering to his posterity. No wonder that infidelity abounds, when the professed defenders of the Faith maintain that we are *guilty* of Adam's sin. There is no intelligent man, with an unbiased mind, who will believe that he is guilty of a sin committed by another, and that, too, thousands of years before he was born. It is this and similar absurdities that have driven so many of our intelligent and inquiring young men into the ranks of a hopeless infidelity."

man, or his parents, that he was born blind?" "Neither," said
the Master. Yet it is true that much of the evil in the world is
directly or indirectly the result of sin. Says Mark Hopkins,
than whom our century has not had a clearer or profounder
thinker on man's moral nature and relations, "Evil from acci-
dent, or misfortune, or from the laws of nature as regarded
impersonal, is not punishment." Many good people are sorely
perplexed in their faith simply because they refer to a "mysterious providence of God" sufferings that arise from their own
mistakes, from the wills of other people, or otherwise are incident to the state of things of which man, a finite and fallible
creature, is a part.

2. Humanity, in this earthly state, is a great rational, moral,
sentient economy in which the well-being of each is largely
dependent on the will and behavior of others. In the nature of
the case, which we must regard of divine ordaining, this principle of interdependence and representation is of the widest
prevalence, and we are constrained to believe that it is not
limited to the sentient creatures of this little sphere. In the
case of husband and wife, parents and children, ruler and subjects, we see the operation of this principle under relations
which make the well-being of some necessarily and very largely
dependent on the knowledge and virtue of others; but nowhere
do we see the operation of that principle which is involved
in what speculative theologians have attempted to fasten
upon the teachings of God's word under the name of "*imputation.*"

Holding firmly, then, by the plain teaching of God's word,
that "by one man sin entered the world;" and that from the
original transgressor corruption of moral faculties passed to his
posterity; and that death came by sin, since, because of inherited depravity, "all have sinned," and so death passed to all
men; and since man in this fallen condition is under moral
weakness because of depravity, and under just condemnation

for actual sin, we are led to consider the divine and merciful provision for man's restoration through

5. *A covenant of grace.*

" Man, by his fall, having made himself incapable of life by
that covenant (of works), the Lord was pleased to make the
second, commonly called the covenant of grace, wherein he
freely offers unto sinners life and salvation by Jesus Christ,
requiring of them faith in him that they may be saved." (Confession, section 23.)

A covenant implies, (1) parties, (2) promise, (3) conditions, (4)
penalty. Man was originally a *party* to what is usually called
the "covenant of works," God being the other *party*. God
promised the reward of life, on *condition* of obedience, and fixed
the *penalty* of disobedience. This covenant is styled also the
" covenant of life," as it promised life, and the " legal covenant,"
because the condition was obedience to *law*.

But the first parents failed to obtain life and blessedness under
the first covenant, and involved themselves in guilt which justly
exposed them to penal sufferings while they also rendered the
race subject to physical death, and involved them in moral
depravity which rendered spiritual life and blessedness morally
impossible. Man's dire necessity is God's stupendous opportunity to demonstrate, not to man only, but, in providing deliverance for man, to show to all his universe of moral subjects, that
he is gracious and merciful, not willing the death of his rational
creatures, and capable, in his infinite wisdom, of so providing
for the redemption of man, as to more than secure all the moral
ends which demanded the death of the transgressor.

Here we reach another of the vital points wherein Cumberland Presbyterian doctrine differs materially from Westminster
theology. The latter system teaches, according to Hodge's
Commentary on the Confession, " that God *having determined to
save the elect* out of the mass of the race fallen in Adam,
appointed his Son to become incarnate in our nature, and as the

Christ or God-man Mediator, he appointed him to be the second
Adam and representative head of redeemed humanity, and as
such entered into a covenant with him and with his seed in him.
In this covenant the Mediator assumes *in behalf of his elect seed
the broken conditions of the old covenant of works* precisely as
Adam left them. Adam had failed to obey, and therefore forfeited life; he had sinned, and therefore incurred the endless
penalty of death. Christ therefore suffered the penalty and
*extinguished in behalf of all whom he represented the claims of the
old covenant,* and at the same time he rendered a perfect vicarious obedience, which was the very condition upon which eternal
life had been originally offered. All this Christ does as a principal party with God to the covenant in acting as the *representative of his own people.*"

We have indicated by italics the more prominent parts of the
foregoing which contrast Westminster theology with that of our
own Church. The following paragraph from Hodge's Commentary contains language that is certainly remarkable, and such
as we must think scarcely any believer in the God of the Bible
could use unless in extenuation of a theory abhorrent to reason:

"Subsequently, in the administration and gracious application
of this covenant, Christ the Mediator *offers* the blessings secured
by it to all men on condition of faith—that is, he bids all men to
lay hold of these blessings by the instrumentality of faith, and
he promises that if they do so they shall certainly enjoy them;
and he, as the mediatorial surety of his people, insures for them
that their faith and obedience shall not fail."

"The Calvinistic view," as Dr. Hodge designates it, and as he
has briefly sketched it for us, teaches: (1) that God "determined
to save the elect out of the race fallen in Adam; (2) that he
appointed his incarnate Son to be the second Adam and representative head of redeemed humanity" (the elect); (3) that "the
Mediator assumes in behalf of his elect seed the broken conditions of the old covenant of works," and so "suffered the

penalty and extinguished in behalf of all he represented the claims of the old covenant," and "rendered (for the elect) a perfect vicarious obedience," or fulfilled "the very condition upon which eternal life had been originally offered;" (4) that the rest of mankind were passed by, as not being elect, and were not included in those for whom Christ covenanted, suffered, and obeyed; (5) that, consequently, all the guilt of Adam's sin, as imputed to them, and of their personal transgressions remains against the non-elect, without any propitiation whereby it would be possible for these sins to be forgiven or for the non-elect to be saved; and yet, (6) in the administration and gracious application of this covenant Christ the Mediator "*offers* the blessings (secured by the covenant) to all men on condition of faith!"

Christ "*offers*" the non-elect the blessings of the covenant of grace, says Dr. Hodge. What does Dr. Hodge mean, what can he mean by his emphasized "*offers*" them the blessings of the covenant, save that it is an offer without any thing offered? Is Christ chargeable with such mockery? Having unconditionally excluded a portion of the human race from the covenant, and left them without power to repent or believe, Christ now, according to this Calvinistic theology, "bids all men to lay hold of these blessings" by faith. That is to say that Christ, denying to a portion of humanity the power to believe, bids them believe and so "lay hold on" blessings neither provided nor designed for them! If this is Calvinism, as one of its eminent expounders states, can we wonder, that, as Rev. John Miller declares, Calvinism has successively died in seven of its great doctrinal centers?—We notice finally:

6. *The fullness and universality of the covenant of grace under the New Testament dispensation.*

The administration of the scheme of redemption has been a progress at once grand and wonderful. Is it possible for the student of history to believe that no other will and no other power than man's has guided and effected the long series of events which culminated in the dissolution and removal of the Judaic state, and the ushering in of this simpler, fuller, and universal dispensation of what is called the gospel? The race has no better, no higher hope than this gospel of love. In the moral sky there is no Sun of Righteousness but the center of this gospel administration. This is "the dispensation of the fullness of times," in which believers of all nations are to be gathered into one brotherhood of peace and good will, that these and the family of God in heaven may be united under Christ, to reign with him in the new heavens and new earth wherein only the righteous shall dwell.

CHAPTER IX.

FREE WILL—THE MORAL LAW—MORAL GOVERNMENT—MAN'S FREEDOM CONSISTENT WITH GOD'S SOVEREIGNTY.

" 34. God, in creating man in his own likeness, endued him with intelligence, sensibility, and will, which form the basis of moral character, and render man capable of moral government.

" 35. The freedom of the will is a fact of human consciousness, and is the sole ground of accountability. Man, in his state of innocence, was both free and able to keep the divine law, also to violate. Without any constraint from either physical or moral causes, he did violate it.

" 36. Man, by disobedience, lost his innocence, forfeited the favor of God, became corrupt in heart and inclined to evil. In this state of spiritual death and condemnation, man is still free and responsible; yet, without the illuminating influence of the Holy Spirit, he is unable either to keep the law or lay hold upon the hope set before him in the gospel.

" 37. When the sinner is born of God, he loves him supremely, and steadfastly purposes to do his will; yet because of remaining corruption, and of his imperfect knowledge of moral and spiritual things, he often wills what in itself is sinful. This imperfect knowledge and corruption remain, in greater or less force, during the present life; hence the conflict between the flesh and the spirit."—*Confession of Faith.*

" *There is nothing good or evil, save in the will.*"—*Epictetus.*

" *To deny the freedom of the will is to make morality impossible.*"—*Froude.*

I. FREEDOM OF THE WILL.

ALIKE in their pulpit ministrations and in their doctrinal discussions, Cumberland Presbyterians have plainly taught and strenuously insisted on the freedom of the human will. In their theological system, freedom is a basic and essential truth. Freedom denied, human conduct is divested of every trace of a moral phase, and the term virtue can stand for no such reality as the common sense of mankind attaches to it. " I do not perform an act," says Le Devoir, "I do not pronounce a word, which does not suppose a belief in my liberty and in that of others. . . . . Deny the belief in liberty, and society falls to pieces." With the ancient philosopher whose sentiment we have cited above, and with Mr. Froude, Mark Hopkins tells us that "all virtue is from the will, as all knowledge is from the intellect." To these opinions of profound thinkers we must add the common judgment of mankind, of which a judicious writer observes that "a *fact so universal* has many chances of being in conformity with reality."

It is well known, however, that the denial of the freedom of the will, in one form or another, and by positive assertion or logical inference, has found place alike in religious creeds and philosophical systems. Fatality, necessity, determinism, or the denial of freedom, by whatever name, has been also a favorite refuge of atheists and infidels. Of the atheist of his day, Jeremy Collier says: "If you will take his word for it, an atheist is a very despicable mortal, ... no better than a heap of organized dust, a stalking machine, a speaking head without a soul in it. . . . . He has no more liberty than the current of a stream or the blast of a tempest; and where there is no choice there can be no merit."

Greek and Roman philosophy had its "destiny" (*fatum*) whereby the events of every human life evolved along a course irreversibly predetermined. Pantheism and Mohammedanism alike bind man's action by a power that excludes the idea of freedom. The materialist tells us that volitions only seemingly proceed from free will, while they are simply necessary movements dependent on states of the brain, which states are in turn dependent on influences external to the body. The evolutionist will have it that man is "the resultant of his ancestors," and that so his will is but the effect of many and long continued causes, in the grasp of which causes it is "tied to its course by a law of nature, as a planet to its orbit or a plant to the soil on which it grows."

Of the old idea of "destiny," a recent vigorous thinker on psychological subjects says, "Even in the Christian religion there remain some traces of this conception of destiny, presented, it is true, under the feature of a personal God, the absolute master of all the events of the world. . . . . In some Christian sects, belief in predestination has become a dogma;" and by predestination is meant, the author quoted tells us, a "purpose formed by God from all eternity to cast away certain men and to save others." Similarly, as the same author hints, the idea of "grace," in the sense of divine assistance needful to the accomplishment of good and the sanctification of the soul, granted to some and refused to others, "has direct relations with fatalism."

Against this theological dogma, whether the fatality implied is made to depend on an eternal predestination of every individual of the race to a specific doom from which escape is impossible, or upon a limited atonement, or upon the denial of the grace without which salvation is impossible, Cumberland Presbyterians protest, as they do also against all theological premises which by logical inference lead to such a dogma. The men who were instrumental in organizing the Church accepted the Westminster Confession of Faith as a doctrinal standard "so far as they believed it consistent with the word of God," meaning thereby that they excepted the doctrine of fatality.

The fact of the freedom of man in willing is assured to him through consciousness. Not only is he conscious of putting forth volition, but conscious of doing it freely, and conscious of power to refrain from the choice made. Free will is man's power, as Condillac well said, "of doing what he does not do, and of not doing what he does do." He who does not reverence the name of God has power to do so; and he who desecrates the Sabbath and deals fraudulently has power *not* to do these things. Nothing short of this idea of moral freedom can afford any basis for merit, responsibility, or rewards and penalties.

To say that man wills freely what he does will, but could not will otherwise than what he does will, is to give him only the freedom of the water in the flowing stream.

Further, it is Cumberland Presbyterian doctrine that while through disobedience man became "corrupt in heart and inclined to evil," yet is man not by this depravity under a fatal necessity of sinning, but is "still free and responsible by virtue of the gracious influences of the Holy Spirit." God wills not the death of any, and as he "commands all men everywhere to repent," we must believe that men are capable of the repentance required of them. The wrath of God is not manifested against the ungodly because of an unconditioned appointment of them to wrath, on God's part, nor because of any fatal impotency of will in them, but "because knowing God they glorified him not as God, nor gave thanks; but became vain in their reasonings, and their foolish heart was darkened."

Cumberland Presbyterians not only preach a gospel designed for all men, but believe that they preach to men who have the power to accept this gospel by exercise of the ability that is in them to will to turn away from sin, to accept Christ as their Savior, and to keep the commandments of God. This view of the gospel and of man's ability, under the dispensation of the Spirit, to accept the gospel, should be constantly pressed upon the sinner's attention. "Fallen man can," says Rev. Robert Donnell, "upon the gospel plan choose life or death, blessing or cursing. This is abundantly evident from the word of God: 'Choose ye this day whom ye will serve' (Josh. xxiv. 15); 'Ye will not come unto me that ye might have life' (John v. 40); 'Whosoever will, let him take the water of life freely' (Rev. xxii. 17)."

It is true, as the Confession asserts, that "when the sinner is born of God he loves him supremely, and steadfastly purposes to do his will;" but it is not to be inferred that Cumberland Presbyterians teach, therefore, that until one is born again he can put forth no effort to comply with the terms of the gospel. To those yet unconverted, the exhortation is, " *Choose* ye this day whom ye will serve." Of men who were not yet "born again " the Master said, when commanding the eleven to go into all the world and preach his gospel, "he that believeth and is baptized shall be saved." Man must *choose* the service of God— must *choose* salvation as offered in Christ, and not passively wait to be "born again " in order to be able to choose.

The doctrine of "irresistible grace," the doctrine of an " effectual call," in the sense that some receive such, and others receive only "common " or necessarily ineffectual "operations of grace," and the doctrine that man is passive until born again, as to the matter of personal salvation, are errors which have wrecked multitudes of souls, and errors against which the earlier Cumberland Presbyterian ministers frequently protested with great earnestness and power of logic.

Cumberland Presbyterian theology, with its fundamental premises of the impartial goodness of God, a general atonement, the offer of life to all men, the general operation of the Spirit through which man is enabled to repent and believe, and the freedom of the will, is a theology of common sense, conformable, on the subjective side, to the normal conscious experiences of the soul, and opposed to fatality and every species of religious mysticism.

It is scarcely possible for us to overestimate the importance of correct views of the freedom of the will as a co-ordinating principle in a rational system of theology and of religion. Equally important is it in its relations to religious experience and practical godliness. It is *choosing* to repent of and forsake sin, *choosing* the salvation offered in Christ, *choosing* to accept the commandments of Christ as the rule of life, *choosing* to consecrate himself to God's service and human welfare, that makes a man a Christian ; and it is *choosing* to continue steadfast until death that causes his path to shine more and more unto the perfect day, and crowns him with eternal life. And yet it is "all of grace" that he is called, that every one is called, thus to "*seek* after glory, honor, and immortality." "By faith Moses, when he was come to years, *refused* to be called the son of Pharaoh's daughter, *choosing* rather to suffer affliction with the people of God than to enjoy the pleasures of sin for a season, for he *had respect* to (looked to) the recompense of the reward." If much of the preaching of to-day does not lay too much stress on the idea of *getting* religion, it certainly does lay too little stress, the Bible being witness, on the idea of *choosing* religion, *living* religion, *doing* religion.

Between the teachings of hyper-Calvinism and the phenomena of mind as attested in man's consciousness there is an irreconcileable antagonism. Calvinism sweeps away the principles that must underlie all just conceptions of moral government, utterly divesting man of that self-determination which is the sole faculty through the conscious exercise of which it is possible for him to give himself to God or to rebel against God's righteous claims. Not the heathen philosophy which exalted "destiny" to the throne of the universe as a power swaying irresistibly the wills of gods as well as of men, nor the baldest materialism of to-day, which regards matter as eternal and all phenomena, those of mind included, as but links in an endless chain of fatalistic causation, is more subversive of rational ideas of virtue and of moral government than is that theological system of *necessity* which the genius of Augustine and afterward that of Calvin attempted to fasten on the thought of the Christian world; and in their efforts to aid the mind in emancipating itself from these shackles Cumberland Presbyterians have rendered useful service to the cause of evangelical truth.

The professed belief, on the part of Calvinists, of what are irreconcileable contradictions is a puzzling psychological phenomenon. For instance, what more could an Arminian say than is said in this passage from a Calvinistic writer: "Let none presume ever to suppose that God can be wanting on *his* part, or to cast the blame of his own negligence and impenitence on the predestination of God. He will have all to be saved, and calls upon all men to come unto Jesus that they may have life; and it were blasphemy to suppose that he offers for the acceptance of his creatures a gift which he had *causatively* foreordained that they should be unable to receive. He is ever working by his spirit *for good—and for good only*, and strives with every man until he, by his own obstinate resistance, has destroyed within himself the susceptibility of renewal and done despite to the Spirit of Grace." The same writer, amazing as the fact seems, still clings to his Calvinistic premises—the eternal unconditional decree of whatsoever comes to pass—that some of the human race are unconditionally chosen in Christ unto everlasting glory, and the rest of mankind passed by and doomed to wrath, for whom, according to Dr. Hodge, Christ did not assume " the broken conditions of the old covenant of works precisely as Adam left them," as he did for the "elect seed," and, worse still, if possible, the guilt of Adam's sin is imputed to those for whom Christ did not assume the conditions of the covenant broken by Adam, and this imputed sin of Adam is made "the cause of the loss of original righteousness and the acquisition of original sin." If for a sin committed by another, and unconditionally imputed to him by a Sovereign Will, a human being is unconditionally passed by and ordained to wrath, that human being is not a victim of fatality, we fail to conceive what is meant by fatality.

Calvinistic "decrees" and "predestination," of logical necessity, lead to the doctrine of fatality. The distinction between causative will and permissive will, says Dr. Forbes, "Calvin would not hear of." "Why do we say God *permits*," asks Calvin, "but just because he *wills?*"

"Calvin was afraid," says Dr. Forbes, "that if he conceded any originating power whatever to the creature's will the sovereignty of God would thereby be infringed," and justly adds that "he (Calvin) does not see by the repulsive aspect he gives to this attribute in pressing it beyond its legitimate sphere, and by making the sovereignty of God override all his other attributes, he throws an obstacle in the way of the cordial acceptance of this most important and humbling, yet consolatory, truth."

Only within the sphere of freedom—the power to choose the end for which he will live, and to subordinate ten thousand volitions to the realization of the generic choice, can responsibility attach to man. This sphere of freedom is the domain of moral law, of virtue, of moral government; and we may proceed to notice how out of man's nature as a rational creature capable of happiness and suffering, and endowed with self-determining power, there issues what is at once the *law of his constitution* and the *will of his Maker*, namely,

II. THE MORAL LAW.

When we assert that the moral law is but the law of man's constitution, it is meant that it is simply the rational way of acting for a being endowed with man's powers and susceptibilities, and existing for the end for which man is conceived to exist. Given, that *end*, and man's constitution, as endowed with intelligence, sensibility, and will, and reason affirms a law of action for man, and that law of action is the moral law.

It is only in view of an "end" for which man is conceived to exist that a law of action can be predicated. Not only an end, but a highest end must be conceived as conditioning the idea of law for a being endowed with knowledge and freedom. As endowed with sensibility, man is capable of enjoyment, of happiness, of *good*, and of good that may come to him through numerous sources. But his constitution reveals a supreme good, a *summum bonum*. It is in view of ends, as higher or lower, which man apprehends, and from which he can freely choose for himself a supreme end of his life endeavors, that issue moral law, man's responsibility, and his approval or disapproval of self, in accordance with the choice made. At this point it is that destiny is in man's own hand. Whatsoever he soweth, that shall he reap. If he choose as an end the gratification of the flesh, or the acquisition of wealth, or worldly fame, he chooses unworthily, and not only misses the supreme good, but brings upon himself the retribution of his own outraged moral nature. " Man's chief end is to glorify God, and to enjoy him forever." Whether we study man's faculties and susceptibilities, appeal to his experience, or accept the teaching of the Bible, the Catechism is found to harmonize with the profoundest philosophy as to man's well-being. Only when man seeks happiness through obedience to the will of his Maker does he find his true end, the highest good of which he is capable.

Viewed only as proceeding from man's constitution, or as learned from his experience, moral law is but the rule by which man attains the highest good. "A law," says Mark Hopkins, "tells us what to do, and commands us to do it, but becomes law only as it is enforced by a penalty, or by punishment." Unless a law be " supposed to express the will of God with his authority lying back of it, it will be, as men now are, of small force for controlling the appetites and passions."

The Creator, infinitely wise and good, not only made man for the happiness that comes through virtue, but wills that man shall attain this end; and thus the law divinely impressed upon man's constitution is also the positively revealed will and command of the Creator. God says to men through his inspired word, Thou shalt, and thou shalt not. Man is free to obey and to disobey. Yet a voice within him says, This you *ought* to do, that you *ought not* to do. So there is within man's breast that which makes him " a law unto himself "—that something which separates man from the brute by what one has called " the greatest difference in the universe "—that something within us, though no part of us, which the greatest of German philosophers declared equally wonderful with the starry heavens above us—the MORAL LAW.

III. MORAL GOVERNMENT.

No man liveth unto himself only. Every individual is a member of a great social and moral economy. God's purpose in the creation of beings rational and sentient, is the diffusion of happiness through a vast moral economy. Every subject in this great economy is bound, not only to choose his own highest well-being, but with regard to the purpose of God that all shall attain their end, and, first of all, with respect to his obligations to his Maker. Not only in striving to realize the end for which he was made is man to glorify God and enjoy him, but he is under obligation to be a worker together with God in the promotion of the highest good of the whole moral economy. Within limits of their capacity to enable man to attain his end, both the family and the state are of divine appointment—powers " ordained of God " for human well-being.

God, by creation and preservation, is the rightful King whose dominion rules over all. But over man and other subjects of moral law, he rules by a system of rewards and punishments. The fundamental law of his kingdom is, *Thou shalt love the Lord thy God with all thy heart, and thy neighbor as thyself.* " Love is the fulfilling of the law." And the " love " we are required to exercise toward the neighbor in kind and measure as toward self, consists in *choosing* and *seeking* for the neighbor the attainment of his end. The general prevalence of this law of God's kingdom in the hearts and lives of men would result in what one has rightly called " the highest earthly conception "— a " vast Christian commonwealth instinct with order."

The view we have taken of free will enables us to see how man can rationally yield himself to God through the exercise of that freedom, and the poet uttered a truth accordant with philosophy and religion in saying, " Our wills are ours, to make them thine ; " for only through the will can man give himself or any thing else to God. But the power to give ourselves to God freely, is the power also to withhold ourselves from and to rebel against God.

"If God would be a Father and a Moral Governor," says Mark Hopkins, " he must have children and subjects in his own image, and with the prerogative of choosing or rejecting him as their supreme good. Control by force, or by an impulse from without, is the opposite of control by love, and of order from a rational choice, and the highest duty of man is to give himself in the spirit of a child—that is, by faith, to God."

It is because man has turned away from God, and seeks happiness through the choice of other than the right end, that the world is full of unrest, sorrow, and suffering. Such a choice is sin.

In the light of the general principles we have thus attempted to make plain, it will not be difficult to understand how

IV. GOD'S SOVEREIGNTY AND MAN'S FREEDOM

harmonize in that moral government which God exercises over his creature man.

True it is, indeed, that the profoundest thinkers have been perplexed over the problem we have here pronounced not difficult to understand. Calvin solved the problem, as Dr. Forbes tells us, " by denying there is any to be solved "—" by eliminating entirely the conflicting element on the opposite side of the question, and merging man's will wholly in God's will. The common sense of mankind has been in error in considering that man's will could originate any thing—even *sin*. God is the originator of all, even of *sin*." Such, a professed Calvinist being judge, is the conclusion Calvin deduced from his own premises. The ceaseless unrest of Westminster theology grows out of the fact that it accepts Calvin's premises with a " so as thereby " the conclusion does not follow—an attempt to disjoin ideas which are by logical necessity inseparable.

Calvinistic necessitarians charge the advocates of free-will with a denial of the scriptural doctrine that salvation is of grace; but such a charge is unjust; more still, if man be not free in the sense and measure we have supposed, then would it be impossible for salvation to be by grace, for grace is favor to the undeserving, but if not free, man is neither deserving nor undeserving.

The all-wise Creator saw fit to bring into being a vast moral economy. It was his sovereign will to create such intelligences, and to govern them according to the nature he gave them. Here on the earth, as an actuality, we find such a moral economy, the subjects of which do, through civil government and in a thousand other ways, treat one another as endowed with freedom of will and action, and therefore as responsible.

Had not an omnipotent Creator power to create such a being as we have supposed man to be? If in the exercise of his sovereignty he has created such a being, wherein is his sovereignty denied? If when in rebellion and deserving only the divine displeasure man is saved by divine interposition, how is "grace" denied as being the procuring cause of salvation? It is not denied.

CHAPTER X.

REDEMPTION IN RELATION TO THE HEATHEN AND THOSE INCAPABLE OF FAITH.

" There is a wideness in God's mercy,
  Like the wideness of the sea;
There 's a kindness in his justice
  Which is more than liberty;
For the love of God is broader
  Than the measure of man's mind;
And the heart of the Eternal
  Is most wonderfully kind."—*Faber*.

THE subject of the last preceding chapter leads us, by obvious connection, to inquire whether salvation is possible to those who live and die without knowledge of Christ's atoning work, and, if it is possible, on what conditions. It is matter for regret that the discussion of a question of so much interest must, by the limits prescribed for this volume, be restricted to a few pages. A brief summary of the great doctrines of redemption will suitably bring the question before us:

1. In the exercise of freedom of will, which "is the sole ground of accountability," man brought sin into the world, and death by sin.

2. "Jesus Christ, by his perfect obedience and sacrifice of himself, became the propitiation for the sins of the whole world."

3. That the legal aspect of this merciful provision, which sprang wholly from God's sovereign grace, is comprised in the fact that all the benign ends of God's moral government that could have been attained by the punishment of the transgressor,

can be attained through the sufferings and death of Christ as displaying God's disapprobation of sin and his supreme regard for holiness and for the happiness of his creatures.

4. Atonement takes away no one's sins except in the sense, (1) that God can justly and does forgive the sins of those who repent of sin, and choose obedience, and (2) that it provides the gracious influences whereby the sinner may experience moral and spiritual regeneration, if he submit himself to those influences. Pardon, justification, salvation, or the blessings which come to man through Christ, by whatever word expressed, must mean, in a general sense, (1) deliverance from the penal consequences of sin, By pardon, made morally possible through atonement, and (2) restoration to holiness and, thereby, to blessedness.

5. Christ's atoning work is for humanity, lifting the race into a new and gracious probation, and, as the Bible certainly teaches, thus secures to every human being the possibility of attaining that spiritual blessedness in which consists the supreme good for which man was made.

In the application of these doctrines to the problem of actual salvation, we distinguish three classes :

(a) Those who, by early death or by natural impotence of mental faculties, in this life know nothing of Christ. Of this class Cumberland Presbyterians say, "All infants dying in infancy, and all persons who have never had the faculty of reason, are regenerated and saved."

Knapp is certainly incorrect when he declares that " none have really ever doubted the salvation of those dying in infancy ; " for the damnation of some of this class is an unavoidable inference of the doctrine of unconditional election and reprobation—of what a Presbyterian judicature lately stigmatized as " *the horrible doctrine of preterition.*" While our Confession teaches that all dying in infancy are " regenerated and saved," the Westminster doctrine, consistently with its dogma of unconditional decrees, is that "*elect* infants" dying in infancy are saved.

(*b*) Those to whom the gospel is offered.

(*c*) That large class—as yet by far the larger part of our common humanity—who have lived to years of moral accountability, and passed from this probationary stage, without knowledge that Christ tasted death for them.

A consistent Calvinist holds, as Dr. Briggs admits, that this life is not in any proper sense a state of probation, since, according to Calvinistic doctrine, by eternal decree of election or preterition every man's destiny is determined before he is born. Cumberland Presbyterian doctrine makes the blessings of the gospel available to all humanity—wide as the curse is the offer of the remedy.

Whatever may be the extent of the knowledge of duty to which man may attain without the light of revelation, the Scriptures clearly teach that only for the right use of what he hath shall man give account. Peter never opened his mouth to more reasonable utterance than when, in audience of those present "to hear all things commanded of the Lord," he said (Acts x. 35): "Of a truth I perceive that God is not a respecter of persons; but in every nation he that fears him, and works righteousness, is accepted of him."

So Paul declares, that there is no respect of persons with God," asserting—

" For whenever the Gentiles who have not the law
Do by nature the things of the law,
These, having not the law, are a law unto themselves;
Who show the work of the law written in their hearts,
Their conscience also bearing witness,
And their thoughts meanwhile accusing or excusing one
another."

And so, speaking of the light of nature as the source of a knowledge of God and of duty, he declares: " For, from the creation of the world, his invisible things are clearly seen, being perceived by the things that are made, even his eternal power and Godhead; so that they are without excuse." And so, as justifying God's displeasure at the wickedness of heathendom, Paul says of such sinners, "Who, *knowing the judgment of God*, that they who do such things are worthy of death, not only do them, but have pleasure in those who do them."

There can be no question as to the fact that the heathen world lieth in abominable idolatries and other wickedness—and that it is a just reproach to Christianity that it has not caused all the world to hear the glad tidings designed for all ears—yet it is true that even in heathen lands there have been illustrious examples of lives noble and virtuous, and of moral and religious teaching very like to portions of the inspired word. St. Clement says: "Let us look steadfastly upon the blood of Christ, and see how precious his blood is in the sight of God, because, being poured out in behalf of our salvation, it has procured for the whole world the gift of repentance." In like manner is Christ declared "the true Light which lighteth every man that cometh into the world." The prophet Haggai announced the coming Messiah as "*the Desire of all nations.*" That the early teachers of Christianity understood that present good and the possibility of salvation and eternal blessedness came through Christ to the whole human race, "even as from Adam malediction came upon all," the following passage from Irenæus is proof: "For it was not merely for those who believed on him in the time of Tiberius Cæsar that Christ came, nor did the Father exercise his providence only for men who are now alive, but for all men, who from the beginning, *according to their capacity*, have in their generation feared and loved God, and practiced justice and piety toward their neighbors, and have earnestly desired to see Christ and to hear his voice."

Whether the good exhibited in the lives of men not under the influence of the published gospel is due simply to the natural powers of the human soul, as the vestiges of the moral likeness broken by the fall, or to be ascribed to gracious influences coming upon man through Christ's assumption of humanity in his incarnation is an old controversy upon the consideration of which we need not enter, it being sufficient for our purpose to say that the latter view is the one sanctioned by such passages as the following:

"God sent not his Son into the world to condemn the world, but that the world through him might be saved." Certainly it is possible for the world to be saved.

"I exhort, therefore, first of all, that supplications, prayers, intercessions, and giving of thanks, be made for all men—for kings and all that are in authority, that we may lead a quiet and peaceable life in all godliness and decorum; for this is good and acceptable in the sight of our Savior God, who desires that all should be saved and come to the knowledge of the truth." It must mean that salvation is possible to all, and that all are open to the influences of prayer.

"As the Eternal Son became our Redeemer, Mediator, and effectual Intercessor, so," says a most thoughtful writer, "to complete the work which he began, to make effectual for our salvation his sacrifice, mediation, and intercession, the Holy Ghost was sent to dwell in the hearts of men; to be the agent of reunion between God and man; to be the source and beginning of that *new life, from which comes the capacity of holiness, the power to know and to love God, and to obey and love his commands.*"

In every human life there is that *experienced conflict* between good and evil, between the flesh and the Spirit, which led a heathen philosopher to declare that he was possessed of two souls arrayed against each other. It is in the power of man, raised to a new probation in Christ, to follow the promptings of the Spirit; and in his power to resist the Spirit, to live in the "flesh;" and which he chooses determines his destiny. "The gospel tells us whence that goodness proceeds," says the writer above quoted, "which we find everywhere to co-exist with the evil in the heart of man," adding in another connection, " the scriptural testimony to this great fact of the indwelling of the Spirit in the hearts of all men in all ages, is emphatic and conclusive." St. Paul affirms that "the manifestation of the Spirit is given to every man to profit withal."

Of high ideals of virtue in the lives and the teachings of men who had not the gospel, many illustrations could be given, but the following must suffice:

On the *examination of conscience* Seneca gives this admirable advice: "We should every day call our conscience to account. Thus did Sextius. When his daily work was done he questioned his soul, Of what defect hast thou cured thyself to-day? What passion hast thou combated? In what hast thou become better? What more beautiful than this habit of going thus over the whole day? . . . . I do the same, and, being thus my own judge, I call myself thus before my own tribunal. When the light has been carried from my room, I begin an inquest of the whole day; I examine all my actions and words. And why should I hesitate to look at any of my faults when I can say to myself: Take care not to do so again—for to-day I forgive thee?"

How many professed Christians there are—how many ministers, perchance—who could learn from Seneca, and profit by his example! Yet Seneca lived in a time of abounding wickedness and fell a victim to the malice of Nero (A.D. 65), observing, when the sentence came, "I might have long expected such a mandate from a man who had murdered his own mother and assassinated all his friends."

Equally remarkable, and of a more religious character, are these words of Epictetus, a Greek moralist of whom a contemporary said, "I thank the gods for Epictetus, from whose writings I can collect wherewith to conduct life with honor to myself and advantage to my country: " " If we had an understanding, ought we not," says Epictetus, "both in public and in private, incessantly to sing and praise the Deity, and rehearse his benefits? Ought we not, whether we dig, or plow, or eat, to sing this hymn to God? Great is God who has supplied us with these instruments to till the ground; great is God, who has given us hands and organs of digestion; who has given us to grow insensibly, and to breathe in sleep. These things we ought forever to celebrate, and to make it the theme of the greatest and divinest hymn, that he has given us the power to appreciate these gifts, and to use them well. Were I a nightingale, I would act the part of a nightingale; were I a swan, the part of a swan. *But since I am a reasonable creature, it is my duty to praise God.* This is my business, ... and I call on you to join in the same song."

Not a few Christian scholars have believed some of the great moralists of the heathen world to have been inspired. Of Socrates, Plato, and Sakyo Mouni, Farrar says (in his *Early Days of Christianity*), "These, too, were enabled to shed some light on the problems of sin and sorrow, because they had kindled their torches at the Sun of Righteousness," and adds that, "in the deliverance of the one great revelation, even the heathen have borne their share." The "Apologists of the second century, and the philosophic Greek Christians of the third, never hesitated," he further alleges, "to recognize the truth that the influences of the Holy Spirit are as the wind which bloweth where it listeth, and that the poets and the philosophers of the heathen are often the conscious and the unconscious exponents of his inward voice." But it is not to be overlooked that Christianity appeared at a time when the world's moral sky was one of almost unbroken gloom, a star like Seneca appearing only here and there, and that Stoicism, the best philosophy heathendom had produced, "amid the terrors and temptations of that awful epoch utterly failed to provide a remedy against the universal degradation."

Account for the fact as we may, it is of vast significance in this connection, that coextensive with man's conscious sense of moral unworthiness, which seems world-wide, there is a belief that the favor of God is dependent on sacrifice. Symington, in his work on Atonement, says that " every such sacrifice may be regarded as pointing directly to the one perfect sacrifice of the Son of God." Further, as the same able writer adds, " every part of the Gentile world is familiar with the idea of substitution, and the very terms which this principle suggests the use of, are found in almost every language on earth."

These views of the relation of Christ's atoning work, and of the accompanying influences of the Spirit, to humanity as a whole, have direct bearing on the obligation and the encouragement of those who now have the gospel to endeavor to give it to the yet less favored portion of the race, which, through the quickening influence of the Spirit, is endued with power to believe on him of whom it waits to hear, who tasted death for every man. Through this one sense of need, this one atoning sacrifice for all, this one quickening Spirit striving with all, all willing subjects receive power to become sons of God and heirs of everlasting blessedness.

One of the ablest Christian thinkers and writers of the century declares that modern skepticism is a natural result of the narrowness of the popular theology. We come to the close of this cursory view of some of the leading doctrines of the gospel with a like belief ; and likewise with a profound conviction of the substantial correctness, and, therefore, of the immense value of the rational statement of scriptural doctrine, contained in the plain and brief Confession of Faith of the Cumberland Presbyterian Church. To so interpret Christianity as to make it discordant with reason, with man's consciousness, or with the obvious facts of human experience ; to make the issue of the gospel depend on an unconditional decree of God which, out of the same humanity, elects some to salvation and passes by and ordains others to wrath ; to make the remission of sins dependent on the prayers and intercessions of priest or pope, or the blessings of salvation dependent on any baptism or other outward form, is to offer a Christianity from which the growing intelligence of the times will revolt. Never before did more solemn obligation rest on the ministry and all other religious teachers, to speak the things which become SOUND DOCTRINE, even THE FAITH ONCE DELIVERED TO THE SAINTS, for thereon depend the power and destiny of the Church of the living God, itself THE PILLAR AND GROUND OF THE TRUTH.

CHAPTER XI.

SIN—ATONEMENT—PARDON—RESTORATION.

"27. Jesus Christ, the only begotten Son of God, was verily appointed before the foundation of the world to be the Mediator between God and man, the Prophet, Priest, and King, the heir of all things, *the propitiation* for the sins *of all mankind*, the Head of his Church, the Judge of the world, and the Savior of all true believers.

"28. The Son of God, the second person in the Trinity, did, when the fullness of time was come, take upon himself man's nature, yet without sin, being very God and very man, yet one Christ, the only Mediator between God and man.

.   .   .   .

"31. Jesus Christ, by his perfect obedience and sacrifice of himself, which he, through the Eternal Spirit, once offered unto God, became *the propitiation for the sins of the whole world*, so God can be just in justifying all who believe in Jesus.

"33. *Jesus Christ tasted death for every man*, and now makes intercession for transgressors, by virtue of which the Holy Spirit is given to convince of sin and enable man to believe and obey, governing the hearts of believers by his word and Spirit, overcoming all their enemies by his almighty power and wisdom, in such manner and ways as are most consonant to his wonderful and unsearchable dispensation."—*Confession of Faith.*

"God, out of his mere good pleasure, did provide salvation for all mankind."—*Catechism, Ans. to Ques.* 22.

"And he is a propitiation for our sins; and not for ours only, but also for the whole world."—1 John ii. 2.

"For God so loved the world, that he gave his only begotten Son, that whosoever believeth on him should not perish, but have everlasting life."—John iii. 16.

"When the fullness of the time was come, God sent forth his Son, ... to redeem them that were under the law."—Gal. iv. 4, 5.

THE section of the Confession on CHRIST THE MEDIATOR is clear, full, and, as it seems to us, thoroughly scriptural. Any thing like a complete development of its teachings would far transcend the limits that must be observed in this chapter.

Only a few leading points can be brought under consideration, and these will be more clearly seen in their logical relations if we make brief reference to truths set forth in the last chapter.

We have seen that man, endowed with intelligence, sensibility, and will, is by his constitution a subject of moral law. Capable of good as a sentient creature, and possessed of conscious self-determining power, with ability to see the results of his behavior in their relation to his own and other's well-being, man is a person, a self-conscious rational *ego*, intrusted with, and responsible for, the destiny of the spiritual selfhood, which has capacity for sharing the bliss of heaven, and of suffering the torments of the lost. Moreover, the law which issues from his moral nature his Creator proclaims by revelation, *Thou shalt love the Lord thy God with all thy heart, and thy neighbor as thyself,* and thus man finds himself a subject of a moral government whose Head has a right to command the homage and obedience of all creatures, and will, as wise and good, reward the obedient and punish the disobedient.

Taught to believe that man was made in the "image of God," we find his actual state one of rebellion against his God. Instead of loving, he hates, defrauds, kills his neighbor. Instead of realizing his end, to glorify and enjoy God, man has altogether turned aside, and has utterly corrupted his way through willful and continued rebellion against the law of his own moral constitution and the proclaimed will of his Maker. Sin reigns unto universal moral corruption and condemnation.

On the fact of *sin*, man's guilt and ruin, is conditioned the remedial system called the "gospel." God loved the world, and, "out of his mere good pleasure," of his infinite compassion, let us say—"did provide salvation for all mankind." This is the great event of time! The wonderful economy which prepared the way for the coming of the Redeemer looked forward to Calvary, and all subsequent time looks back to Calvary, for there was "lifted up" the God-man who is drawing the

world unto himself. Though it may seem folly to the philosopher and still "scandal to the Jew," yet more and more is the
world coming to receive this salvation that is through atonement, and to look upon it as the one event prophetic and pro-
ductive of a grand issue, a divinely appointed issue, to which
the moral creation moves.

The Scriptures teach, not only that redemption comes to man
through atonement, but that without atonement there could be
no redemption; and also that the *death* of Christ was for some
reason, essential to atonement. "Christ died for the ungodly."
Speaking of his death, Christ said, "I lay it (my life) down of
myself." "Who his own self bore our sins in his own body on
the tree." "Christ also hath once suffered for sins, the just for
the unjust, that he might bring us to God." "Redeemed . . . .
with the precious blood of Christ, as of a lamb without blemish
and without spot."

When it is asserted that on moral grounds a thing is *necessary,*
it must be meant that it is necessary in view of some end.
God's purpose to redeem man from sin and its consequences, as
an end proposed, rendered an atonement necessary. In other
language, divine justice, in view of the ends of the divine
government, could redeem man only on condition of the substitution of something in the place of the death of the sinner that
would equally well secure the ends of the divine government.
The necessity, nature, and efficiency of the atonement can be
understood only as viewed through man's moral condition as a
transgressor of law, and as dead in sin.

We may be sure that the well-being of God's rational
creatures requires the punishment of sin, else sin would not be
punished. "Punishment," says Mark Hopkins, "is the infliction of a previously declared penalty by the will of the lawgiver
for the sake of sustaining the authority of the law." "Obviously, the penalty must express, and that only can," says
Hopkins, "the estimate by the lawgiver of his own rights, and

of the rights of others that are in question, and also his *benevolent desire to present the highest moral motives the case will admit to prevent the infraction of law.*" Right views in this connection are of the utmost importance, not only as to right theory of atonement, but in the matter of the soul's acquiescence in the wisdom and love of the God whose government over us appoints that *the wages of sin is death.* " The proper ground of punishment under any government is not the violation of obligation— that is, guilt as such," continues the same author, " but only the violation of obligation, as that violates rights . . . . In the divine government. . . . punishment is not in view of the guilt as such, but as it is guilt that violates the rights of others. . . . and hence, even though guilt may have been incurred, if the rights of all be perfectly preserved and secure, punishment may be righteously omitted."

In the light of these fundamental principles we may present a plain illustration of man's condition, of what an atonement does for him, and how it does it: The subject of a good king has committed a crime for which he has been sentenced to die, and, by persistent rebellion against righteous authority, has contracted such proneness to evil as makes it morally certain that were sentence *not* executed he would remain a wicked, unhappy rebel. Such is man's condition. He is under condemnation, and moral depravity fills him with enmity to the law of righteousness, to which his carnal mind is not subject and can not be. The subject of the king needs (1) pardon and (2) restoration to right voluntary attitude to his king and to righteous rule. And such are the needs of the sinner in view of his relation to God and God's law. Pardon, or the removal of the sentence, and restoration to holiness the sinner must have in order to salvation. The wise king will say that as he loves his subjects he must punish rebellion in order to preserve obedience, harmony, and happiness. If it is not possible to substitute in the place of the death of the offender some expedient that will equally well secure the ends of righteous rule, the transgressor must (by moral necessity) suffer the penalty.

If we are to regard atonement as a great verity in God's dealing with the human race, we certainly find in it the two elements of a moral condition rendering pardon safe, and such a reinforcement of the spiritual energies of the soul of man as puts pardon and renewal within his power through submission to God and the use of the gracious means supplied. What human governments may not be able to do, the wisdom and love of God fully accomplished in providing a ransom for those under just sentence of condemnation. Nay, more, we may suppose that the sufferings and death of Christ will do more to promote holiness and happiness throughout Jehovah's vast moral empire—for we can not affirm that the knowledge and influence of Christ's work are limited to mankind—than the everlasting punishment of the millions of the redeemed would have done. The "advent" which brings to earth peace and good will, and is glad tidings of great joy, fills heaven, we may suppose, with a joy otherwise unknown.

The view of the atonement thus briefly outlined is, we believe, the generally accepted one among Cumberland Presbyterians. It is at once rational and scriptural. It honors God, harmonizes with man's nature and spiritual needs, and so justifies itself to his understanding as to leave without excuse its willful rejectors. The very ideas herein expressed, as to the nature of the atonement, were the substance of that wonderful system of sacrifices antedating and typical of the great offering to be made in the fullness of time, and with efficacy in itself to justify man's pardon and procure his restoration to holiness. On this point the following words are excellent: "The service of the temple, with its incessant lessons of sin and redemption, foreshadowed the forgiveness of guilt through a Savior to come. The need and assurance of God's forgiving mercy were written in the propitiatory sacrifices from the beginning. When we read in Leviticus or in Numbers and Deuteronomy, the arrangement of types and typical services foreshadowing the great redemption for mankind, and note the part which each individual Hebrew had to perform with them—priest, ruler, and all the common congregation alike required to lay their hand on the head of the sin-offering, confessing their guilt, . . . it is as if we heard the sweet hymn of Watts rising on the air of the desert :

> 'My faith would lay her hand
> On that dear head of Thine,
> While like a penitent I stand,
> And there confess my sin.'

" They brought their own offerings, and slew the victims with their own hands, acknowledging their guilt, and casting themselves on God's forgiving mercy."

As the sin and the trespass offerings were *for the expiation of the sins* of those offering them, so, " the blood of Jesus Christ, his Son," meritoriously and in fact, " cleanseth us from all sin," being in itself, as synonymous with his sufferings and death, a consideration on account of which God can be just in justifying, or treating as free from guilt, every soul that accepts Christ and walks in newness of life through him.

As evidence of the harmony of these views with the current doctrinal views of the Church, the following passage from Rev. J. M. Hubbert's tract, entitled, *The Atonement,* is cited with much satisfaction : " Sin deserves punishment, and God could not let it go unpunished, without appearing to be unrighteous, or unjust. And yet he was graciously inclined to spare the sinner. Here was the problem, therefore, how to pardon the transgressor, and at the same time show the divine justice. Through the death of Jesus both objects are accomplished, God manifesting his justice while justifying him that believes in Jesus. God's righteousness is thus shown to be sin-condemning and at the same time sin-forgiving."

Dr. T. C. Blake thus sums up his views of "*the necessity of the atonement :* " (*a*) to show God's abhorrence of sin ; (*b*) to exhibit God's regard for the moral law; (*c*) necessary—*absolutely* necessary to man's salvation; (*d*) from the fact that atonement has actually been made. But these leave untouched the fundamental question as to *why* it was necessary for God to show abhorrence of sin and regard for moral law. It must be a question as to an end or to ends, which finds a rational solution in the idea that the end of God's government, namely, the highest well-being of all his rational creatures could be conserved only through atonement, if the sinning were to be redeemed. Certainly God abhors sin and regards moral law, because the former destroys and the latter promotes the happiness of his rational universe.

Rev. James Craik, D.D., in his admirable work entitled, *The Divine Life*, presents a scheme of the way of salvation through atonement, which we thus briefly state : "(1) The entire race of man is by nature fallen, degenerate, dead. (2) The universality of redemption—' The Lamb of God taketh away the sins of the world.' (3) Christ hath sent the Holy Spirit to be the Teacher, Monitor, and Guide of the souls for which he died, and to dwell in the hearts of men, the principle of a new and divine life— the bond of re-union between God and man. (4) This redemption from death, and this consequent gift of life, are as extensive and as universal as the previous condemnation which had come into the world by sin. (5) The divine life thus given to every man is a germ which does not necessarily destroy and take the place of the carnal nature, but co-exists with it, and enters into conflict with all that is evil and depraved in the natural life, and, if properly nurtured, will ultimately overcome all the evil, and substitute for that evil purity, goodness, and every divine affection."

There has been recently on the part of some of our theological teachers and writers a disposition to discard the idea that the sufferings and death of Christ were in any sense needful to remove *legal* obstructions from the way of man's pardon—that the atonement did not on any account render more safe the display of divine mercy to sinners, but that its aim, as an illustrious example of love and self-sacrifice, is solely to move the heart of man to penitence, love, and obedience. The theory looks to the life and the death of Christ, to find soul-inspiring example, and not to his agony and the offering of himself as an expiation or atoning sacrifice. Such a view is chargeable, in our judgment, with greatly detracting from the glory and significance of the atonement, and it affords no adequate explanation of the " mysterious agony of dread and terror which befell the Savior in the olive garden of Gethsemane," when he certainly bowed beneath a pressure greater than ordinary mortal anguish under outward circumstances like those surrounding the Savior. Certainly the Scriptures favor the idea that in the Temptation, the Transfiguration, the sorrow in Gethsemane, and in Calvary's agony and darkness we are taught that the Mighty Deliverer was "verily drinking our cup of sorrow, and sweating drops of blood in the vicarious endurance of our load of sin, that it was the weight of the sins of the world under which he was staggering which made him breathe out, in the exhaustion of his agony, 'If it be possible, let this cup pass from me.'"

A *general* atonement, or that Christ's atoning work was, in the same sense, *in behalf of all men*, has ever been a prominent tenet of Cumberland Presbyterian theology. That Christ died for all men, that God's impartial love wills the salvation of all, that the Spirit strives with all, and the freedom of will whereby it is in him who hears the gospel to determine whether he will accept it or will reject it, are great themes prominent in the preaching of the first Cumberland Presbyterian ministers, and handled by them with great force of logic and often in power and demonstration of the Spirit. The following passage from a lecture by Dr. Burrow, delivered while he was a professor of theology in Bethel College, indicates the clear and positive manner in which those ministers insisted on the doctrine of a general atonement:

" There are not a few' who, while they agree with us that Christ suffered and died in our room and stead—for us in the full and true sense of that term—and that we are justified and saved alone through his righteousness, at the same time differ with us widely as to the extent of the atonement. For while we believe that Christ died for all in the same sense and to the same extent, there are many who hold that he died for only a part. . . . We feel well assured that the same amount of Scripture testimony which goes to prove the doctrine of the atonement, and that Christ died for sinners, goes with equal force to prove that it was for all. . . . One truth must be plain to impartial readers of the Bible: That if Christ ever did bear the sins of any part of the world in his body on the tree, and did suffer and die in their room and stead, he did the very same for the whole world, without distinction, partiality or respect of persons; and we may confidently rely upon it as being the universal, uncontradicted, harmonious testimony of God's word, and it is so believed and taught by Cumberland Presbyterians."

From *The Doctrines of Grace*, by Rev. Milton Bird, D.D., who wrote copiously, vigorously, and most logically on the doctrine of the atonement, we take one illustrative passage: "The atonement is the only channel through which man receives life and favor from God. If so, his existence and the mercies enjoyed by him most plainly show that he is embraced in its gracious provision. The whole human race take their existence under a dispensation of mercy; the atonement is the ground of this dispensation, and therefore embraces all in its saving design. The atonement is not a provision for particular persons chosen out of the general mass· none are passed by and left without remedy under the law, to inevitable damnation. In its design, a door of hope and the way of salvation are opened to all the fallen race of man; a foundation is safely and firmly laid in the divine law, government, and perfections for the forgiveness of sins, which is as extensive as the family of man. . . . . The neglect of the great salvation is the only reason why any perish in their sins."

In like manner did Rev. Finis Ewing with great power and clearness teach that Christ died in the same sense for all mankind. Citing John iii. 16 in support of his view, he says, " I am aware that some explain this text as meaning the elect world; but such explanation is unsound. Let us paraphrase the passage agreeably to that explanation, and see how it will do: ' God so loved the *elect*, that he gave his only begotten Son, that whosoever of the elect believe, should not perish, etc.; consequently that part of the elect world that do not believe must perish.' The absurdity of this will at once appear." " The very commission that Christ gave his disciples implies," he says, " the same thing; ' Go ye into all the world and preach the gospel to *every* creature,' etc. ' He that believeth and is baptized shall be saved; and he that believeth not shall be damned.' What! damn a soul for not believing a non-truth! Would it not be a non-truth for a sinner to believe in Christ if he had not died for him ? "

It is among the recollections of the writer's boyhood that Cumberland Presbyterian ministers produced in Western Pennsylvania a profound impression as they proclaimed with great earnestness the impartial love and mercy of God, and that he had manifested these by giving his Son to taste death alike for all men, and to the intent that all might turn to the stronghold thus available for all. The preaching of the Presbyterian pulpit of the locality had been largely about " decrees," " predestination," and " election ; " and wherever it was proclaimed gladly did the people hear of the impartial grace of God which bringeth salvation and has appeared in behalf of all men, and many were they who found in the messages of those earnest

preachers "glad tidings of great joy" for which their souls
were thirsting; for no other truths can so inspire men with
hope or so move them to gratitude and the consecration of self
to God, as can the doctrine of God's impartial love as displayed,
alike in behalf of Jews and Gentiles, rich and poor, high and
low, through the gift of his own Son, who tasted death, the one
Redeemer for the one humanity, that whosoever believeth
should not perish but have everlasting life.

As an illustration of the stern—but consistent, we must say—
Calvinistic teaching in the early part of the century, may be
cited this passage from article ix. of a " Declaration and Testimony " which the Associate Presbytery of Pennsylvania "found
it necessary" as they believed, to publish "for the doctrine and
order of the Church of Christ: Our Lord Jesus Christ was a
representative and surety for the elect only, he died for them
only, and for none else in any respect; and all for whom he died
shall infallibly be saved. God is just and will not require
double payment for the same debt: had satisfaction been made
by Christ for the sins of all men, none would have perished
under the curse; death, the wages of sin, would not have been
due to any, if Christ had suffered it for the whole human race."

About half a century earlier the Associate Synod of Edinburgh (Scotland), "seeing their people in danger of being led
astray by fair but seducing pretences, did in a few propositions,
state, explain, and defend the Scripture doctrine concerning the
suretyship and death of Christ, 'That he was a surety for the
elect only, and died for none but those who were given him out
of the world; that his intercession is for the elect only,'" etc.
The historian tells us that "on this occasion one minister
belonging to the synod dissented from his brethren strongly,
insisting that Christ died, in *some sense*, for all mankind; though
what that sense was, he never could distinctly tell." It is added
that, as "he refused to forbear teaching such an opinion,"
though " earnestly entreated," "the synod found no other way

to preserve unity of doctrine, but by deposing him from the ministry of the gospel, which they accordingly did."

Whoever will set out with the proposition of an eternal, unconditional decree of election and reprobation, will find himself involved in hopeless logical contradictions if he professes to believe the doctrine of a general atonement; and he will be found saying that Christ did die for all, and he did not; that the non-elect can receive Christ, and that they can not, and thus on to the end.

The Cumberland Presbyterian Church has found a glorious mission in proclaiming the impartial love of God as manifested in the great provision whereby whosoever will may take of the water of life. In this respect, certainly, our denomination has accomplished a good work, contributing its part to that true progress of Christian thought away from the frigidity and fatality of Calvinism into the clear sunshine of the Bible doctrine of God's love for all mankind. Nor can we overestimate the influence or the benefit of such progress in hastening the recognition of the great brotherhood of humanity as the offspring of one loving Father of all. Objects of so great a love, we feel within us a constraining power. We love him because he first loved us. As we receive his spirit, so a new power within us makes us workers together with him, and so through the willing subjects of his grace is God bearing to men the message of his love, that the ends of the earth may look unto him and be saved. Nor may we suppose that even the Christian has yet come to an adequate conception of the measure or of the constraining power of DIVINE LOVE,

> "For the love of God is broader
> Than the measure of man's mind;
> And the heart of the Eternal
> Is most wonderfully kind."

Two great facts touching the Atonement Cumberland Presbyterians must firmly hold, if they would be orthodox as tested by the Scriptures and by the teachings of our fathers:

20

1. That Christ, as a Lamb without spot, "by sacrifice of himself once made," "taketh away the sin of the world." In other words, the true idea of Atonement is inseparable from the sufferings and death of Christ. It was in order "that he by the grace of God might taste death for every one," that he was "made for a little while lower than the angels (Heb. ii. 9). "But now once, in the end of the ages, he has been manifested for the putting away of sin *by the sacrifice of himself*" (Heb. ix. 27). "So also Christ, having been once *offered to bear the sins* of many, will, to those who look for him, appear a second time, without sin," that is, "without being a sacrifice, to expiate sin " (Heb. ix. 28). "In which will we have been sanctified, through the offering of the body of Jesus Christ once for all " (Heb. x. 10).

2. That the sufferings and death of Christ are *expiatory* in their relation to man's redemption.

By this proposition is meant, not that the atonement was needful to render God merciful, but to *render pardon safe.* If we are to believe that in any proper sense of the term, God exercises government over his rational creatures, we must believe that penalty is annexed to disobedience. But we must remember that it is *love* which prompts to penalty in God's administration over his moral creatures. Penalty is a feature of God's administration for good, without which feature *highest well-being could not be secured.* By *atonement*, then, we are to understand such a substitution for the infliction of the penalty upon the guilty as will fully as well secure that for which the divine goodness inflicts penalties—the highest well-being of his universe of creatures rational and sentient.

The Atonement is, on one side, an infinitely efficacious expression of God's disapprobation of sin, and of the destructive nature of sin in his moral empire; and, on the other hand, of God's infinite compassion for his creatures made in his own image. It was because God so LOVED the world, that atonement was provided, and it is for the same love of the happiness of his creatures that God can not forgive sin without an expedient that will, equally well with the infliction of the penalty of the law, promote obedience, moral order, and happiness. To promote happiness, God's empire of rational creatures was spoken into being. These principles are clearly applicable in the family and in the state—which are but phases and modes of his government over rational creatures—and there seems no valid reason why we may not say that they are applicable throughout his vast empire of moral agents. While we are taught that it is for every member of the human race that Christ, by the grace of God, tasted death, we may reasonably suppose that this display of infinite compassion and his atoning work make a deep and lasting impression for good throughont the moral universe, and thus is of boundless value in promoting the end for which God creates and governs subjects of moral law.

The foregoing view of the subject is perfectly consistent with the doctrine of atonement for all men, while it does not involve us, on the one hand, in the error of Universalism, nor, on the other, shut us up to the Calvinistic dilemma of the partial exercise of God's mercy in a limited atonement, or of an atonement for that part of humanity which his mercy passed by and ordained to wrath.

The remark of Ralph Wardlow has great force : " The entire word of God bears us out in believing it to have been atonement by sacrifice—in other words, by substitution and vicarious suffering. Of this the Bible is full. To the mind that can contrive, to its own satisfaction, to strip the Bible of the doctrine of atonement by vicarious suffering, it might, in my apprehension, be safely pronounced impossible to convey a divine discovery at all."

It seems to the writer to be of the utmost importance that as Cumberland Presbyterians we adhere to the teachings of the fathers of the Church on this vital doctrine of atonement. This ground abandoned, we are wanderers without compass, liable to divisions and strifes engendered by dogmas which heterodoxy substitutes for God's revealed truth. The passage in Heb. ix. 24– 28, and its connections, as indeed the whole espistle, seem to leave no ground for doubting that the sufferings and death of Christ are, according to the Scriptures, the indispensable condition of man's deliverance from the penal consequences of sin : " But now once, in the end of the ages, hath he (Christ) appeared to do away sin by the sacrifice of himself. And as it is appointed unto men once to die, but after this the judgment, so *Christ was once offered to bear the sins of many* (Isa. liii. 12), and unto them that look for him shall he appear a second time without sin unto salvation." The last clause, " and unto them that look for him," etc., signifies, as the best expositors agree, that Christ " will not appear as *a piacular victim to expiate sin*," etc. The drift of this very important passage is faithfully stated, it seems to us, in the following comment by Moses Stuart : " It is plain that the sense attached in Scripture to bearing any one's sins is the actual suffering of the consequences due to sin. . . . The sentiment, then, is, that Jesus by his death endured the penal consequences of sin. By which, however, we are not to understand that the sufferings of our Redeemer were in all respects an exact equivalent; but, that vicarious suffering is here designated seems to be an unavoidable conclusion, both from the *usus loquendi* of Scripture, and the nature of the argument in chapters viii., ix."

Atonement was not through Christ's holiness of life, or perfect obedience to the law man had violated, as Anselm taught, and as Hodge seems to teach, in saying that Christ literally fulfilled the covenant of works in the stead of the elect, but, as Paul certainly teaches, it is in the *death* of Christ we find the fulfillment of the sacrificial types, the great expiation whereby God can be just in the justification of the sinner who repents and returns, through regenerating grace, to holiness of life. Christ's death is not a ransom paid to the devil, as Gregory taught, for man's release. That wondrous spectacle, Jesus suffering, dying on Calvary, is atonement because a display to men and to angels, of God's holy displeasure at sin and of his infinite regard for the ends of his moral government over rational creatures. Atonement does not make God merciful, but it renders it morally possible for God, consistently with the ends of his righteous government, to exercise mercy by pardoning the transgressor on condition of repentance and return to obedience. It saves no human being absolutely, but does make all men prisoners of hope through him who is the propitiation for all. Through this Atonement mercy and salvation are for all, as the air and the sunshine are for all, and the regenerating and sanctifying influences needed for man's restoration to life and holiness flow from and accompany this gracious dispensation through Atonement. In its inception, its execution, its application, it is all of *grace*. As heaven opened its glories to the beloved disciple when exiled on rocky Patmos, he saw Jesus standing before the throne as a "lamb newly slain," and heard ten thousand times ten thousand of the redeemed, in sounds louder than mighty waters, chanting, "Blessing, and honor, and glory, and power unto him that sitteth on the throne, and unto the Lamb forever and ever," and the burden of "the new song" was, "Thou art worthy to take the book, and to open the seals thereof; for thou wast slain, and hast redeemed us to God by thy blood out of every kindred and tongue and people and nation."

CHAPTER XII.

THE GENIUS OF THE CUMBERLAND PRESBYTERIAN CHURCH.

THIS volume having already outgrown the limits designed by those at whose request it has been written, it is necessary to omit the discussion of "Repentance Unto Life," "Saving Faith," "Justification," and a few other topics which, like the ones named, are essential parts of a system setting forth the way of salvation to man through the person and work of a Redeemer. For the same reason this concluding chapter must be entirely briefer than would otherwise have been consistent with the interest and importance of the subject to which it relates.

The Cumberland Presbyterian Church, like the kingdom of God of which it claims to be a part, came not with "observation." It did not march out of a great denomination a powerful *exodus* numbering thousands, with leaders, discipline, and ample equipments. On the contrary its humble origin was the organization of a presbytery by three ministers little known to the world, but men of earnest piety, and of deep convictions of duty in relation to teaching and defending what they believed to be God's truth. The work thus humbly begun has, through the blessing of God, as we must believe, continually enlarged, holding on its way through a desolating war, and standing forth to-day, at the end of eighty years, as a recognized branch of the Presbyterian family of Churches, with a membership of one hundred and sixty-five thousand, an earnest ministry, colleges, missions, periodicals, publishing house, and other agencies of an aggressive denomination. Surely, an inquiry into the characteristics of a body that has, in a period comparatively so short, achieved results comparatively so great, could not prove uninteresting or unprofitable. What account, then, may we truthfully give of this member of the Presbyterian family? First, then, to correct some false statements made through lack of information or of a sense of justice, we believe that it may be truthfully said that we are:

1. Not charactered by "doctrinal unsoundness." Of this charge, repeated throughout our history, we plead not guilty, and appeal to our doctrinal symbols in justification of the plea. It is at least circumstantial evidence of our innocence, that thousands of the strongest divines and laymen in the Presbyterian Church are to-day demanding just such a modification of the Westminster Confession as will substantially harmonize with ours.

2. Not a Presbyterian Church that "believes in an uneducated ministry." This accusation, so often made in the way of disparagement, should be sufficiently refuted, to the satisfaction of all candid persons, by the numerous colleges, universities, and other institutions of learning our Church has founded and is supporting. We do hold that there are circumstances under which it may be right and even very needful, to license men who have not had what is usually meant by a collegiate education. The founders of the Church believed that they lived at a time when such a step was justified by the wants of the section of country in which they labored. Their policy with respect to this matter has received the sanction of not a few of the wisest and best men of the mother Church. In the great demand for preaching in the revival of 1800, our fathers saw and deeply felt only what Rev. Dr. Cuyler recently declared so well in the columns of the *Evangelist*, when he said: "Three truths are as solid and indisputable as the rocks of yonder mountain. First, we must have more preachers of the gospel of salvation. Second, when the Holy Spirit moves a Christian man to preach

Christ Jesus we must not tie him fast with the ecclesiastical red tape. Third, *when ministers enough can not be got into the pulpit by the long regulation roads we must open shorter roads.*"

3. Not a band of ecclesiastical warriors, or Ishmaelites with our hands against all other denominations. In fact it is barely possible that any Church is more ready than are Cumberland Presbyterians to fraternize cordially with all other evangelical bodies. In this respect our spirit is truly catholic and magnanimous. The circumstances of its origin imposed on the founders of the denomination the necessity of much doctrinal preaching, and of frequently explaining wherein we differ from Calvinists on one side and from Arminians on the other. Accused of "doctrinal unsoundness," portrayed in books as holding "tenets congenial to men in the flesh," and ridiculed as being "in favor of an ignorant ministry," what else could our ministry have done consistently with legitimate self-defense and with their obligations to what they believed God's truth and the path of duty, but to explain and defend the doctrines and aims of the new denomination to which they gave their labors with a zeal that bordered on inspiration. They did not believe, nor do we to-day believe, that they were disputing about doctrinal differences in themselves insignificant and practically of no consequence, but that they were condemning pernicious error, and contending for great verities vitally related to the salvation of men. That there is to-day in the Presbyterian Church a large party who reject the teaching of the Westminster Confession on all the points on which Cumberland Presbyterians reject it, and that they consider the changes demanded as of the gravest importance, the pending discussion of the question of "revision" has most clearly and fully demonstrated.

Out of the vast amount of material from which we could draw proofs of the last assertion in the foregoing section, we select the following report of the action of the Rochester Presbyter, as it was given through the press in the autumn of 1891.

More complete indorsement or more triumphant vindication of the preaching and polity of our fathers would be scarcely possible. History certainly does repeat. Could Finis Ewing, Robert Donnell, John Morgan, and their compeers, from whose lips thousands received with great joy the message of God's impartial love, now return to the Church militant, they would certainly be alike amazed and delighted to find how nearly a great body of divines and laymen of the mother Church are asserting the very truths and using the very words for which they themselves were half a century ago called dangerous errorists. A few sentences being omitted for the sake of brevity, the action of the Presbytery is as follows:

"The principal change proposed and desired by this Presbytery is in connection with section 7, which declares that 'the rest of mankind God was pleased to pass by, and to ordain to dishonor and wrath.' Some changes in this section have been made by the committee, but its most objectionable feature still remains. The words, 'God was pleased to pass by' have been changed for, 'God was pleased not to elect.' . . . . This can be regarded only as an attempt to cast a softening veil over the *horrible doctrine of preterition.* It was held and voted, therefore, that the whole of this seventh section, both in its original and in its altered form, be omitted from the Confession of Faith, for the following reasons: 1. Because it is the one *dark and dreadful item* against which more than a hundred presbyteries lifted their united voices. 2. Because it is a doctrine *nowhere taught in the Scriptures,* and a doctrine repudiated by some of the foremost authorities in our denomination, such as Drs. Crosby, Van Dyke, and A. A. Hodge, the last pronouncing it '*unscriptural* and *immoral.*' 3. Because it is a doctrine no one preaches and *no one can preach either to the edification of saints or sinners.* . . . 4. Because it contradicts the sacred word, aye, and the solemn oath of Almighty God. The section asserts that 'God was pleased to ordain to dishonor and wrath' a multitude of his creatures; but God himself lifts up his voice and swears, 'As I live I have no pleasure in the death of the wicked.' 5. Because it is contrary to the tenor and spirit of the gospel throughout, which declares, in divers manners and sundry places, that God would have all men to come to a knowledge of the truth and be saved. 6. Because *it turns to hollow mockery the free and universal offer of salvation* as set forth in the reviser's new chapter on that subject. 7. Because, in the estimation of multitudes of pious and intelligent people, it belies the tears of the adorable Savior, which, in the deep compassion of his soul, he shed over the most incorrigible of sinners, the inhabitants of Jerusalem.

In view of all these facts the presbytery voted to recommend the omission of this seventh section, both in its original and revised form, and the adoption of the following as a substitute for it:

The decrees of God concerning all mankind, are to be so construed as to be in harmony with these declarations of Scripture, namely: *that Christ is the propitiation for the sins of the whole world, and that God is not willing that any should perish, but that all should come to repentance and live.*

" This presbytery further recommends that in chapter 6, section 2, the statement " defiled in all the faculties and parts of soul and body" should be modified. Also that in section 3 of the same chapter, the clause " the guilt of this sin was imputed " should be omitted, for the following reasons: that the guilt of Adam's act could not in reason or in righteousness be laid to the charge of his children, who were yet unborn; that to say " we all sinned in Adam " is to say what is *utterly unintelligible and inconceivable*: that we can no more become subjects of guilt before we have existence than we can become subjects of reward or punishment before we have existence; and that the whole idea is contrary to natural justice and to the express decision of Scripture, ' The son shall not bear the iniquity of the father.'"

The following sentiments from the pen of Rev. S. G. Burney, D.D., LL.D., the venerable professor of Systematic Theology in our university at Lebanon, Tenn., states his view of the relation of our theology to other systems:

"I think our theology is a distinct system in itself. It is not intermediate in the sense that it consists in part of Calvinistic, and in part of Arminian tenets. It is intermediate in the sense that it avoids the extreme *monergism* of the former, and the extreme *synergism* of the latter. These views are indicated in the 40th section of our Confession of Faith. Our people have always given more prominence to the doctrine of regeneration, than any other denomination in this country. They have also urged with more emphasis than others the necessity of trusting in Christ, rather than in creeds, the sacraments, ritualistic observances, etc."

As our denomination is locally a Western and a Southern Church, we must look to those sections for information respecting the labors and the spirit of the generation of men now passed away. In a recent article on the "Effect of the Early Preaching and Life of Our Church Upon the Religious Interests of the World," Rev. E. P. Henderson, D.D., who himself had extensive personal knowledge of that early preaching and life of our Church, states a number of facts highly interesting in themselves, and illustrative of the subject under review. He informs us that "Drs. Blackburn and Nelson, and Rev. James Gallagher (Presbyterian ministers) have left written testimony in favor of our preachers and their work," and cites from Mr. Gallagher's *Western* Sketch-Book the following passage:

"There are among them many strong men; workmen that need not be ashamed. And their blessed Master has been with them in every part of that wide field where they have labored, and has made his gospel the power of God unto salvation to many thousand believing souls. From my inmost soul I honor those men, and I will speak of it in the presence of the Church of my God. I have no hesitation in declaring my belief that during the last forty years no body of ministers in America, or in the world, have preached so much good, efficient preaching, and received such small compensation (financially). That Church now stands before heaven and earth a monument of God's great work in the revival of 1800."

The following is cited by Mr. Henderson, the author of the many "historical facts" illustrative of that wonderful "power of God unto salvation" exhibited by the gospel as preached by men whose like would seem not to be found to-day:

"Rev. James Bowman, of the Presbyterian Church, seeing the wonderful results of camp-meetings among the Cumberland Presbyterians, resolved to hold a camp-meeting in his congregation. But his brethren in his presbytery were nearly all on the old side, and would have nothing to do with camp-meetings. The few favorable to the revival had other engagements. Bowman could get no help. The ecclesiastical authorities of the mother Church had forbidden its people either to recognize the preachers of the Cumberland Presbyterian Church, or to commune with its members. Notwithstanding this, Mr. Bowman invited Rev. J. B. Porter to assist him at his camp-meeting. This was a new departure. Porter agreed to assist on two conditions: First, that he should be allowed to preach his own doctrine. Second, that there should be no tokens used at the communion service, but that all Christians be allowed to participate. His conditions were accepted. . . . While Porter preached from the text, 'Turn, ye prisoners of hope,' the mighty power of God swept over the vast assembly; sinners fell like men slain in battle. The meeting was protracted from day to day, until there were one hundred and twenty-five professions. Fifteen of the converts became ministers of the gospel."

When so much of interest in this connection might be said, it is occasion for regret that we have space for so little. Having spent his life on the very border of the Church, and coming into the Church, though in his youth, quite after its introduction into Pennsylvania, the writer felt the need of assistance, in this part of the work, from those better situated to form a correct judgment, and hence, by personal interviews and by correspondence, has endeavored to arrive at the true spirit of the Cumberland Presbyterian Church, and to learn what beside it may possess as entitling it to the claims of individuality among the Protestant bodies of America. While other kind responses must be omitted, we give place to the following scheme from J. L. Goodknight, D.D., a minister of wide observation in relation to the affairs of the Church, and one born and reared in its bosom :

"THE GENIUS OF CUMBERLAND PRESBYTERIANISM.

" 1. The denomination of the country masses, by the country masses, and for the country masses. So far it has not been a denomination of the cities, by the cities, for the cities. The phenomenal growth and truth disseminating power have been largely the result of its touch with the rural population. The men born and brought up on the farms and in country towns have controlled and do yet control the mercantile pursuits and thought and legislation of the United States.

" 2. The denomination of a free gospel—without money and without price. No other ministry has done as much gospel work for so little financial pay or temporal advantage, as have Cumberland Presbyterian ministers. The same with equal truthfulness may be said of the men and women who have given themselves to the educational work of this denomination.

" 3. No denomination has kept more in touch and sympathy with the changing conditions of moral advance or has done more proportionally to promote it. It has led in such advance moral reforms in the true Pauline spirit. The faith of the denomination has been, that when society is truly saturated with gospel teachings and principles, then all wrongs and iniquities will be and must be righted.

" 4. The denomination has shown great power and capability of advance and of adaptation to the growing demands and needs of its own people, and the peoples in whose midst it has done and does its work.

" 5. Its flexibility and adaptability have made it peculiarly the denomination molding and molded to the genius of the United States and her institutions. It is the child of the conditions and needs of the United States Republic ; and so has developed along the lines of the polity and policy of our distinctive Americanism.

" 6. The denomination has been eminently apostolic in its methods of home mission work. Its evangelists have gone everywhere preaching the gospel at their own charges. No denomination has contributed more to the upbuilding of other denominations than Cumberland Presbyterianism. This was especially so in the early history of the denomination, when its evangelists cared more for, and especially emphasized, the saving of the people, rather than the organization of new congregations or the propagation of their own peculiar ism.

" 7. This denomination is peculiarly the John Baptist among denominations, crying: Prepare ye the way and make plain paths, so that the creeds of modern Christendom shall be in harmony with the Bible, rather than with a system of logic or of philosophy. The denomination has been the pioneer of creed revision in modern times. It is the first denomination since the apostolic days, whose formulated creed is based upon pure Bible teaching. The whole Protestant Christian world is drifting toward its formulated doctrinal creed as interpreted in harmony with vicarious atonement and the universality of the gospel provision.

" 8. It is capable inherently of indefinite expansion and growth. Its essential gospel principles are those which are sooner or later to permeate the world wide Protestantism."

If Cumberland Presbyterians can not claim the distinction of leading the way, they are certainly among the foremost denominations in the recognition of the obligation of the Church toward moral reforms. The great questions of to-day which so vitally affect the interests alike of society and of the Church, and the numerous deliverances by ecclesiastical courts, pertaining to these questions, practically illustrate our meaning. As a leading religious journal recently expressed it, "Jesus Christ came into the world not merely to save individuals for future felicity, from a present hopeless wreck, but to revolutionize and reorganize society." "The Church is passing," says the journal, "from the one theology to the other." It is in this awakening, and in this transition of the Church from the narrow conceptions of the past as to the functions of Christianity, with the quickening of the Christian conscience in relation to the public welfare, that is to be found a guarantee of the future well-being of society, the nation, and the Church itself.

According to its spirit, its teachings, and its declared mission, Christianity lays the ax at the root of every tree which brings not forth good fruit, whether such tree be found in social customs, political creeds, civil codes, or false systems of religion. Among these evil trees, and greatest of all, is the "all-blasting upas" of the drink traffic, which "rains its plagues on men like dew," corrupts legislation, and like a very Antichrist obstructs the work of the Church. The greatest and the most needed awakening that can come to the clergy and the laity of the Church of to-day is that of an aroused conscience in relation to the Christian's duty of using his means, his personal influence, and his prerogatives as a citizen for the removal of this and other great evils tolerated and protected by legislation, but which, as the Bible expressly declares, the Son of God was manifested to destroy. If in these closing paragraphs we may express a great and most earnest hope respecting our Church, it is that, next to holding firmly to its sound doctrinal formula, it may be awakened to a sense of its obligation to the great moral movements which ameliorate the conditions of society and open the way for the coming of the kingdom of God. The Church will not instrumentally have achieved the mission for which it was organized, and for which Christ came into the world, until it shall have so imbued all human institutions with his teachings that the government shall be upon his shoulders, instead of being, as at present it so largely is, upon the shoulders of the evil one. Born herself because of a needed reform in theological teaching, and from the very beginning adopting a policy required by the needs of the masses hungry for the bread of life, the Cumberland Presbyterian Church should, through an untrammeled pulpit, an earnest and consecrated ministry, and a well-instructed and devoted membership, rise in its spiritual power to the measure of the demands on it in this crisis of both Church and State.

Its past success and its present condition justify the pleasing assurance that the Church will come to the close of its first century in the full tide of prosperity, and enter upon the second century with resources of men and means and institutions, which, through the blessing of its great Head, will secure for it an honored place among divinely appointed agencies for the world's salvation.

> "Round her habitation hovering
> See the cloud and fire appear,
> For a glory and a covering,
> Showing that the Lord is near."